Conflict Resolution

AN INTRODUCTORY TEXT

Desmond Ellis
Dawn Anderson

2005
EMOND MONTGOMERY PUBLICATIONS LIMITED
TORONTO, CANADA

D0814325

Printed in Canada.

We acknowledge the financial support of the Government of Canada through the Book Publishing Industry Development Program (BPIDP) for our publishing activities.

Acquistions editor: Karen Davidson
Marketing director: Dave Stokaluk
Production editor: Jim Lyons, WordsWorth Communications
Production assistant: David Handelsman, WordsWorth Communications
Proofreader & indexer: Paula Pike, WordsWorth Communications
Cover designer: Susan Darrach, Darrach Design

Library and Archives Canada Cataloguing in Publication

Ellis, Desmond
    Conflict resolution : an introductory text / Desmond Ellis, Dawn Anderson.

Includes index.
ISBN 1-55239-156-6

    1. Conflict management—Textbooks.   I. Anderson, Dawn
II. Title.

HM1126.E44 2005   303.6'9   C2005-905344-5

For Donna

Contents

Preface xi

{1} CONFLICT: DEFINITIONS 1
Chapter Objectives 1
Conflict Is Normal 1
Functional and Dysfunctional Conflict 2
Conflict and Its Terminology 3
What Is Conflict? 4
    Objective Interaction Definitions 6
    Subjective Feelings Definitions 7
    Integrative Definition 8
Types of Conflict 11
    Interest Conflicts 13
    Value Conflicts 14
    Cognitive Conflicts 17
    Identity Conflicts 19
    Realistic and Unrealistic (Personality) Conflicts 21
Conflict Analysis 22
    Discovery 22
    Prominent Source 25
    Solution 26
Conflict Analysis Illustrated 27
    Is There a Conflict? 27
    What Is the Conflict Really About? 27
    Who Are the Parties and What Is Their Relationship? 28
    Prominent Source 28
    Caveats 29
Chapter Summary 29
Recommended Reading 29
Films, Videos, and DVDs 30
Websites 30

{2} RESOLVING CONFLICT: STRUGGLE AND NEGOTIATION 31
Chapter Objectives 31
Approaches to Conflict Resolution 31
Struggle 32
    Evaluation 36
Negotiation 37
    Impression Management 37
    Distributive and Integrative Negotiation 39
    Impression Management in Integrative and Distributive
        Negotiation 41
Models of Negotiation 41
    Positional Bargaining 42
    Principled Negotiation 50
    Cyclical–Developmental Negotiation 61
Why Negotiations Can Fail 73
    Beyond Failure: Conflict Escalation 75
Chapter Summary 76
Recommended Reading 76
Films, Videos, and DVDs 77
    Struggle 77
    Negotiation 77
Websites 78

{3} MEDIATION, ARBITRATION, AND ADJUDICATION 79
Chapter Objectives 79
Mediation 79
    What Is Mediation? 79
    An Overview of Principles and Procedures 82
    Roles 83
    General Ground Rule 83
Models of Mediation 84
    Rights-Based Mediation 84
    Interest-Based Mediation 90
    Transformative Mediation 98
    Narrative Mediation 102
    Co-mediation 109
Mediation Ethics 110
Arbitration 113
    Binding and Non-Binding Arbitration 114
    Judges and Arbitrators 114
    Arbitration and Mediation 117

Baseball Arbitration 118
Evaluation 119
Mediation–Arbitration 120
Evaluation 122
Adjudication 122
Mini-Trial 124
Evaluation 125
Guidelines for Selecting Procedures 126
Chapter Summary 130
Appendix 3A: Uniform Mediation Act Principles 131
Appendix 3B: A Summary of the Ontario Arbitration Act, 1991 132
Recommended Reading 135
Films, Videos, and DVDs 135
Websites 136

{4} POWER 137
Chapter Objectives 137
Definitions of Power 137
Unidimensional Definitions 137
Multidimensional Definitions 138
Distinguishing Unidimensional (Resources) from
    Multidimensional (Process) Definitions 138
The Parties' Use of Resources 139
Relational Definitions 140
Resource Theories of Power 141
Scope of Power Resources 141
Process Theories of Power 143
Gulliver's Process Theory of Power 144
Modifications to Gulliver's Process Theory of Power 148
Application of the Ellis Process Theory of Power 150
Conflict Between the Cree and Hydro-Quebec 151
Resources 151
Use of Resources 152
Outcomes 153
External Factors and Outcomes 154
Case Study Postscript 154
Effects of the Balance of Power Between the Parties 155
Practical Implications of Power Balancing 156
Assessing Power Imbalances 157
Resource Differences 160
Use of Resources 161

Ethical Considerations in Power Balancing 164
The Power of a Mediator 165
Evaluation of Resource Theories 166
Chapter Summary 167
Recommended Reading 167
Films, Videos, and DVDs 168

{5} CULTURE 169
Chapter Objectives 169
Cultural Relativity 169
Definitions of Culture 170
Cultural Definitions of Conflict Resolution 171
Cultural Theories 171
Value Orientations Theory: Collectivism and Individualism 172
Communications Theories: Meanings and Styles 183
Situational Factors 187
In-Groups and Out-Groups 187
Ethnocentrism and Stereotyping 189
Ethnocentrism 189
Stereotyping 191
Cultural–Situational Theory 193
Advice for Practitioners 194
Keep a Dual Focus on Cultural and Situational Factors 194
Facilitate Information Sharing and Alternation 194
Reconcile Interests 194
Be Sensitive to the Nuances of Culture 195
Abandon Ethnocentrism, But Uphold the Rule of Law 195
Assist the Parties in Abandoning Stereotypes by Abandoning
    Them Yourself 195
Use the Elicitive Model of Conflict Resolution Where
    Appropriate 196
Evaluation of Cultural Theories of Conflict Resolution 196
Strengths 196
Weaknesses 197
Chapter Summary 197
Recommended Reading 198
Films, Videos, and DVDs 198

{6} GENDER 199
Chapter Objectives 199
Definitions of Gender 199

Theories of Gender 200
    Socialization Theory 201
    Interactionist–Situational Theory 203
    Structural Theory 204
Application of Gender Theories to Conflict Resolution 205
    Struggle 205
    Negotiation 206
    Mediation 212
    Adjudication 215
Evaluation 217
    Socialization Theory 217
    Interactionist–Situational Theory 217
    Structural Theory 218
Implications for Practice 218
Chapter Summary 219
Recommended Reading 220
Websites 220

{7} PERSONALITY 221
Chapter Objectives 221
Definition of Personality 221
The Five-Factor Theory of Personality 222
Personality and Negotiations 223
    Personality in Actual Negotiations 223
    Personality in Simulated Negotiations 224
Situational Factors 228
    Motivational and Interpersonal Orientations 228
    Level of Aspiration 230
    Social Value Orientations 232
Personality and Struggle 233
    The June Bug Study: Situational Factors 234
Evaluation 237
    Personality Theory and Research 237
    Situational Theory and Research 237
Chapter Summary 237
Appendix 7A: The "Big Five" Personality Traits 238
Recommended Reading 240

REFERENCES 241
INDEX 267
ACKNOWLEDGMENTS 273

Preface

Human beings seem to know much more about starting conflicts than they do about resolving them. Perhaps this is why there are few if any university or college courses with titles such as *Starting Conflicts: Theory, Research, and Practice*. There are, however, many courses on conflict resolution. The universities that Dawn and I teach at offer such courses, and we are among the instructors who teach them. In that capacity we have reviewed numerous texts to use in these courses, and it was because none of the books met all of our selection criteria that we decided to write this book. We have sought to write a book that

- is interdisciplinary;
- includes an interesting variety of Canadian case studies and examples;
- is relatively easy to understand for students new to the topic of conflict resolution;
- is comprehensive with respect to contemporary conflict resolution procedures;
- integrates theory and practice;
- provides a sound basis for more advanced degree, diploma, and certificate courses; and
- organizes the content into three interrelated segments—conflict, conflict resolution, and generic factors.

In chapter 1, we define conflict. More specifically, we compare and critically evaluate subjective (mutually hostile feelings) and objective (mutually harmful interactions) definitions of conflict. The definition we offer integrates subjective and objective definitions and clearly separates conflict from attempts made to settle instances of conflict (conflict resolution). Sources of conflict vary. More than one source may be present in any given conflict. Conflict analysis may reveal that the presence of a predominant source in a particular conflict. A classification based on the predominant source yields four types of conflict. In this chapter we also discuss interest, value, cognitive, and identity conflicts.

We identify five conflict resolution procedures in this book: struggle, negotiation, mediation, arbitration, and adjudication. Struggle and negotiation are procedures in which the parties involved in the conflict attempt to settle it themselves. We define, describe, compare, and critically evaluate these two "self-help" procedures in chapter 2.

Mediation, arbitration, and adjudication are procedures in which a third party who is not involved in the conflict attempts to settle it, albeit in different ways. We define, describe, and critically evaluate these three procedures in chapter 3. We also discuss mediation ethics and guidelines for selecting appropriate conflict resolution procedures in this chapter.

Power, culture, gender and personality are "generic factors" in conflict resolution. That is to say, they are factors that, to a greater or lesser degree, influence the process and outcomes of all conflict resolution procedures. In chapter 4, we describe, compare, and critically evaluate resource and process definitions and theories of power. Then, we apply an integrated resource/process theory of power to a real-life conflict between the Cree of northern Quebec and Hydro-Quebec. We also discuss mediator interventions aimed at balancing power and mediator power.

In chapter 5, we define and theorize culture. Cultural influences on the process and outcomes of negotiation and mediation are important in all societies, but they are especially important in multicultural societies such as Canada. At the same time, the impact of culture increases or decreases depending on the strength of situational factors. We present evidence supporting a joint (cultural/situational factors) or "see-saw" model in this chapter. We also discuss two important cultural influences: ethnocentrism and stereotyping.

In chapter 6, we define and theorize gender and discuss its impact on the process and outcomes of struggle, mediation, and negotiation. One important lesson of chapter 5 is reinforced in this chapter: when situational factors are stronger, the impact of gender is weaker, and when situational factors are weaker, the impact of gender is stronger.

In chapter 7, we define and theorize personality and critically evaluate its application to conflict resolution procedures. The important lesson of the chapters on culture and gender is further reinforced in this chapter. When situational factors are stronger, personality effects are weaker, and when situational factors are weaker, personality effects are stronger.

Desmond Ellis
Oakville, Ontario
July 2005

CHAPTER ONE

Conflict: Definitions

> **Chapter Objectives**
>
> *Define conflict as a relationship involving specific mutual feelings and harmful interaction.*
>
> *Provide examples of conflict that fit the definition.*
>
> *Describe four major types or predominant sources of conflict.*
>
> *Explain why knowledge of the predominant source of a conflict is helpful to negotiators and mediators.*
>
> *Describe the essential features of conflict analysis.*
>
> *Apply conflict analysis to the Cree–Hydro-Quebec conflict.*

CONFLICT IS NORMAL

Conflict is normal in society because the structural and cultural conditions that give rise to it are present in all societies. A society's structure includes groups that are identified by age, gender, social class, race or ethnicity, and religion. A society's culture includes values, ways of thinking and feeling, and the identities that are learned by members of these groups. Material and social resources—such as money, shelter, food, employment, medical care, and transport—are always scarce in relation to the demand for them made by members of different groups. Scarcity instigates conflict, especially when it creates zero-sum (win–lose) competition for scarce and desired resources, such as land, water, oil, and money. Conflicts that originate in perceived or actual scarcity of material resources are called "interest conflicts." Moreover, in most societies—and especially in large heterogeneous societies, such as Canada and the United States—members of different groups have different, and sometimes opposing, social and religious values, cognitions (ways of thinking), and identities. Opposing and/or shared group values, opposing cognitions, and differing identities can be as reliable as scarcity in instigating conflict.

In any conflict, interests, values, cognitions, and identities may be identified as interrelated causes, but the origin of the conflict can often be traced to one predominant source. For example, Drohan (2004) identifies competition for material resources—such as precious metals, land, and water—as the predominant cause of many, if not most, international disputes that the media refer to as "ethnic conflicts."

Finally, the structural and cultural conditions of most societies change over time. Change is often a source of conflict because it benefits or harms the interests of members of some social groups more than others.

FUNCTIONAL AND DYSFUNCTIONAL CONFLICT

Conflict is said to be functional when it has beneficial consequences for relationships between individuals and groups. Conflict is said to be dysfunctional when it has harmful consequences for relationships between individuals and groups (Merton, 1957). Sociologists such as Durkheim (1947) believe that conflict is present in all societies because it has some positive consequences for society as a whole. Conflict theorists such as Coser (1956, p. 73) state that conflict is functional for relationships when it promotes change in the direction of greater equality.

Simmel (1955) believes that conflict is functional because it establishes relationships between individuals and groups and promotes unity in the latter. Unlike indifference, which keeps individuals and groups separated, conflict links individuals and groups. Bush and Folger (1994, p. 2) view conflict as functional because it presents opportunities for third parties to intervene in ways that remind the antagonists that they are the authors of their own fate and must take the situation of others into account in making decisions that affect them.

Felstiner and Williams (1978, p. 24) describe conflict as functional when it results in "the continuous modification of the conditions of the relationship … through continued confrontation and discussion of the issues by the parties themselves." Scanzoni (1970, p. 75) also associates conflict with changes that help maintain a relationship by removing the sources of conflict. Psychologically, conflict helps maintain relationships by bringing an issue into the open so that it can be settled in mutually beneficial ways through negotiation by the parties themselves or through the intervention of a mediator. Le Baron (2002, p. 286) conceives of conflict as a gift, as "sand in our oysters … nudging us toward who we can become," motivating us to "extricate ourselves from the knots that confine us."

If conflict has all these positive consequences, why don't we promote it? One reason is that conflict can also be dysfunctional—that is, it can cause significant and widespread harm to interpersonal, inter-group, and inter-nation relationships. This happens when conflict results in the mutual use of force by the parties involved. In extreme situations, such as civil war, there is widespread destruction, and the lives of human beings become "solitary, poor, nasty, brutish and short" (Hobbes, 1651, p. 43). For Coser (1956, p. 73), conflict becomes dysfunctional when it harms something as fundamental as the very basis of a relationship. For example, marital conflict is functional when it brings about changes that enhance a marriage, but it is dysfunctional when it leads to divorce.

CONFLICT AND ITS TERMINOLOGY

A review of the literature on conflict reveals terminological confusion. "Dispute" and "conflict" are often used interchangeably, along with synonyms, such as "altercation," "tug-of-war," and "fighting." Sometimes writers treat dispute as the master concept in the sense that they include it in the title of a book or article and simply subsume conflict under it (Felstiner, Abel, & Sarat, 1981; Macfarlane, 2003; Roberts, 1983). Other writers treat conflict as the master concept (Blalock, 1989; Coser, 1956; Simmel, 1955). Writers who use conflict and dispute interchangeably include Ury, Brett, and Goldberg (1993), Le Baron (2002), and Moore (1996). *The Handbook of Conflict Resolution* (2000), edited by Deutsch and Coleman, does not define conflict and does not include dispute in its index. Some writers use the term "conflict" when the parties attempt to resolve contentious issues themselves, reserving the term dispute for situations where third parties are involved (Gulliver, 1979).

To eliminate terminological confusion in this book, we consistently use the term "conflict" to refer to hostile feelings between two or more parties. We view attempts at conflict resolution as existing on the continuum that is set out in figure 1. In figure 1—and throughout the book—the term "process" refers to how a procedure aimed at settling a conflict is implemented. Decisions about procedural rules and who creates them are relevant here. The term "outcome" refers to the results of a conflict resolution procedure. At one end of the continuum (struggle and negotiation), process and outcome are controlled by the parties themselves. At the other end of the continuum (adjudication), a third party controls process and outcome. In mediation, one of the two middle grounds, the parties control outcome, but a third party controls process. In arbitration, the second middle ground, the parties have some control over process, but the outcome is decided by a third party.

FIGURE 1   **Conflict–Control Procedure Continuum**

Struggle and negotiation	Mediation	Arbitration	Adjudication
Process and outcome controlled by parties	Process controlled by third party; outcome controlled by parties	Process control shared by parties and third party; outcome controlled by third party	Process and outcome controlled by third party

WHAT IS CONFLICT?

Killings and assaults "sparked" by "conflict" figure prominently in newspaper reports about violent crimes. For example, in 2004 the *Toronto Star* reported that conflict over the payment of a $10 cover charge at a Toronto nightclub resulted in the fatal shooting of one club owner and the wounding of another. The details of the incident are set out in "Conflict at a Nightclub."

Conflict at a Nightclub

The people who ran First Fridays, including Colin Moore, had posted security personnel at the door to frisk patrons for weapons or alcohol.

On the first Friday of every month, for four years, the 51-year-old father of two had been running the charity dance and social for middle-aged Guyanese Canadians. A popular man who made friends easily and inspired strong loyalties, he attended the community's functions and supported its causes.

On Friday, July 5, 2002, a beautiful summer evening, Colin was in a particularly good mood as he checked the washrooms and chatted with security as patrons started arriving.

When the gunman burst into the kitchen of HHMS Nightclub, Leisa Maillard looked straight into his eyes. "You don't have to do this, you know. If you guys want to fight, just fight," the 39-year-old mother of two pleaded. "He has a wife and kids."

But the killer pointed his pistol at her: "Shut your blood clot before I kill you," he growled, using a Jamaican insult.

Seconds later, the gunman and an accomplice shot eight .38 calibre and 9 mm slugs into Colin Moore. His brother Roger Moore escaped with a graze to his head.

The year Moore was killed, 2002, nearly half the city's 60 homicides were caused by firearms. Then, as now, the majority involved some aspect of gangs, guns and drug activity.

But the slaying of Martin Colin Moore was different in several key respects, according to the crown.

It was not a dispute between rival gangs.

It was not a drug deal gone bad. It was sparked, Crown Attorney Robin Fluerfelt told the jury, by a dispute over a $10 cover charge. Moreover, there were lots of witnesses willing to step forward, in contrast to many nightclub shootings where fear lets killers get away with murder, the prosecutor said in his final summation this week.

And there was evidence rarely heard in a Toronto courtroom. Two dramatic 911 calls that provided the jury with a haunting, first-hand account of Moore's execution in the club's small windowless kitchen.

Yesterday, after Ontario Justice David McCombs finished his charge, the jury left to begin deliberations in the trial of Gary Eunick, 29, and Leighton Hay, 21, who have pleaded not guilty to first-degree murder in Moore's death and not guilty of attempting to murder his brother Roger.

Police who investigate homicides say they are dealing with a new breed of killer today.

They're young, armed and can be set off over something as inconsequential as a perceived "dis" or being searched before entering a club. Disputes once settled with fists are now finalized with guns, with lethal consequences.

Source: Powell and Small (2004, p. B1).

A review of newspaper articles about interpersonal and inter-group conflicts published during the past three years reveals the presence of the following two elements:

1. mutual feelings of anger or hostility originating in a mutual experience of events perceived to be
   a) harmful (for example, disrespectful, frustrating, or threatening to identity), and
   b) intentionally inflicted by the other party with whom there was a fleeting or a more permanent relationship; and
2. harmful interactions (fights, assaults, and killings) resulting from angry or hostile feelings aimed at settling the conflict or expressing the feelings.

Stories of conflict that appear in the media are worthy of attention because they describe real situations in contemporary society. They are also reflected in the work of some of the social scientists whose definitions are presented in this chapter. In addition, they highlight the relationship between conflict (mutual feelings of anger or hostility) and conflict resolution (interactions aimed settling conflict). Third parties attempt to achieve durable resolutions by helping the parties in conflict reduce or eliminate their underlying hostile thoughts and feelings for each other; they do not focus exclusively on achieving agreements that merely alter conduct. Most well-informed third parties understand that the media tend to identify struggle involving assaults and killings as the usual (or invariable) method of resolving conflicts because it is far more newsworthy than other (and more frequently used) ways of attempting to settle conflicts, such as walking away or negotiating.

A review of the relevant scholarly literature on conflict reveals the presence of two frequently cited answers to the question "what is conflict?" The first answer defines conflict in terms of the thoughts and feelings of human beings. This is a *subjective* definition. The second answer defines conflict in terms of the interactions or relationships among parties that overtly express the thoughts and feelings identified by advocates of the first answer. The interaction or relationship definition is *objective*.

Objective Interaction Definitions

Interaction definitions of conflict focus on the aversarial or harmful actions exchanged by two or more persons or groups. Prominent sociologists who offer interaction definitions include Blalock and Coser. Blalock (1989, p. 7) defines conflict as "the intentional mutual exchange of negative sanctions or punitive behaviours." For Coser (1956, pp. 8, 37), conflict is "a struggle over values and claims to scarce status, power and resources in which the aims of the opponents are to neutralize, injure or eliminate rivals." Coser also states that hostile feelings increase the likelihood of conflict but do not define conflict, because conflict involves an actual struggle—that is, the use of force, fraud, or other harmful means—and because conflict "always takes place in interaction between two or more persons."

In our view, there are two problems with Coser's definition. First, practitioners guided by it would focus on one manifestation of conflict—namely, mutually harmful interactions—rather than the conflict itself—that is, the mutual subjectively experienced feelings of hostility. As a result, practitioners would attempt to achieve, or to help the parties achieve, ceasefires. Ceasefires are settlements that end harmful interactions, as opposed to more durable resolutions that change underlying thoughts and feelings and end mutually harmful interactions.

Second, while hostile feelings and thoughts are invariably present when parties engage in mutually harmful interactions, the reverse is not necessarily true. Professional boxing comes to mind. This indicates that hostile feelings rather than mutually harmful interactions are at the heart of conflict.

Seven concepts are interrelated in the legalistic relationship definition formulated by Felstiner, Abel, and Sarat (1981). The seven concepts are a perceived harmful event or incident, angry feelings, a grievance, naming, blaming, claiming, and rejection. The following example illustrates the interrelationship among these concepts. A supervisor makes a sexually explicit offer to a subordinate employee (*incident*), who is angered and upset (*feelings*) by her perception of the incident as a personal affront (*grievance* and *naming*) and an intentional violation of social and legal norms (*blaming*). She wants a transfer to another department, an apology, payment of $12,000 for the pain and suffering she experienced, and compensation for the week's wages she lost when she took time off work to recover from the effects of the incident (*claiming*). The supervisor becomes enraged (*feelings*) when he discovers the subordinate employee's allegation against him, and flatly rejects her claims. He challenges her version of the incident and dares her to take the matter to the firm's complaints committee (*rejection*). In the Felstiner, Abel, and Sarat definition, conflict emerges not when the supervisor and subordinate employee experience angry or hostile feelings toward each other, but after the subordinate employee makes claims and the supervisor rejects them.

The analysis of Felstiner, Abel, and Sarat would also support an argument that the conflict between Germany and Britain that resulted in World War I arose only after Germany rejected Britain's demand that it respect Belgium's neutrality. For Felstiner et al. (1981, p. 47), a conflict relationship emerges only following "the rejection of a claim in whole or part."

This definition also suffers as a result of its neglect of feelings. Claims grounded in an incident that a party perceives to be harmful are made and rejected, or perceived to be rejected, without engaging the feelings of the parties involved. By contrast, perceptions and feelings are central to scholars who offer subjective definitions.

Subjective Feelings Definitions

Social psychologists Pruitt and Rubin (1986, p. 4) define conflict as "perceived divergence of interests or belief that the parties' current aspirations cannot be achieved simultaneously." Feelings are associated with such perceived divergences, and sociologist Aubert (1963, p. 25) includes them in his definition of conflict as "a relationship characterized by the presence of inflicted frustration or hostility." For Aubert, feelings of frustration, antagonism, or tension are invariably present in a conflict relationship between two or more persons or groups. Although the source of these feelings is "action taken by one party which frustrates the other," Aubert excludes action and interaction from his definition of conflict. Specifically, he defines conflict as "[the] state of tension or hostility between two (or more) parties irrespective of how it originated and how it is terminated."

Simmel also defines a conflict relationship in terms of "antagonistic feelings," not in terms of antagonistic conduct (Coser, 1956, pp. 59-60). Antagonistic or hostile feelings may be useful to those who experience them, because they motivate or justify actions taken to reduce their intensity or to eliminate them. In Simmel's view (1955, p. 34), it is expedient to have hostile feelings toward opponents or enemies. For contemporary lawyer-mediators such as Bennett and Hermann (1996, p. 108), "Conflict is a state of ... tension between individuals or groups of people." This state of tension may be reduced or eliminated through the use of conflict resolution tactics that explicitly acknowledge feelings or emotions and accept their regulated expression (Bennett and Hermann, 1996, pp. 94-99; Fisher, Ury, & Patton, 1991, pp. 29-32; Gulliver, 1979, pp. 35-140; Stone, Patton, & Heen, 1999, pp. 85-108).

The subjective definitions presented so far emphasize feelings. By contrast, the subjective definition presented by Wilmot and Hocker (2001, p. 400) emphasizes cognitions or perceptions. Thus, Wilmot and Hocker define conflict as "an expressed struggle between at least two interdependent parties who perceive incompatible goals, scarce resources, and interference from others in achieving their goals." In this definition, conflict exists when the perception of scarcity, incompatible goals, and/or frustration in achieving these goals are *communicated* to each other by the interdependent parties. Here, the communication of perceptions of harm inflicted against each other by the parties creates a conflict relationship or transforms non-conflict relationships into interpersonal (or inter-group) conflict relationships. Parties who perceive mutually inflicted incidents and events as harmful but who do not communicate their perceptions to each other will not be engaged in a conflict relationship unless or until they do so. If the parties subsequently communicate with each other, the manner in which they convey their perceptions can either resolve or escalate the conflict by increasing its intensity and generality. Methods of communication include the conflict resolution techniques of struggle, negotiation, mediation, arbitration, and adjudication.

Integrative Definition

We like Wilmot and Hocker's definition because it

- situates conflict in a relationship;
- separates conflict from the strategies and tactics used in attempting to resolve conflict; and

- identifies communication as the mechanism that creates, expresses, and manages conflicts.

These attributes make this definition more useful to practitioners than the subjective and interactive definitions we have reviewed to this point. We believe that the usefulness of this definition can be increased in two ways. First, practitioners can identify perceptions of inflicted harm as the trigger for hostile feelings that lie at the core of conflict (Aubert, 1963; Simmel, 1955). In our view, conflict is present when hostile feelings aroused by perceptions of inflicted harm are communicated, and hostile feelings are present to a greater or lesser degree in all conflicts, not just "destructive conflicts." Second, practitioners can recognize that conflict resolution literature defines struggle not as conflict, but as a technique aimed at ending conflict by any means, including force or fraud (Carnevale & Pruitt, 1992). Wilmot and Hocker seem to be confounding conflict with conflict resolution when they include "expressed struggle" in their definition of conflict.

With these thoughts in mind, we propose the following definition of conflict: *a conflict relationship is a relationship characterized by mutual feelings of hostility instigated by perceptions of incompatible goals, scarce resources, and interference from others in achieving these goals.* Here conflict refers to a relationship in which divergences create feelings of anger, hostility, or frustration that the parties attempt to reduce or eliminate through action, interaction, or avoidance. Our definition integrates objective interaction and subjective feelings definitions.

Note that our integrative definition does not cover divergences that do not instigate negative feelings. These divergences we define as *disagreements*. To clarify our notion of disagreements, consider an example that involves co-owners of a cookbook store. The owners have opposing views about the kinds of books they want to sell in the future. One wants to stock the store mainly with cookbooks that promote healthy eating, while the other wants to continue to sell a wide variety of cookbooks. Both cite business-related reasons for their decisions. The co-owners negotiate an amicable agreement to end the partnership and go their separate ways. They were friends before they became business partners, and they remain friends after their business relationship ends. This example falls within our definition of disagreement and outside our definition of conflict. An example of a conflict, this one played out on a baseball field, is described in "Conflict on the Diamond."

Conflict on the Diamond

The Toronto Blue Jays and the Tampa Bay Devil Rays were angry at each other because a Rays player publicly accused the Jays of being "quitters." Angry feelings were expressed when pitchers on one team hit batters on the other team with the ball. Before a game on September 23, 2002, the umpire warned the players on both teams that he would not tolerate a pitcher's intentionally hitting an opposing player with a ball. When the Jays' ace pitcher, Roy Halladay, subsequently hit a Rays' batter, Rocco Baldelli, with a pitch, the umpire ejected Halladay from the game. A ceasefire ensued, and the players exchanged no more hits during the remaining innings of the game.

The conflict between the teams was still present, however (Baker, 2002a, p. C1). Hostilities erupted during the game played the next day. Four pitchers were ejected for hitting batters. Players from both teams rushed at each other ready to fight (Baker, 2002b, p. C1). Had the umpire called a time out during the first game, mediated the conflict, and helped the players on both teams reach an agreement that pitchers would stop hitting batters, the escalation of conflict might have been avoided. The process and outcome of mediation might have resulted in the dissipation of angry feelings and the cessation of harmful interactions. If this had happened, conflict between the two teams might have evaporated.

In applying our integrated definition of conflict to the hostilities described in "Conflict on the Diamond," perceptions of inflicted harm aroused mutual feelings of anger and frustration in members of both teams. The exchange of mutual harms instigated by these feelings maintained or escalated these feelings. It is possible that simply thinking constantly about angry feelings and their sources also maintained or escalated these feelings (Rusting & Nolen-Hoeksema, 1998). Harmful interactions may end because a party is no longer capable of retaliating, as happened when the umpire expelled the pitcher from the game. However, as long as mutually hostile feelings exist, harmful interactions may have ceased, but conflict is still present, as was evident at the game following the one in which the pitcher was removed.

Having described the difference between conflict and disagreement, we draw attention to the fact that disagreements can become conflicts and conflicts can become disagreements. Consider an example of the former: a union and management disagree about the size of a wage increase, but during negotiations emotions are aroused and negotiators on both sides make accusations that result in mutual feelings of hostility. Now, consider an example of the latter: parties bring feelings of mutual hostility with them to mediation but the mediator permits the regulated expression of emotion and redirects the attention of the parties to settling issues that are the source of their disagreement. Although conflict and disagreement are defined differently, they have something in common: the same conflict resolution procedure can be used in attempting to settle them. Examples are provided in chapter 2.

Deutsch (1973) makes a useful distinction between *manifest* and *latent* conflict. Manifest conflict refers to interactions expressing hostile feelings caused by perceptions of inflicted harm. Latent conflict refers to underlying hostile feelings caused by perceptions of inflicted harm that have not yet been overtly expressed. In our view, latent conflict is conflict. In the baseball example, it refers to mutual feelings of hostility between members of the two baseball teams.

It is possible for feelings of hostility to lie buried for years and for contemporary incidents to bring them to consciousness. This appears to have happened in China recently. Japan's current attempts to challenge China's hegemony in Asia by trying to obtain a permanent seat on the United Nations Security Council, establish closer security relations with the United States that would commit it to defending Taiwan in the event of an attack by China, and drill for oil in locations China regards as part of China, coupled with its replacing the word "massacre" with the word "incident" in textbooks that refer to Japanese troops' killing over 250,000 civilians in Nanking in 1937 "has brought old grievances to the boiling point" (Cohn, 2005, p. A2). These actions have also resulted in harmful measures being taken against Japanese people and businesses located in China. As a result, relations between China and Japan are now characterized by mutual feelings of hostility.

In sum, the integrated definition of conflict we offer builds on the subjective feelings definitions and the objective interaction definitions presented earlier by

- conceiving of perceptions of inflicted harm as causes of hostile feelings,
- identifying hostile feelings as central to the definition of conflict, and
- separating hostile feelings (conflict) from interactions aimed at eliminating them or reducing their intensity (conflict resolution).

TYPES OF CONFLICT

Many, if not most, conflicts are characterized by the perceived presence of two or more of the following instigators of hostile feelings:

- different or opposing values or ideals (in relation to such matters as democracy, security, and women's rights);
- divergent interests (in tangible things, such as land, water, and money);
- different or opposing cognitions (such as understandings of history, interpretations of statements, and perceptions of actions); and

- identity threats (such as challenges to a person's sense of self as an individual or group member who feels entitled to respect).

As an example, consider the antagonistic feelings and communications that arose between musician Paul McCartney and artist Yoko Ono, executrix of husband John Lennon's estate. McCartney and Lennon were a song-writing duo and members of the Beatles, a popular singing group. Details of the conflict that arose between Ono and McCartney after Lennon's death are set out in "Ono and McCartney in Conflict."

Ono and McCartney in Conflict

Antagonism between Ono and McCartney arose from a variety of sources:

- *Divergent interests*. McCartney and Ono disagreed about royalty payments. McCartney felt that Ono was earning more than was fair from the song *Yesterday*, which he wrote, while Ono felt that McCartney should honour the royalty payment arrangements included in the Beatles contract.
- *Divergent cognitions*. Ono felt that Lennon, as lyricist, made a significant contribution to the popularity of songs such as *Yesterday* and *Hey Jude*, but McCartney, who wrote the melodies, felt that he alone was responsible for the songs' success.
- *Identity threats*. McCartney wanted history to recognize his individual creativity and contribution to the Beatles. Ono felt that McCartney's reversal of the 40-year songwriting credit line "Lennon–McCartney" to "McCartney–Lennon" was an affront to John's identity.

On June 4, 2003, McCartney ended the conflict by agreeing not to change the Lennon–McCartney credit on some of the best-known and loved Beatles songs. McCartney is reported to have said, "Lennon and McCartney is still the rock and roll trademark I'm proud to be part of—in the order it has always been" (Scott, 2003, p. A10).

If conflict usually emerges from many causes, why have scholars and practitioners identified four different types of conflict on the basis of a single cause: values, interests, cognition, and identity? The answer to this question has three parts.

First, in some conflicts, one of these causes may be far more prominent than others. For example, many commentators characterize the antagonism between Ono and McCartney as an identity conflict because identity was the most prominent concern to both parties (Goddard, 2002, p. A43; Pritchard

& Lysaght, 2002). Second, the intensity with which antagonistic feelings are subjectively experienced varies with the kind of cause that is most prominent. Third, the conflict resolution techniques that are likely to be most effective in muting or eliminating antagonistic feelings vary with the cause that is most prominent.

Interest Conflicts

For sociologist Aubert (1963, p. 26), "a conflict of interest stems from a condition of scarcity. Both [parties] want the same thing but there is not enough [of it] for both to satisfy their wants." For Rothman (1997, p. 10), interest-based conflicts "are everyday, routine forms of ... conflict that contain elements that are relatively obvious, observable and tangible ... concrete and clearly defined and the outcomes each side seeks are bounded by the resources at stake: more or less land, wages and benefits, or military and economic power." Based on the results of her study of "armed conflict around the world," Drohan (2003, p. A15) concludes that most, if not all, of the international conflicts she studied were interest conflicts "started by greed (for timber, gold, diamonds, oil, water, tax revenues) than by historical [ethnic] grievances."

Interest-based conflicts commonly erupt as a result of feelings of anger or frustration in the field of labour relations. Union representatives frequently demand fair wages for their membership, only to find that their demands are rejected by management as unreasonable in the face of a company's poor earnings. In this example, the source of the conflict is money, which is in scarce supply relative to the needs of workers and the desires of the company for more of it. In another example, northern and southern Sudan have a significant interest in water and are involved in a conflict over the distribution of water from the Nile. The amount of water is scarce in relation to the demands of northern and southern Sudan, both of which claim they need more water than they are diverting from the Nile (Deng, 1993). For other examples of interest conflicts over scarce water and land resources, see Faure and Rubin (1993) and Kelly and Homer-Dixon (1995).

Scarcity is included in the preceding definitions of interest conflict. However, scarcity is not essential to the definition because interest conflicts can occur in the absence of scarcity or perceived scarcity. Consider an everyday conflict between a landlord and tenant. The tenant has made many complaints to the landlord about the late-night noise coming from the apartment above him, but the noise continues unabated. The tenant responds to the landlord's perceived inaction by withholding the rent. The landlord has a legitimate interest in receiving a rent cheque, and the tenant has a legitimate interest in having a quiet apartment at night. Here the parties want different, but related outcomes: a rent cheque and quiet. The parties are not involved in a conflict over the same resource that is scarce in relation to their demands for it. Yet, it is an interest conflict because the tenant's interest in quiet is threatened by the landlord's inaction, and the landlord's interest in the rent cheque is threatened by the tenant's actions. With this example in mind—and many conflicts of this kind happen every day all over the world (Fisher, Ury, & Patton, 1991; Gulliver, 1979)—we define interest conflicts as *conflicts over valued tangible resources between parties whose interests in them are divergent*. This definition includes conflicts over all tangible resources that are scarce in relation to demands for them.

Value Conflicts

Two elements are usually present in value conflicts: perceived divergences in the recognition and evaluation of cultural elements or culture as a whole, and depth of associated feelings. Aubert (1963, p. 25) defines a value conflict as being "based upon a dissensus concerning the normative status of a social object." Where the "social object" is a religion, nation, or ideology, dissensus over values contributes to religious, nationalistic, or ideological conflict.

It is relevant to point out that what sociologist Aubert defines as "values"—such as safety, freedom, peace, and justice—scholars who are trained in psychology or law refer to as "interests." Thus, psychologists Pruitt and Rubin (1986, p. 10) state that they "use the term interests where others use values or needs," and they define interests in the same way that sociologists define values—that is, "as peoples' feelings about what is basically desirable. They tend to be central to peoples' thinking and action, forming the core of their attitudes, goals and intentions." Lawyers Fisher, Ury, and Patton (1991, p. 48), authors of the influential text *Getting to Yes*, define interests in the same way that sociologists define values. None of these scholars distinguishes between ultimate and proximal (or instrumental) values.

Ultimate and Proximal Values

Sociologists define values as "ultimate ends" or "general evaluative standards about what is desirable" (Stark, 1985, p. 42). Ultimate ends are ends in themselves. Individuals and groups are motivated to achieve them solely for their own sake. Religious and nationalist values are ultimate values. *Ultimate values* are not only ends in themselves; they are also ideals that people are willing to die for or to embrace at great personal cost. For example, Jehovah's Witnesses may be willing to die if the medical interventions that would save their lives, or the lives of their children, are forbidden by their religious values. As another example, a few of the many people who embrace the religiously grounded value of the "right to life" are willing to kill doctors who demonstrate their commitment to the value of the "right to choose" by performing abortions.

Proximal values are values or ideals that are used as a means to achieve other ends. In other words, they are instrumental values. For example, the early Calvinist precursors of modern-day capitalist entrepreneurs viewed business success as desirable because it was a sign of being among the "elect" who would be "saved." Here, business success is the instrumental or proximal value; salvation is the ultimate value (Weber, 1956).

More recently, economists with the Federal Reserve Bank of St. Louis conducted a cross-national study aimed at discovering why some nations are richer than others. One of their major findings was that nations in which most or many citizens believe in and fear going to hell are richer than nations in which a minority of citizens believe in and fear going to hell. Avoiding hell is an ultimate value; wealth is a proximal value in this instance (Reuters News Agency, 2004, p. E3).

These two examples are cited to illustrate the difference between proximal and ultimate values. They should not be interpreted as evidence that suggests that religious values are responsible for the development of capitalism in Western Europe or for societal differences in economic development (Diamond, 1999; Fukuyama, 2005, p. 35).

Proximal value conflicts are conflicts over divergent values that are associated with interests that can be compromised or reconciled. Many examples of proximal value conflicts are described in *Getting to Yes*. Consider now one that was observed by Ellis during his study of the Ontario Human Rights Board mediation service. A worker whose sense of identity was threatened by the sexual advances of a supervisor was paid $17,500 by the supervisor to compensate her for pain and suffering. In this case, a human right—freedom from sexual harassment in the workplace—was arguably a proximal rather than an ultimate value for the claimant. If the right to freedom from sexual harassment, which is included in the Ontario *Human Rights Code*, was an ultimate value, she could have responded as another claimant did in a similar case. That is, she could have refused to accept the compensatory funds offered by the respondent without admitting his guilt, rejected a mediated agreement, and pursued the matter all the way to a hearing before the Human Rights Board, where her allegations would be considered on their merits.

In proximal value conflicts, values are used as a means of satisfying interests, or as a cover for them. Here, values are known to and communicated by the opposing parties. Thus, teachers who go on strike and education authorities who lock them out both cite "the welfare of students" as the reason for their actions. A similar situation exists when members of other occupations,

such as nurses, professors, janitors, airline pilots, prosecutors, police officers, and firefighters, are engaged in negotiations with their employers.

In sum, ultimate value conflicts are less likely to involve interests, whereas
proximal value conflicts usually or invariably involve interests. Interest conflicts, on the other hand, do not usually involve dissensus on values, and
may actually involve consensus on values. Thus, hostile feelings may be
present between two parties who value money, land, or water equally highly
and want a greater share of it than the other party (Aubert, 1963).

Settling Value Conflicts

In analyzing and attempting to settle value conflicts, it is important not only
to determine whether the conflict involves ultimate or proximal values, but
also to identify the kinds of values—for example, ethnic, religious, class, or
gender values—that are being used by the parties to rally support. Thus, in
the conflict in Sri Lanka involving the primarily Hindu Tamil Tigers, an
ethnic minority, and the Buddhist Sinhalese, an ethnic majority, members
of both groups use common ancestry and culture, rather than religion, to
rally support. Therefore, this conflict is primarily an ethnic, rather than a
religious, conflict.

Ultimate value conflicts involving different or opposing religious, class,
and gender values are of great historical and contemporary significance. In
analyzing conflicts over ultimate values, three points are worth noting. First,
ultimate value conflicts can involve parties who share the same religious
values. One example is the civil war in the Darfur region of Sudan between
opposing forces who both claim to be followers of Islam (Lacey, 2004).

Second, ultimate values can be used as a means of mobilizing support for
actions taken to achieve or preserve political and economic objectives. An
example is US President George W. Bush's use of national security values,
which were threatened by the 9/11 terrorist attack on the World Trade
Center, to mobilize support for attacking Iraq (Kirn, 2004).

Third, history may offer clues to settling conflicts about ultimate values.
Thus, in an analysis of the ages-old conflict between Christendom and Islam, we may search for the causes of peaceful relations during the 300 years
when Christians lived under Muslim rule, and during the 300 years when
Muslims lived under Christian rule. The historical details of these periods
are set out in "A Period of Peace."

A Period of Peace

Under Muslim rule in Andalusia (southern Spain) during the seventh
to tenth centuries, Jews, Muslims, and Christians lived in communities
that were physically and culturally separated from each other. The

result was a segmented social structure with zones occupied by majority group Muslims, minority group Jews, and minority group Christians. Pragmatic arrangements that included trading between members of the three communities and the common use of market-places, water sources, and roads linked the three communities and also brought them together in areas that were common ground. The cultural norm of *convivencia* (living together) supported these arrange-ments and the segmented social structure. As long as the society allowed minorities to live and worship as Jews and Christians, there was peace. However, when the Christian community's geographical, cultural, and especially religious barriers were breached during the 15th century, there was civil war or internecine strife between Muslims and Christians.

When Christians ruled as the majority group from the 15th to the 18th centuries, the sources of peace and internecine strife were almost identical.

Source: Wheatcroft (2004, pp. 71-75).

Cognitive Conflicts

Cognition can be implicated in conflict in three ways: through misunder-standing, disagreement over facts, and opposing world views or plans for achieving results (Provis, 1996). Cultural conflicts are an example of con-flict through misunderstanding (Brislin, 1993; Faure & Rubin, 1993). Con-sider the example in "The Feasts of Mohawk and Cree," which is described in greater detail by Brant (1990), a Mohawk psychiatrist.

The Feasts of Mohawk and Cree

The Cree are hunters and the Mohawk are farmers. The Mohawk invited the Cree to a feast. Acting in conformity with their cultural norm, the Mohawk offered their guests more food than the guests could eat, intending to preserve the leftovers for the future. The Mohawk were, after all, prudent farmers who were uncertain about how the weather would influence their food supply. The Cree, acting in conformity with a Cree cultural norm that required them to avoid offending their hosts by eating everything they were served, consumed all the food. The Mohawk were offended by the gluttony of the Cree. The Cree were offended by the Mohawk, who they believed had forced them to eat more food than was healthy. After a number of feasts with the Cree, the Mohawk learned to offer only the amount of food that the Cree could eat at a sitting. This settled the conflict.

Evidence cited by Schafer (2000) indicates that email messages are a significant source of hostile feelings and misunderstandings between senders and receivers. Email-induced cognitive conflicts are facilitated by the brevity, informality, and speed of electronically communicated messages. Unlike face-to-face communication, which is characterized by non-verbal cues, and the opportunity to rephrase or restate depending on how information is received, email communication lacks verbal fluidity and the opportunity for response by the party who receives the message. In some workplaces, the adverse consequences of email-induced conflicts have reached the point where time for face-to-face discussion is deliberately built into workspaces, and email is reserved for utilitarian communications, such as scheduling meetings.

Disagreement Over Facts

Cognitions can also be implicated in conflict through disagreement over facts. In *Bully for Brontosaurus*, Gould (1992, pp. 79-93) provides a historical context for and an example of a cognitive conflict between the US postal service and informed members of the public. The latter protested against the US postal service for failing to use the correct scientific name to refer to a dinosaur depicted on one of its stamps. The postal service labelled the stamp *Brontosaurus* (thunder lizard), whereas the dinosaur's correct scientific name is *Apatosaurus ajax* (deceptive lizard). Perhaps the postal service was confused by the fact that the paleontologist who discovered the dinosaur bones gave both names to the same dinosaur. In this case, disagreement over the facts—the correct scientific name—aroused antagonistic feelings in members of the public and the postal service.

Opposing Plans or World Views

Opposing plans for achieving desired results and differing views about the world can also lead to cognitive conflict. When, for example, the head coach and the defensive coach of the Hamilton Tiger Cat professional football team offered opposing plans for winning more games, the owners of the team settled the conflict by firing the defensive coach (Naylor, 2004, p. 3).

Huntingdon (1993, pp. 24-25) defines a civilization as "the highest level cultural grouping of people and the broadest level of cultural identity people have short of that which distinguishes humans from other species." Consider, for example, the Islamic civilization, which includes different Arabic and Islamic nations, as well as ethnic and religious groups within them. Similarly, Western civilization includes, but is not limited to, Germany, France, Britain, and Italy. According to Huntingdon, the quest for cultural dominance by civilizations will be the major source of global conflict in the near future. Conflicts between civilizations are rooted in different world views about the "relations between God and [human beings], the individual and the group, the citizen and the state, parents and children, husband and wife, as well as differing views of the relative importance of rights and responsibilities" (Huntingdon, 1993, pp. 24-25). At the present time, Israel and Palestine are proxies for Western and Islamic civilizations, respectively. However, if member nations that constitute the two civilizations become directly engaged in the conflict between Israelis and Palestinians, a clash of civilizations will ensue.

Gender, social class, and racial or ethnic conflicts within societies are examples of conflicts between social groupings that hold different world views. These views are, or may be, related to economic or political interests (Marx & Engels, 1948; Sydie, 1987).

Identity Conflicts

Tyler et al. (1998, p. 138) include maintaining identity as one of the three goals that parties in conflict aim at achieving. (The other two are achieving particular results and maintaining relationships.) Identity is defined in terms of reputation, esteem, and "face"—that is, preserving a valued face or image. Identities vary across cultures. In cultures that are based on collective ideals, "identity is defined by relationships to groups of others" (Tyler et al., 1998, pp. 138-139). In individualistic cultures, identity is defined "by what one has, owns or has accomplished" (Triandis, 1989, p. 82). Identities also vary within collectively and individualistically oriented cultures. For example, an individualistic cultures, such as Canada or the United States, some commentators believe that women's identities tend to be defined in terms of their relationships with others, and men's identities tend to be defined in terms of individual achievement (Cross & Madson, 1997).

Stone, Patton, and Heen (1999, p. 112) define identity as, "the story we tell ourselves about ourselves [about who I am or we are]." Racial or ethnic, class, gender, and national identities exist within cultures; members of cultures learn these identities from the media and through interactions with parents, teachers, religious leaders, and peers. The stories people tell themselves about themselves have a personal and a collective referent. Most people tell themselves that, at the very least, they are worthy of recognition and respect as individuals, and that the national, racial or ethnic, gender, religious, and family groups they belong to are also worthy of respect and recognition. When recognition and respect are not forthcoming—or are replaced by lack of recognition and disrespect or, in an extreme situation, stigmatization and demonization—hostile feelings arise. Disrespectful words and actions threaten identities that people value.

Frequently, people respond to threats to their identity by themselves threatening the valued identities of those who have threaten them. The result is a collective identity conflict, such as the one currently engaging the United States and the Democratic Republic of North Korea. The latter is described as part of an "axis of evil" by the president of the United States and an "Orwellian Stalinist regime ruled by a sociopath" by a prominent US senator. The United States is described as a "capitalist aggressor," a "warmonger seeking world domination," a "nuclear first striker," and a "pirate" by North Korea's leaders.

In Koring's analysis (2003, p. 7) of the sources of hostile feelings between the United States and North Korea, America's perceived lack of recognition and disrespect for North Korea underlies the value conflicts (socialism versus capitalism, inequality versus equality), and interest conflicts (control over the territory of North Korea) between the two countries.

Rothman (1997, pp. 6, 11) defines collective or group identity conflicts as "conflicts ... derived from existential (material) and underlying psychocultural concerns that are perceived as threatened or frustrated." Collective identity conflicts are

- rooted in psychological, historical, and cultural factors;
- hard to define because, unlike conflicts over tangible factors, such as land or water, they involve intangible needs that "spring from the heart";
- likely to be present whenever antagonistic feelings between the parties are partly or mainly caused by perceived identity threats that underlie or become associated with value, interest, and/or cognitive conflicts; and
- characterized by rigidly categorical perceptions of the world.

Values (for example, belief systems that regard lands as sacred or statehood, security, and autonomy as desirable), interests (for example, a requirement for territory or water) and cognitions (for example, historical interpretations that justify land claims) are all sources of antagonistic feelings between Israelis and Palestinians. However, according to Rothman (1997), identity conflicts are associated with and underlie these value, interest, and cognitive conflicts.

Rothman's analysis of the Israeli–Palestinian conflict led him to conclude that mutual name-calling (for example, terrorists, state terrorists, murderers, savages, assassins, butchers, criminals), negative stereotyping (for example, ruthless, bullying, immoral, devious, inferior), and demonization (for example, evil, inhuman, religiously fanatical) preceded or accompanied the use of struggle tactics by both parties.

The predominant sources of conflict described here are structural, cultural, and/or situational. Personality as a predominant source of conflict has been ignored. Sociologist Simmel (1955) offers a typology of conflicts that includes personality.

Realistic and Unrealistic (Personality) Conflicts

Coser is the foremost interpreter and modifier of Simmel's work on conflict. According to Coser (1965, p. 172), *realistic conflicts* "arise from specific demands within the relationship and from estimates of gains of the participants, and … are directed at the presumed frustrating object." This definition indicates that realistic conflicts involve the use of strategies and tactics that attempt to achieve specific results or outcomes. Although initiated by antagonistic feelings, realistic conflicts involve some regulation of these feelings in favour of calculating the costs and benefits of using other means of achieving a tangible result. One of these means might include changing the situational conditions that give rise to antagonistic feelings.

Levy (2004, p. B5) describes a realistic conflict between three unions and the City of Toronto. The unions were on strike because the City of Toronto intended to reduce overtime pay for work being done on 85 road projects during the summer of 2004. Both sides expressed antagonistic feelings toward each other. Union leaders calculated the immediate and longer-term costs to their membership of a reduction in overtime pay, and of striking to prevent this reduction. The City of Toronto calculated the monetary cost to the public of continuing to pay overtime at the existing rate (there was the possibility of an increase in car and truck licence fees) versus the cost of a strike to the motoring public. This conflict was eventually settled. The negotiated agreement included a reduction in overtime pay and an assurance that the proportion of road work undertaken by non-union companies would not be increased during the next five years.

Unrealistic conflicts are grounded in the personalities of individuals who are strongly motivated by the need to express feelings of hostility. These individuals do not regulate their feelings in the interest of calculating the costs and benefits of using non-aggressive means to achieve desired outcomes, because outcomes other than the expression of hostile feelings are not relevant to them. Unrealistic conflicts are often associated with marital separation or divorce. In this forum, one party's underlying hostility—a personality dimension—can be reflected in the use of aggressive strategies and tactics (name-calling, swearing, threatening, accusing, belittling) aimed not at settling issues such as child support, access, and property division, but at expressing hostile feelings toward the other party as an end in itself.

CONFLICT ANALYSIS

The discussion of conflict analysis presented here is likely to be most useful to mediators. A mediator is a third party who helps the parties involved in a conflict to settle their differences themselves. The role of a mediator is described in greater detail in chapter 3.

Conflict analysis for mediators has three major objectives: discovery, prominent source, and solution. In order to achieve these objectives, relevant information must be collected, analyzed, and integrated (Moore, 1996, p. 132).

Discovery

With the first objective of discovery in mind, a mediator collects information or data for the following specific purposes:

- to discover whether a conflict exists;
- to discover what the conflict is really about; and
- to get to know, or know better, the parties as individuals and the nature of the relationship between them.

Does a Conflict Exist?

Our integrated definition of conflict defines the conditions under which a conflicted relationship exists between two or more parties. The relevance of determining whether a conflict exists can be illustrated by the following example. Consider a junior high school in which bullying is rampant. The principal hires a mediator to mediate conflicts between the bullies and their victims. Should a mediator, who has expertise in resolving conflicts, intervene in a bully–victim relationship? The integrated definition of conflict suggests that mediation is likely to be ineffective because the bully–victim relationship is not characterized by mutual feelings of hostility; rather, it is characterized by unilateral contempt felt by the bully toward the victim and unilateral fear felt by the victim for the bully (Coloroso, 2002, p. 16). According to Coloroso, neither mediation nor teaching conflict management skills are likely to be effective in decreasing the incidence and prevalence of bullying in schools because bullying "is not about anger and not about conflict, but involves taking pleasure from another person's pain."

Mutual feelings of antagonism, hostility, or anger define a conflict relationship. These feelings are usually revealed by most parties when they tell their side of the conflict story to mediators. During the initial narrative, when each party is listening to the story told by the other, mediators attempt to avoid increasing the intensity of the conflict or prompting retaliation by inviting the parties to use I-statements rather than You-statements. (Contrast the impact of "I felt very angry because I felt I was being cheated"—an

I-statement—with "I am very angry with this jerk because she's a liar and a cheat"—a You-statement, which takes the form of a personal attack (Bennett & Hermann, 1996, p. 96).

If a mediator perceives that one party—for example, a worker—is reluctant to reveal his feelings in the presence of the other party—his employer—either party may call a caucus. A caucus is a private meeting between the mediator and each of the parties in which the mediator attempts to elicit feelings by asking open-ended questions, such as "What are your feelings about the matter that brought you here today?" or "Now that we are in a private meeting, are there any feelings you have about your employer that you are willing to share with me so I can better understand your relationship with her and the direction in which it is moving?"

What Is the Conflict Really About?

According to Moore (1996, p. 132), a reliable answer to this question requires the collection of data from a number of sources, using a variety of methods and then cross-checking the information obtained. Thus, in attempting to discover contemporary instigators of hostile communications between North Korea and the United States, a researcher might read books and articles about the leaders of the two countries, the relationship between them, the social and political systems of the two countries, their culture, their economic and military resources, and their allies. The researcher might also consult an atlas to determine the geographical and geopolitical location of the two nations. He could read media accounts of intentions and motivations attributed to the leaders of one country by the leaders of the other, and examine critical documents such as the *Treaty on the Non-Proliferation of Nuclear Weapons* (1970) that was ratified by both countries. In addition, some researchers might be able to interview leaders in both countries and observe their demeanour and body language when they are talking publicly and privately about each other. In collecting information from the leaders of the two countries, the researcher could conclude that conflict exists in their hearts and minds, and as a result, the objective historical and contemporary "facts" of the case are less relevant than the way the facts are interpreted by them.

Interpretations and feelings are revealed in the narratives provided by the parties involved in conflicts (Winslade & Monk, 2001). The narratives of the parties in a relationship that is characterized by mutually hostile feelings reveal nothing about the conflict between them for at least three reasons:

1. *Loss of memory.* The parties may not remember relevant details.
2. *Lack of awareness of the causes of conflict.* The parties may not know or be aware of the real or underlying sources of the conflict between them.

3. *Partisan information.* The information revealed in the parties' narratives may be selected for partisan reasons. Narratives almost always position the narrator as the one who is endangered by the interest, value, cognitive, or identity threats of the other party. Narratives, then, are usually provided from the perspective of the narrator as victim (Blalock, 1989).

Selective partisan narratives provided by the parties "construct the conflict and its sources in the telling" (Winslade & Monk, 2001, p. 70). Narrators of conflict stories usually construct their narratives to make legitimate both the general position of narrator as victims and the specific positions they take on the issues involved. According to Fisher, Ury, and Patton (1991, p. 41), underlying stated positions are interests or values. The real causes of conflicts are interests (needs, desires, concerns, and fears) that cannot be reconciled. Interests are "the silent movers behind the hubbub of positions," silent because the parties are usually unaware of them. Consider an example of conflict between two neighbours: a 70-year-old widow and a 30-year-old single man who bring their conflict to mediation. The widow's position is that the young man must move out because he has too many noisy parties and creates even more noise by revving his motorcycle. The young man's position is he has tried to keep the noise down but his neighbour persists in complaining about his motorcycle and his noisy friends, who in one instance turned out to be his parents. By asking the widow about why she is concerned about the parties and the noise and the man about why he is concerned about the complaint made by his neighbour, the mediator discovers that the interest underlying the widow's position is fear, and the interest underlying the young man's position is autonomy. He, like the widow, wants to live his life free from what he perceives as harassment.

Whereas narrators voluntarily disclose information about issues and positions, mediators must usually elicit information about underlying interests by asking appropriate questions. In direct questioning, mediators ask the parties why they want or need the outcomes identified in their stated positions. Bennett and Hermann (1996, p. 58) suggest that parties may reveal their underlying interests if mediators ask questions such as the following: Why is this important to you? How will this proposal meet your needs? What are you trying to accomplish by taking this position?

Who Are the Parties and What Is Their Relationship?
Mediators may collect information about individuals and their relationships in the following ways:

- *Research and observation.* Collect relevant background information about the parties and observe them both as one of them is communicating verbally or non-verbally.
- *Listening.* Active listening involves eye contact and concentration on the communicator and what is being communicated. When listening, do not rehearse possible interventions or reach conclusions. Listen without judging the speaker. Be patient, and convey your patience verbally and non-verbally.
- *Questioning.* Question the parties without conveying the impression that you are interrogating them by using open-ended questions, such as "What can you tell me about your relationship before the conflict took place?" and "How important to you is your relationship at the present time?" Also use fact-finding questions, such as "When did you first notice a change in your relationship?" A more challenging form of questioning involves the use of leading questions, such as "Didn't you say that your relationship ended before the incident that brought you here occurred?"
- *Paraphrasing.* Accurate paraphrasing, defined as "summarizing key informational, emotional or especially significant elements of the speakers message shortly after it has been delivered" (Bennett & Hermann, 1996, p. 82), confirms that the mediator has been listening attentively and "clarifies and ensures understanding" of statements made about a relationship (Bennett & Hermann, 1996, p. 91).
- *Summarizing.* Accurate summarizing, defined as "establishing [a] more long-term understanding" of relationship information, "synthesizing and reviewing important [relationship] information ... and making sure that the parties fully understand what has been stated before moving on to consider other issues" (Bennett & Hermann, 1996, p. 91), also confirms that the mediator has been listening.

Prominent Source

A mediator's second objective is to define the type of conflict the parties are involved in. In our view, the mediator meets this objective when she discovers the presence, relative prominence, and intermingling of divergent values, competing interests, different cognitions, and/or identity threats as potential or actual sources of conflicts. Analyzing the data collected by using active listening and questioning skills assists the mediator in discerning the nature of the conflict. The mediator may conclude that one source is clearly prominent when it is

- identified as a source by all parties (consensus);
- referred to more frequently than other sources (frequency);

- referred to with greater emotional intensity than other sources (emotionality); and
- implicit in, or reliably inferable from, several stated positions on the same or different issues (triangulation).

Where the same source underlies a number of stated positions, consensus, frequency, emotionality, and triangulation are the criteria used in determining the relative prominence of the four major sources of conflicts. If one source is found to be clearly prominent, that source defines the type of conflict that the parties are involved in.

Solution

A mediator's third objective is to match the information he has discovered about the individuals involved in the conflict, their relationship, and the type and intensity of the conflict with procedures, strategies, and tactics that are likely to settle or resolve the conflict most effectively (Rothman, 1997, p. 11).

Some scholars and practitioners state that relationship issues underlie all conflicts, and that mediators should use relationship-mending skills before facilitating negotiations that are aimed at solving substantive problems (Winslade & Monk, 2001, pp. 71-72). Others do not give priority to relationship-mending skills; rather, they maintain that people and relationships must be separated from substantive problem solving, and that different skills must be used in addressing relationship and problem-solving issues (Fisher, Ury, & Patton, 1991).

Ultimate value conflicts, including identity conflicts, are difficult to settle or resolve through bargaining and compromise. Scholars such as Rothman (1997, p. 9) advocate a two-stage process in which dialogue precedes negotiations aimed at settling conflicts over tangible resources. Guided by a mediator or facilitator, dialogue reveals "what adversaries care about most deeply and why, [when] disputants ... begin to speak so that their opponents can listen, and listen so that their opponents can speak." Through dialogue, values may be reconciled in practical ways. For example, dialogue that reconciles divergent values relating to safety, control, and identity through acceptance of a superordinate goal—peace—may prepare the way for negotiations that reconcile the divergent interests of Israelis and Palestinians in the distribution of water—a resource that is scarce relative to both parties' demands for it.

Cognitive conflicts rooted in misunderstandings may be settled most effectively by mediators who adopt a "communications frame." These frames are "interpretative schemes that mediators use to make sense of and organize their activities while at work on a dispute" (Kolb & Kressel, 1994, pp. 469, 475). According to these authors, mediators who adopt a communications frame view no or poor communication as the major cause of misunderstanding and antagonism. Mediators attempt to increase understanding by getting the parties to communicate with each other, or to communicate more effectively. The expected outcomes of improved communication are "better understanding and cooperation" (Kolb & Kressel, 1994, p. 469) aimed at settling substantive problems.

CONFLICT ANALYSIS ILLUSTRATED

The conflict analysis that follows was based on information provided by *Power: One River, Two Nations* (1998), a film produced by the National Film Board of Canada.

In 1971, Hydro-Quebec, an organization created and supported by the government of Quebec, implemented phase 1 of the James Bay project. The purpose of this project was to generate large amounts of hydroelectric power by damming the Le Grande River, which flowed through Cree land. The Cree signed a contract with Hydro-Quebec that permitted it to dam the river in return for monetary compensation. The damming flooded vast amounts of land and caused a great deal of damage to the environment. In addition, it destroyed communities and traditional ways of life. In 1989, phase 2 of the James Bay project was scheduled for implementation. This phase proposed to dam the Great Whale River and to sell a significant amount of the electricity it generated to New York and Massachusetts.

Is There a Conflict?

Analysis of relations between the resident Cree and Hydro-Quebec reveals that a conflict did exist because the relationship between the parties was characterized by mutual frustration and antagonism. These feelings were rooted in Hydro-Quebec's perception that the Cree—a small nation of 15,000—were frustrating Quebec's economic development, upon which the lives of over 7 million Quebecers depended. The feelings of the Cree were rooted in both process and outcome. Their land and their lives were going to be changed by a unilateral decision to dam the Great Whale River. Moreover, they believed that the harmful social and environmental consequences of the first phase of the James Bay projected would be inflicted upon them again if phase 2 were implemented. Hydro-Quebec was well aware of the adverse consequences, and yet it was determined to proceed.

What Is the Conflict Really About?

Hydro-Quebec's position was grounded in a rationale that emphasized the benefits of economic development for all Quebecers, including the Cree.

The Cree's opposition was grounded in a rationale that emphasized the preservation of land that they regarded as sacred and that supported their traditional lifestyle.

Underlying these polarized positions was the ultimate value of national autonomy. The Cree regard themselves as a nation, and nations decide matters relating to the development of their own land. Hydro-Quebec, like the separatist Parti Québécois government in power at the time, regarded Quebec as a nation that included Cree land within its borders. The underlying cause of the conflict then was dissensus over the value of national status for the Cree and Quebec.

Who Are the Parties and What Is Their Relationship?

The parties are the Cree of northern Quebec and Hydro-Quebec, an organization created and supported by the provincial government. Matthew Coon Come was grand chief of the Cree and a leader of the Cree negotiating team. Le Hir was the CEO of Hydro-Quebec and leader of its negotiating team. Hydro-Quebec regarded its relationship with the Cree as contractual because both parties had signed the contract governing phase 1 of the James Bay project in which the Cree received monetary compensation in return for permitting Hydro-Quebec to produce hydroelectric power. The Cree perceived the relationship with Hydro-Quebec as one in which they were victims of manipulation and exploitation by Hydro-Quebec.

The relationship between the Cree and Hydro-Quebec is a continuing one. With the election of Jacques Parizeau and a separatist government in 1994, the relationship between the Cree and the Quebec government changed. Quebec became far more sensitive to the wishes of the Cree because it needed Cree support for its separatist aspirations. One result of this changed relationship was the indefinite postponement of the second phase of the James Bay project by the Quebec government in 1995.

Prominent Source

Consensus, frequency, emotionality, and especially triangulation reveal that this is a value conflict. This conclusion is validated by the "nation-to-nation" agreement between the Cree and the separatist government of Quebec that was in power when the agreement was signed seven years after the conflict ended. Under the terms of this agreement, a hydroelectric project will be constructed on the Rupert and Eastmain rivers in the James Bay area, and the employment and other economic benefits will be shared between two "fully autonomous partners." According to Bernard Landry, premier of Quebec at the time, the agreement between the Quebec government and the Cree Grand Council "opens the way to a new era of a nation-to-nation relationship between the Crees and Quebec" (Seguin, 2002).

Caveats

Before embarking on any conflict analysis, a mediator should keep two caveats in mind:

1. A conflict can actually be about what the parties say it is about.
2. Conceptions of conflict influence the attempts of negotiators and mediators to deal with instances of conflict. Therefore, a mediator should be fully aware of how he conceives of conflict in general, as well as how he conceives of the specific conflict before him.

CHAPTER SUMMARY

This chapter began with an introduction to the topic of conflict, drawing attention to its normality, its beneficial and harmful consequences, and the terminological confusion between "conflicts" and "disputes." We eliminated this confusion by consistently using one concept—conflict—in this book, and we defined this concept. We discussed two types of definitions, both of which viewed conflict as existing in the context of a relationship. Objective definitions focused on mutually harmful interactions between parties. Subjective definitions focused on mutual feelings of hostility between parties. The integrated definition we formulated included both hostile feelings and harmful interactions. We then identified four types of conflicts: interest, value, cognitive, and identity conflicts. Because these four factors are often intermingled, we introduced conflict analysis, which is aimed at identifying which factor dominates any given conflict. Finally, we applied conflict analysis to a contemporary conflict between the Cree of northern Quebec and Hydro-Quebec.

RECOMMENDED READING

Breashears, D. (1999). *High exposure: An enduring passion for Everest and unforgiving places.* New York: Simon & Shuster. This book identifies the sources of conflict among climbers on the slopes of Mt. Everest and describes how conflicts are settled.

De Villiers, M. (1999). *Water.* Toronto: Stoddart. This book describes how values and interests are implicated in conflicts over water, and concludes that water will become one of the major sources of international conflict in the 21st century.

Ellickson, R. (1991). *Order without law: How neighbours settle disputes* (2nd ed.). Cambridge, MA: Harvard University Press. This book describes how conflicts between ranchers in Shasta County are settled by the ranchers themselves, even when the conflicts involve violations of the law.

Wrong, D. (1995). *The problem of order: What unites and divides society.* This prize-winning book identifies and analyzes the fundamental sources of conflict and coercion in society.

FILMS, VIDEOS, AND DVDs

Conflict in the school community: Vignettes. Available from triune@triune.ca or http://www.triune.ca.

The lofters. Video describing a violent attempt to settle a conflict that emerged during the taping of a "reality show." Available from desellis@yorku.ca (60 minutes).

Neighbourhood conflicts. Available from CBS, *48 Hours* (60 minutes).

Sexual harassment: Crossing the line. Available from http://www.films.com (30 minutes).

War of the Roses. Feature film directed by Danny DeVito, starring Michael Douglas and Kathleen Turner (130 minutes)

WEBSITES

Alliance for International Conflict Prevention and Resolution. http://www.aicpr.org. This website provides information about international peace building.

Appalshop. http://www.appalshop.org. The Kentucky Appalshop website provides access to videotapes of real-life conflicts in North America.

Association for the Socioeconomic Analysis of Development and International Conflict. http://www.geocities.com/sociohistory/asadi.htm. This website focuses on international conflict and links it with economic development.

International Crisis Group. http://www.crisisweb.org. The Brussels-based group's website offers monthly summaries of current or potential conflicts all over the world and assesses the likelihood of settlement or escalation.

CHAPTER TWO

Resolving Conflict: Struggle and Negotiation

> **Chapter Objectives**
>
> *Define struggle.*
>
> *Describe the advantages and disadvantages of using struggle to settle conflicts.*
>
> *Define negotiation.*
>
> *Describe the advantages and disadvantages of using negotiation to settle conflicts.*
>
> *Differentiate between distributive and integrative negotiation.*
>
> *Describe positional bargaining, and identify its strengths and weaknesses.*
>
> *Describe principled negotiation, and identify its strengths and weaknesses.*
>
> *Describe cyclical–developmental negotiation, and identify its strengths and weaknesses.*

APPROACHES TO CONFLICT RESOLUTION

In *Getting Disputes Resolved* (1993), Ury, Brett, and Goldberg introduce three approaches to resolving conflicts. The first approach is "reconciling interests." Conflicts can be resolved when the needs, concerns, fears, and wants underlying the stated positions of the parties are addressed and reconciled. The second approach is "determining who is right." Conflicts can also be resolved when the stated positions or claims of one party are supported by legal requirements, social norms, or other legitimate standards, such as "accepted industry practice." The third approach is "wielding power." Conflicts can also be resolved when one party inflicts more personal, material, or social harm on the other than the other can inflict on it, thereby forcing it to give up or give way.

We build on Ury, Brett, and Goldberg's (1993) widely cited approaches to conflict resolution in four ways:

1. *Adding positional bargaining.* We add positional bargaining, also referred to as distributive negotiation in this book (Barry & Friedman, 1998; Fisher, Ury, & Patton, 1991) to the list of approaches. Positional bargaining aims at reconciling positions. It is the most widely used approach to settling conflict (Gulliver, 1979).

2. *Adding the cyclical–developmental model.* We add Gulliver's (1979) "cyclical–developmental" model of negotiation, which reconciles both interests and positions. This model is cross-cultural, and it identifies mechanisms within negotiation that propel the parties toward agreement.

3. *Replacing power with struggle.* All approaches to conflict and conflict resolution view power as a significant component. Power involves more than "acts of aggression such as sabotage or physical attack, and withholding benefits that derive from a relationship, as when employees withhold their labor during a strike" (Ury, Brett, & Goldberg, 1993, p. 8). It can also involve one party's achieving her goals by rewarding the other party (Gulliver, 1979).

   When a party involved in a conflict attempts to prevail by doing more damage to the other party than the other party can do to him, we define the situation as "struggle," following Carnevale and Pruitt (1992). In this book, then, struggle (mutually punishing acts) replaces power (rewarding and punishing acts) as an approach to settling conflicts. We include struggle in our description of conflict resolution because of its historical and contemporary significance as a means of settling conflicts.

4. *Treating third-party procedures separately.* Mediation—a non-adversarial approach—and adjudication—an adversarial approach to conflict resolution—are not included among the three approaches identified by Ury, Brett, and Goldberg (1993). We describe conflict resolution procedures involving third parties—mediation, arbitration, and adjudication—in chapter 3. In this chapter we focus on the two procedures in which the parties themselves attempt to settle conflicts: struggle and negotiation.

STRUGGLE

Carnevale and Pruitt (1992, p. 532) define "struggle" as a process or procedure that "can take the form of physical combat (military battles, strikes), wars of words (shouting matches), political contest (vying for allies) or taking unilateral advantage (theft)." In *Guns, Germs, and Steel: The Fates of Human Societies*, Diamond (1999, pp. 289-291) acknowledges that wars, engaged in for a variety of motives, "have been a constant part of history." During the past 13,000 years, however, evidence indicates that coercive amalgamation emerged as a significant spur to the use of struggle tactics. Coercive amalgamation is a process in which larger groups coerce smaller groups into merging with them to form societies "under the threat of force or by actual conquest" (p. 289). Within and between societies, then, struggle involves the threat or mutual use of force and/or fraud.

Civil wars in Somalia, Sudan, Congo, and Bosnia, fighting between Israelis and Palestinians, and US-led wars against Iraq may be located at one extreme of the continuum of struggle. At other points on this continuum, we can locate reciprocal killings and woundings by members of organized crime and street gangs aimed at settling conflicts over territory, money, or affronts to honour, and homicides and assaults by other members of society aimed at settling arguments over these and many other matters. We can also locate strikes by workers and lockouts by management aimed at "winning" workplace conflicts, and name-calling and threats made by parties who are motivated to settle conflicts through intimidation.

Can struggle—at any point on the continuum—produce agreement? Yes it can, and without discussion of the issues or sources of the conflict. In Hobbes's *Leviathan* (1651, p. 143), the routine use of force and fraud by citizens produces a contract or covenant. This covenant establishes a sovereign (the state) that keeps the peace by the actual or threatened use of overwhelming coercive and punitive force. Today, criminal law, enforced by agents of the state such as police officers, is used to deter violent and economic crimes. Struggle can also help end conflicts by revealing the need for third-party intervention. Thus, a costly airline strike that results in violence on the picket line may move the government to intervene by coercing the parties to arbitrate an end to the conflict. In a different context, among the Azande in Africa, one or both parties involved in a conflict may resort to violence in order to have the conflict mediated by a tribal elder (Black, 1983).

In addition to producing peace by necessitating third-party intervention, struggle, according to the Luttwak thesis (1999, p. 36), can also produce peace "when all belligerents become exhausted or when one wins decisively." Ceasefires, imposed or otherwise brought about by third parties, help prolong conflict, according to this thesis, by allowing "belligerents [to] reconstitute and rearm their forces."

Luttwak's thesis has been criticized on moral and empirical grounds (*The Economist*, 1999, pp. 36-44), but the author makes a valid point to this extent:

parties involved in conflicts frequently use struggle as a means of establishing their relative power and often continue struggling until they reach a point when one or both find giving in, or giving way, preferable to perpetuating their struggle. Not infrequently, struggle follows negotiation, which follows struggle, with the outcome of the negotiation being influenced by the outcome of the struggle that preceded it. In labour relations conflicts, struggle tactics—such as strikes and lockouts—are used to determine the relative capacities of the parties to inflict punishment on each other and to endure the punishments inflicted by the other side. The parties' punishment-inflicting and punishment-enduring power are often reflected in their opening positions and the results of the negotiations that inevitably follow (McCarthy, 1995).

The reciprocal use of punishing struggle tactics can be observed in the 2002–2003 conflict between the Toronto Catholic School Board and the Ontario English Catholic Teachers' Association (OECTA). The details of this conflict are set out in "Punishing Struggle Tactics: Fallout from a Strike and Lockout." Note the serious consequences suffered by people who are not otherwise involved in the conflict.

Punishing Struggle Tactics: Fallout from a Strike and Lockout

Teachers employed by the Toronto Catholic School Board had been working without a contract since August 31, 2002. The parties had been in negotiation for almost nine months, with the teachers asking for an increase in pay and benefits that amounted to nearly 9 percent over two years. The board was offering a 6 percent increase over two years because the provincial government was funding only a 3 percent annual increase.

Displeased with their failure to negotiate an increase that exceeded 6 percent, OECTA started a work-to-rule campaign on May 4, 2003. Working to rule involved "no supervision of extra-curricular activities, including graduations and field trips and overseeing standardized provincial tests" (Kalinowski, 2003). On May 14, 2003, the board threatened to lock the teachers out if they did not return to the bargaining table and negotiate a settlement by May 15. Negotiations resumed, but the parties failed to reach a settlement before the deadline arrived. On May 16, the board locked the teachers out.

Teachers were losing money because the strike pay they received from their association was far lower than their usual salaries. Sixty-nine thousand students had no classes to go to, and their parents were scrambling to make arrangements for the care of their children. Both sides were punishing each other, and it appeared that the side that was less able to absorb the punishment would initiate a return to the bargaining table, unless the provincial government intervened by requiring the parties to arbitrate an end to their conflict. Government intervention of this nature was unlikely because the government believed poll results that showed greater public support for legislation to prevent teacher strikes and board lockouts, than for respecting the current labour relations process. Hence, the government was more likely to legislate the teachers back to work, prohibit them from working to rule, and send the conflict to binding arbitration.

In July 2003, the case was sent to mediation–arbitration. (Mediation–arbitration is discussed further in chapter 3.) Negotiations yielded an agreement that covered three years and included a 3 percent salary increase in the first and second year and a 2 percent increase in the third year. OECTA's opening position was 9 percent over two years, and its members received 8 percent over three years. (The board's opening position was 6 percent over two years.) Terms of the agreement also included changes in supervision duties desired by OECTA.

Instead of alternating between struggle and negotiation, should governments refuse to negotiate and simply use struggle tactics, such as shooting hostage takers? Following the September 2004 Beslan hostage-taking incident in Russia in which over 330 children, parents, teachers, and Chechen hostage takers were killed, Russian President Vladimir Putin preferred to use struggle tactics over negotiation. "No one," he stated, "has a moral right to tell us to talk to child-killers" (Contenda, 2004, p. A3). Putin justified the "collateral damage" at Beslan—over 16 parents, children, and teachers killed for every hostage taker killed or captured—on the grounds of specific and general deterrence. Specific deterrence was aimed at deterring the hostage takers who actually participated in the event from engaging in further hostage takings. General deterrence was aimed at deterring other hostage takers from using hostage taking as a means of achieving their goals.

A number of newspaper editors, researchers, and analysts based in Moscow, France, England, and Germany contend that the use of struggle tactics increases the likelihood of more serious hostage-taking incidents (Contenda, 2004). They point out that the shooting and capturing of Chechen hostage takers has not stopped hostage taking by Chechen separatists. Wines (2004) cites other evidence supporting negotiation over struggle as a way of ending hostage takings. In the Wines article, Picco, a hostage negotiator for the United Nations, states that negotiation is likely to peacefully settle hostage-taking incidents if hostage takers have specific short-term tactical objectives, such as the release of jailed comrades. He believes it is unlikely to settle conflicts if the hostage takers have generalized long-term strategic goals, such as "the destruction of Western values." Struggle can settle both tactically and strategically motivated hostage takings with loss of life, injuries, and destruction of property.

Where struggle does not actually occur, its shadow can influence the course and outcome of negotiations. Hostage negotiations where heavily armed police officers surround or seal off the location in which negotiations are taking place provide an extreme example of negotiations conducted in the shadow of struggle (Freed, 2003). More generally, force and fraud are ever-present possibilities in social interaction in the wider society and in interaction aimed at ending conflicts.

Two factors increase the likelihood of struggle:

1. *Absence of rules.* The absence of struggle-regulating rules and/or an effective rule enforcement body increases the likelihood of struggle. Inter-state conflicts, civil wars, and internecine struggles within organized criminal groupings are examples of situations that lack rules (Asbury, 1927).
2. *Win–lose conflicts.* Territorial conflicts between nation states or criminal groups are examples of conflicts that are, or are perceived to be, win–lose conflicts (Henderson, 1997).

Evaluation

The struggle tactics used by Israelis and Palestinians (Ross, 2004), Ontario teachers' associations and school boards (Contenda, 2004), and union and management in the Caney Creek coal mines (Ury, Brett, & Goldberg, 1993) do not support Luttwak's "give struggle a chance" hypothesis. Based on his experience as a Middle East peace envoy for the elder George Bush and Bill Clinton, Ross (2004, p. 779) reached the following conclusion: "The Israelis with all their military power cannot extinguish Palestinian aspirations. The Palestinians with all their anger and use of terror will not succeed in forcing the Israelis to submit through violence." In fact, the use of struggle tactics by parties involved in conflicts seems to escalate them. For example, Ury, Brett, and Goldberg (1993, p. 101) found that the use of struggle tactics over a two-year period escalated a coal-mining conflict to the point that it was likely that the mine would shut down and a national coal strike would ensue.

Based on these findings, we propose the following modifications or extensions to Luttwak's thesis:

1. War may eventually produce and maintain social order if one party has far greater military and economic resources and is willing to use them to impose order.
2. The hegemony or rule of the winning party is legitimated by time and the gradual amalgamation of the cultures of the winning and losing parties.

Where the parties' ability and willingness to punish each other are relatively equal and where the parties perceive their conflict to be win–lose in nature, the use of struggle tactics will result in mutual harm and, in the extreme, mutual annihilation.

Compared with negotiation, the major disadvantage of struggle is the cost that it exacts on the parties in terms of time, stress, and money, for example. Struggle has higher transaction costs than negotiation because the parties use more of their finite resources in exchanges designed to damage each other. Included in the damage is the harm done to relationships. In addition, win–win outcomes are more difficult to discover than win–lose outcomes. Minimizing transaction costs and discovering win–win situations tend to be less important to persons, groups, and nations that

- mistrust each other;
- believe that struggle will reliably or quickly produce the result they want, directly or indirectly;
- cannot or will not communicate with each other; and
- place a high value on "loss of face," and associate struggle with achieving or demonstrating "face."

Taken together, the motivational, cognitive, value, attitudinal, and situational factors noted here help account for the widespread choice of struggle as a way of ending conflicts (Hanson, 2003). However, most people who work in the conflict resolution field regard struggle as an undesirable way of attempting to end conflicts. They must be pleased to learn that worldwide the number of major wars decreased from 33 in 1991 to 19 in 2003, and that fewer people were killed in 2003 (20,000) than in any year since World War II ended in 1945 (Stockholm International Peace Research Institute, 2004).

NEGOTIATION

What is negotiation? Before embarking on our discussion of various answers to this question, we would like to describe "impression management." This is a technique engaged in by negotiators everywhere, regardless of the type of negotiations in which they are involved.

Impression Management

Communication is a generic social process. People communicate during conversations, debates, and dialogues. They use communication as a means of participating in meetings, games, seminars, and negotiations. Negotiation differs from other forms of communication in a number of important ways, but it also shares with them a motivational orientation that is heightened in negotiation. Goffman (1959) calls this orientation "impression management."

When they communicate verbally and non-verbally, human beings are expressing themselves. There are two fundamentally different kinds of human expression: the expression that individuals *give*, and the expressions they *give off*. Expressions that people give are verbal communications that can be controlled or manipulated, or that others believe can be controlled or manipulated. Expressions that people give off are non-verbal communications or spontaneous verbal communications that are, or that others believe to be, less subject to control or manipulation. Knowing that individuals tend to give expressions that favour themselves, others use the expressions that individuals give off—expressions that are less easily manipulated or controlled—to check on the truth or validity of the expressions that they give. Knowing this, individuals sometimes try to control or manipulate the "uncontrollable" expressions they give off in order to more reliably create and maintain impressions that favour themselves. Thus, writes Goffman (1959, p. 4), "When an individual appears in the presence of others, there will usually be some reason for him to mobilize his verbal and non-verbal intentional and unintentional activity so that it will convey an impression to others which is in his interest to convey." An example of impression management appears in "Impression Management While Dropping in for Tea."

Impression Management While Dropping in for Tea

When a neighbour dropped in to have a cup of tea, he would ordinarily wear at least a hint of an expectant warm smile as he passed through the door into the cottage. Since it was possible to observe the visitor unobserved as he approached the house, islanders sometimes took pleasure in watching the visitor drop whatever expression he was manifesting and replace it with a sociable one just before reaching the door. Some visitors in appreciating that this examination was occurring would adopt a social face a long distance from the house, thus ensuring the projection of a constant image.

Source: Goffman (1959, p. 8).

Impression management characterizes all negotiations, but the impressions conveyed are different during the phases of negotiation. As you will see below, some negotiations—such as divorce negotiations between cooperative parents—are mainly integrative; others—such as those involving commercial transactions—are mainly distributive. Impressions conveyed during negotiations that are mainly integrative and negotiations that are mainly distributive also tend to be different.

Distributive and Integrative Negotiation

Why Choose Negotiation?

Unilateral action can settle conflicts. The prime minister of Israel, Ariel Sharon, has stated that the unilateral actions he initiated—building a security barrier to separate Gaza and the West Bank from Israel and withdrawing settlers from Gaza—will help settle the Israeli–Palestinian conflict. It may settle the conflict, as Gee (2004) suggests, but the settlement may not be a durable one because it was not the product of a negotiated agreement. This conflict has lasted for over 50 years, and a number of attempts have been made to negotiate a peaceful settlement. Presumably, Sharon has now decided that the conditions favouring negotiation over unilateral action no longer prevail.

Negotiation is often chosen when both parties

- believe they cannot get what they want unilaterally,
- have some conflicting and some shared interests,
- are in a stalemate that harms them both, and
- perceive negotiation to be the best way of attempting to end the conflict.

If the parties decide to negotiate, their negotiations will usually involve two phases: integrative and distributive. Some negotiations, however, may be primarily or exclusively distributive or integrative.

Distributive Negotiation

Distributive negotiation is a process aimed at achieving outcomes desired by each participating party where the parties are relatively indifferent to the outcomes achieved by the other parties (Barry & Friedman, 1998). The results of distributive negotiations can be positive for both parties. For example, Party A may give way on an issue that is important to Party B, and in return, Party B gives way on an issue that is important to Party A. An example, from Canadian party politics is set out in "Distributive Negotiations in Party Politics."

Distributive Negotiations in Party Politics

During negotiations aimed at merging the Canadian Alliance and Progressive Conservative parties, Stephen Harper, leader of the Alliance, wanted the votes of riding associations with more members to carry greater weight in electing the leader of the new party. Peter MacKay, leader of the Progressive Conservatives, wanted the votes from each riding association to be given equal weight in electing the leader. Harper accepted MacKay's proposal, but in return he wanted MacKay to accept his proposal that the new party's policies would be decided by the Alliance's usual one person/one vote method and the support of a majority of the party's provincial associations. MacKay agreed, believing his chances of being elected leader would increase if each riding association had equal voting weight. Harper accepted MacKay's proposal, believing his insistence on traditional Alliance voting procedures would increase his chances of being elected leader, even if the riding associations had equal voting weight (Laghi & Fagan, 2003, p. 1). This agreement produced symmetric, or win–win, outcomes for Harper and MacKay because they each achieved the result they desired.

The Harper–MacKay negotiation also yielded asymmetric, or win–lose, outcomes for other parties. For example, David Orchard, a member of the Progressive Conservatives who opposed the merger with the Alliance, perceived it to be a win–lose outcome, with the Progressive Conservatives being the loser and the Alliance being the winner.

Distributive negotiation is called "distributive" because it segregates, rather than integrates, the needs and interests of the parties involved. For David Orchard, in the Alliance–PC negotiations described in "Distributive Negotiations in Party Politics," negotiations that led to the merger were distributive because the values and interests of the two parties were different and opposing (segregated); moreover, the negotiated agreement reflected Alliance, rather than Progressive Conservative, values and interests.

Distributive negotiation is a process that emphasizes

- strategic disclosure and manipulation of information by the parties;
- each party's concern with it's own interests;
- distribution of value (getting a larger slice of a pie that is perceived to be fixed in size), rather than creation of value (enlarging the pie);
- competition; and
- bargaining.

Integrative Negotiation

Integrative negotiation is a process aimed at achieving results that serve the interests of all parties. In other words, integrative negotiation is aimed at achieving win–win outcomes. The process is called "integrative" because it integrates, rather than segregates, the needs and interests of the parties. Integrative negotiation, which is more cognitively complex than distributive negotiation, emphasizes

- full disclosure of relevant information by the parties;
- each party's concern with the interests of all parties;
- the creation of value (enlarging the pie), rather than the distribution of value (getting a larger slice of a pie that is perceived to be fixed in size); and
- collaboration.

Distributive negotiation is less cognitively complex than integrative negotiation. It is far easier to distribute value through the manipulation of information and the process of bargaining than to create value through problem solving and distribute it to all parties. At the same time, however, distributive negotiations can yield agreements through the creation of elegant formulas that satisfy the most important interests the negotiating parties, and producing these formulas is a complex task.

Impression Management in Integrative and Distributive Negotiation

Impression management occurs in both integrative and distributive negotiation. However, as we noted earlier, the impressions that integrative and distributive negotiators attempt to convey are quite different.

Principled negotiation (Fisher, Ury, & Patton, 1991) is integrative negotiation. The following is the impression management advice that we pass along to prospective principled negotiators. Manage the information you offer in such a way as to suggest you have a good case on its merits and that you are confident about reaching a satisfactory agreement. Your confidence stems both from the merits of your case and your knowledge that you have alternatives to a negotiated agreement. You would prefer, however, to reach an agreement that would also be satisfactory to the other party because some aspects of the other party's case also have merit. You are as interested in your relationship with the other party as you are in reaching a win–win agreement.

Positional bargaining is distributive negotiation. The following is the impression management advice that we pass along to prospective positional bargainers. Manage the information you convey in such a way as to suggest that your case is better than the other party's, and that you are committed to reaching an agreement that reflects this difference. You are better able to absorb the costs of failing to reach an agreement than the other party. You are perfectly willing to walk away from negotiations because you have better alternatives, and you are as interested in making a deal as in making or keeping friends.

MODELS OF NEGOTIATION

In this section, we explore three models of negotiation:

1. positional bargaining/distributive negotiation;
2. principled negotiation/integrative negotiation; and
3. cyclical–developmental negotiation, which includes both integrative and distributive phases.

Positional Bargaining

The primary goal of positional bargaining is to reach a deal. A deal is an agreement that reflects the power relationship between parties where power is not equally balanced. It often—but not invariably—favours the more powerful party. In Gulliver's cyclical–developmental theory (1979), positional bargaining is part of the more comprehensive process of negotiation. It occurs during the phase of negotiation when there is an "exchange of more or less specific substantive proposals (demand, bid, offer) and counterproposals about the terms of agreement for the outcome of one or more issues" (p. 160). Fisher, Ury, and Patton (1991, p. 4) exclude positional bargaining from principled negotiation, and define it as "successively taking on and then giving up on a sequence of positions." A prototype of positional bargaining can be found in markets or bazaars where negotiations are conducted through the process of haggling. Figure 2.1 illustrates positional bargaining, also referred to as concession–convergence theory, in graphic form.

Fisher, Ury, and Patton use a five-step process in *Getting to Yes* (1991) to describe positional bargaining. The five steps are as follows:

- Take a position.
- Argue for it.
- Make concessions.
- Compromise.
- Reach an agreement.

Compromise and Formula

In positional bargaining, the mechanisms that bring about deals include compromise and a formula. *Compromise* refers to meeting the other party halfway, or accepting terms of an agreement that represent the middle ground between what each of the parties wants. For example, in the case of serial killers Paul Bernardo and Karla Homolka, Murray Segal, the Crown (prosecuting) attorney, negotiated with George Walker, Homolka's lawyer. Walker stated that he wanted "no jail time for [Homolka], but if [she] had to be incarcerated, it should be in a psychiatric hospital," not a penitentiary. Segal wanted her to serve 20 years in prison. Their negotiations led to an agreement, which took the form of a plea bargain reached through compromise. Walker agreed that Homolka would serve time in a penitentiary, fully cooperate with the police in collecting evidence against Bernardo, testify against Bernardo at trial, plead guilty to two manslaughter charges, and waive her right to a preliminary hearing. Segal agreed that Homolka would serve two concurrent (simultaneous) 10-year terms in a penitentiary where "she would be eligible to apply for full parole within two and a half years of her first day in prison" (Williams, 2003, pp. 186-188).

FIGURE 2.1 Positional Bargaining (Concession–Convergence) Model of Negotiation

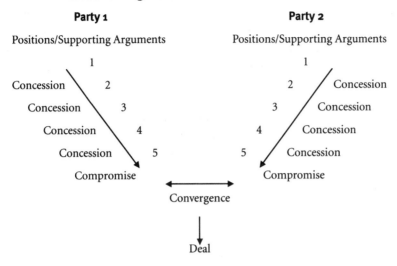

Underlying compromise is the spirit of give and take, a willingness to split the difference in order to make a deal. Deals can settle disagreements and conflicts. "Positional Bargaining During a Car Sale" on the following page illustrates how compromise produces a car sale by settling a divergence or disagreement over the price of a car. Below, we describe how positional bargaining settled a conflict between Israelis and Palestinians.

In a conflict documented in *The Siege of Bethlehem* (Canadian Broadcasting Corporation, 2002), Palestinian militants, including some who were accused of having killed or injured Israelis, took refuge in a church in Bethlehem. Other Palestinians, alleged to be innocent hostages by Israelis, were also in the church, which was surrounded by heavily armed Israeli soldiers. This was the setting in which positional bargaining took place between Israeli and Palestinian negotiators.

These were the positions communicated by the Israeli negotiators:

- All Palestinians inside the church must come out.
- The "most wanted"—that is, Palestinians accused of having killed or injured Israelis—would be taken into Israeli custody.
- The "wanted"—those suspected of being militants—would be exiled from Gaza and be required to move to other parts of Palestine.
- The "not wanted" could return to their homes in Gaza.

The Palestinians communicated the following positions:

Positional Bargaining During a Car Sale

Buyer	Seller
Values	*Values*
• security	• prestige as a salesperson of the year
Position 1	*Position 1*
• 2 percent below dealer price	• 6 percent above dealer price
• sport gearshift	• no
• CD and tape player	• tape player
• upgraded sound system	• no
• metallic paint (silver)	• no
• leather upholstery	• no
• trade-in of $10,000	• trade-in of $5,000
Position 2	*Position 2*
• 3 percent below dealer price	• 6 percent above dealer price
• sport gearshift	• no
• CD player	• no
• upgraded sound system	• no
• metallic paint (any color)	• no
• cloth upholstery	• yes
• trade-in of $10,000	• trade-in of $5,500
Position 3	*Position 3*
• 3 percent below dealer price	• 6 percent above dealer price
• sport gearshift	• no
• upgraded sound system	• no
• non-metallic paint (white)	• yes
• trade-in of $8,000	• trade-in of $6,000
Position 4	*Position 4*
• 3 percent below dealer price	• 6 percent above dealer price
• sport gearshift	• no
• upgraded sound system	• yes
• trade-in of $8,000	• trade-in of $6,000
Position 5	*Position 5*
• 5 percent below dealer price	• yes
• sport gearshift	• no
• trade-in of $7,000	• yes
Compromise	*Compromise*
• will accept $7,000 if sport gearshift is included	• will pay $7,000 for trade-in if buyer accepts yellow car with sport gearshift and moon roof that is now on the lot

Agreement reached

- Those who were "most wanted" by the Israelis would be released into Palestinian custody.
- Those classified as "wanted" and "not wanted" by the Israelis could go back to their homes in Gaza and the West Bank.

In negotiations aimed at persuading Palestinians to come out of the church, the Israelis offered to provide medical treatment to injured Palestinians who came out. A number of Palestinians responded by leaving the church. Then the Israelis offered to return to their homes unharmed any Palestinian teenagers who came out. A number of them responded by leaving the church. The Palestinians requested food. Israeli negotiators responded by offering food in exchange for the release of those who wished to leave the church.

The 38-day siege was ended by an agreement that included the following terms:

- The "most wanted" would be sent into exile abroad.
- The "wanted" would leave the West Bank for Gaza.
- The "not wanted" would be free to return to their homes in Gaza or the West Bank.

The first term was a compromise by the Israelis and the Palestinians. The second term was a compromise by the Palestinians who did not want to leave their homes in the West Bank. No evidence was presented in *The Siege of Bethlehem* indicating that mutual feelings of hostility between the Israelis and Palestinians involved in this conflict were decreased by the agreement.

The process of concession–convergence is one way in which positional bargainers settle conflicts. Another method is the use of a bargaining formula. A bargaining formula is a recipe, blueprint, or code that settles differences or solves problems. In the context of negotiations, a bargaining formula "contains and justifies outcomes acceptable to both parties and provides a series of referents on the specific details of an agreement" (Zartman, 1975, p. 73). Parties can create bargaining formulas out of the building blocks of their positions, common ground, and objectives during their time away from the negotiation table. An example of a bargaining formula is provided in "Bargaining Formulas at Work in the Political Arena."

Bargaining Formulas at Work in the Political Arena

China and Taiwan
In 1958, mainland China and Taiwan were involved in a struggle in which China bombarded the Taiwanese islands of Kinman and Matsu. Taiwan's army bombarded the Chinese mainland with high

explosive shells for 44 days. Together, the parties lobbed well over 400,000 shells at each other, about 10,500 shells per day. Incremental concessions may have reduced the number of shells dropped on each other to 260 per day over a five-year period (1,815 days). Eventually, the parties took time out and jointly created this formula: China would bombard Taiwan with, for example, 10 low-explosive shells on Tuesdays, Thursdays, and Saturdays; Taiwan would do the same thing on Mondays, Wednesdays, and Fridays. Sundays were shell-free days for both parties. The few low-explosive bombs that the parties continued to drop would symbolize entitlement for the Chinese and freedom for the Taiwanese, and far fewer people from both China and Taiwan would be killed or routed from their homes. Although China continued to drop leaflet bombs on its three weekly bomb days until 1978, the parties' bargaining formula led to a desirable outcome more rapidly than would have been the case had the parties relied on the gradual process of incremental concessions and eventual compromise (Cernetig, 1999).

The Morality of Positional Bargaining

In the moral hierarchy established by Fisher, Ury, and Patton, principled negotiation is ranked above positional bargaining (1991, pp. 1-14). The authors provide two reasons for the lower moral standing of positional bargainers: failure to use "decent" tactics and greediness. In asserting that positional bargainers fail to use decent tactics, Fisher, Ury, and Patton compare them with principled negotiators. Principled negotiators, the authors assert, try to "obtain what [they] are entitled to and still be decent"; positional bargainers, however, use relationship-damaging tactics, such as "haggling … tricks and posturing" (1991, p. xviii).

The linking of haggling, tricks, and posturing with relationship damage may not accurately describe what happens in most cases of positional bargaining. Partial disclosure of information and some degree of posturing (making statements or taking positions that were known to be unrealistic) are standard or expected practices. We hypothesize that in the majority of cases, positional bargaining does not damage relationships because parties tend not to use tactics that violate limits set by mutual expectations. Moreover, Fisher, Ury, and Patton present no evidence to support an invariable link between positional bargaining and relationship damage.

There are instances, however, where positional bargaining tactics may inflict further damage on relationships that are already complex and volatile. Ross (2004), for example, cites instances that arose during the negotiations between Israelis and Palestinians that he attempted to facilitate. Damaging tactics that Ross observed included making unconditional commitments and then making them conditional (p. 449), stating a position and then changing it (p. 449), tolerating or condoning violence during negotiations aimed at security (pp. 617-618), manipulation (pp. 333, 688), trickery (p. 688), and lying (p. 465).

Fisher, Ury, and Patton cite greediness as the second reason for placing positional bargaining lower on a moral hierarchy than principled negotiation. Principled negotiators want to share the pie; positional bargainers want most or all of it for themselves. According to Mnookin, Peppet, and Tulumello (2000, pp. 211-216), they are more likely than principled negotiators to use the following "hard bargaining, relationship damaging tactics" to get it:

- extreme claims followed by slow concessions;
- "take it or leave it" offers;
- personal insults;
- bluffing, puffing, and lying;
- threats and warnings; and
- belittling the other side's arguments or alternatives.

The greediness allegation is undermined by the fact that Mnookin, Peppet, and Tulumello ignore compromise as a mechanism that produces agreements reached by positional bargainers. Compromise limits greediness by requiring each party to give up something in order to get something. "Compromise" does not appear in the index of *Beyond Winning: Negotiating To Create Value in Deals and Disputes*. Litigation, however, does appear, and the authors seem to equate positional bargaining with the use of these highly adversarial tactics by lawyers attempting to settle conflicts during the litigation process (Mnookin, Peppet, & Tulumello, 2000, p. 108).

The adversarial tactics identified by these authors may be used by some positional bargainers on some occasions, but positional bargaining cannot validly be defined solely in terms of their use. Still, compared with principled negotiators, who "behave decently" and take the interests of the other party into account (Fisher, Ury, & Patton, 1991, p. xviii), positional bargainers are probably less concerned with the effects of their behaviour on the other party. They are also less likely to "discover possible trades that could have left both sides better off" (Mnookin, Peppet, & Tulumello, 2000, p. 108). Compared with principled negotiators, positional bargainers are probably more likely to "make people contentedly settle for less than they meant to get, in return for more than they meant to give" (Kesterton, 2004, p. A22).

Readers who share the high value that Fisher, Ury, and Patton (1991) place on "amicable relationships" may agree with them and not be swayed by other considerations. On the other hand, they may take one or more of the following considerations into account in reaching a conclusion:

1. Positional bargainers all over the world routinely settle conflicts without using, or with minimal use of, hard bargaining or relationship-damaging tactics (Gulliver, 1979).
2. Positional bargainers may become vulnerable to exploitation by placing an undue emphasis on establishing or maintaining amicable relationships (Barry and Friedman, 1998).
3. Positional bargainers may not be concerned about establishing or maintaining amicable relationships where they have had no previous relationship with other parties or where they have no intention of continuing their relationship after negotiations have ended.

Efficiency and Positional Bargaining

In addition to alleging that positional bargaining is morally inferior, Fisher, Ury, and Patton also allege that it is inefficient compared with principled negotiation (1991, p. 9). Positional bargainers routinely use bottom lines—positions that are not to be changed—as a way of protecting themselves from accepting agreements they should reject. The authors contend (pp. 97-100) that the use of bottom lines is inefficient for three reasons:

1. *Bottom lines prevent learning.* Negotiation is a process of learning and using newly acquired knowledge to increase the likelihood of achieving desirable results. The use of a bottom line prevents learning. If nothing the other parties can say or do will change a negotiator's bottom line, why bother listening and learning at the bargaining table?
2. *Bottom lines inhibit exploration.* The rigidity of bottom lines diverts attention away from mutually agreeable solutions. For example, if a tenant sets a bottom line monthly rental cost of $1,000 for an apartment, and a landlord agrees to rent the premises for $1,100, including hydro, Internet access, and cable television, the tenant may agree to sign a lease, if she finds these additional services desirable. A rigid bottom line would prevent her from even exploring her options.
3. *Bottom lines tend to be too extreme.* When bottom lines are too high or too rigid, they tend to prevent deals from being made.

In addition to protecting themselves from accepting agreements they should reject, prudent negotiators should also protect themselves from rejecting agreements they should accept. Unlike bottom lines, which offer the first type of protection, a best alternative to a negotiated agreement (BATNA) offers both types of protection (Fisher, Ury, & Patton, 1991, p. 99). For example, an applicant for a position of head cashier at a college might achieve the first type of protection by bringing a firm salary expectation of $25,000 with him to negotiations with the director of accounting services.

Another applicant for the same position might achieve both types of protection by bringing to the negotiations an offer of $28,000 from another college in the same city, which offers the same inducements and benefits. We believe that positional bargainers are well advised to replace bottom lines with BATNA.

Fisher, Ury, and Patton also maintain that positional bargaining is inefficient because it

- reconciles the parties' positions but not their underlying interests or values,
- may damage relationships, and
- has higher transaction costs (1991, pp. 5-10).

In some cases, the reconciliation of positions results in the reconciliation of interests. Specifically, some value (or interest) conflicts can be settled by stating positions that include the offer of tangible resources, such as money (Aubert, 1963). For example, in his study of human rights mediation, Ellis (2003) found that values, such as respect, are routinely transformed into sums of money included in the stated positions of claimants and respondents, with the amount determined by positional bargaining. Here, the money paid by respondents to claimants and the conditions attached to the payment—such as letters of reference, letters of regret, no admission of guilt, no publicity, and the posting of human rights cards in workplaces—appeared to reconcile the claimants' interests in vindication with respondents' interests in reputations.

Although it is always desirable to maintain good working relationships during negotiations, negotiators are often involved in conflicts in which they are more interested in achieving tangible results than in establishing or maintaining relationships with each other (McCarthy, 1995; Canadian Broadcasting Corporation, 2002). In these cases, positional bargaining may be more efficient than principled negotiation with its dual focus on relationships and outcomes.

Finally, Fisher, Ury, and Patton (1991, pp. 5-6) allege that positional negotiation may be less efficient than principled negotiation in settling disagreements because agreements reached through positional bargaining are less stable. The deals made by spotters for NASCAR drivers in major races at Talledaga and Daytona exemplify the instability of agreements reached through positional bargaining. At these race courses, horsepower is regulated, and the key to winning a race is "the draft." When "in the draft, two or more cars running together can [go faster than] even the fastest car running alone …. So [without another car alongside] … you are stuck" (Huler, 1999, p. 34). Spotters prepare for making deals during a race by observing the draft provided by others' cars during practice sessions. During the race, spotters use cellphones to make deals with drivers to become draft partners. These deals are respected until several draft partners reach the pack of cars that is leading the race. At this point, deals are routinely ignored or violated by drivers who think they can win the race by abandoning the deals they have made.

A single example is not a sound basis for concluding that positional bargaining produces less stable agreements than principled negotiation. Findings from comparative research on the stability of agreements reached by principled negotiation and positional bargaining in a variety of cases would be needed to justify such a conclusion.

Evaluation

STRENGTHS

Supporters of positional bargaining, even the critics we referred to, agree that positional bargaining

- is relatively simple to participate in;
- is the process most frequently used to settle conflicts in most societies;
- helps the parties communicate what they want and how strongly they want it; and
- provides the parties with an anchor—their stated position—in an uncertain and stressful face-to-face situation.

WEAKNESSES

Positional bargaining also has some weaknesses. It

- has higher transaction costs in terms of stress, time, and money than principled negotiation;
- may produce less stable or durable agreements because of its focus on offers and counteroffers;
- focuses singularly on outcome rather than jointly on relationship and outcome; and
- uses bottom lines instead of BATNA.

Principled Negotiation

Fisher, Ury, and Patton (1991, p. 10) define negotiation as a kind of communication that may or may not occur directly between the parties, which is

- explicit,
- reciprocal, and
- designed to reach an agreement between parties who have some shared and some opposing interests, and who are often frustrated, tense, angry, anxious, and uncertain.

Other definitions of negotiation include the following: "a procedure for resolving opposing preferences" (Carnevale & Pruitt, 1992, p. 532); "a means of doing better by joint action than would otherwise be possible" (Lax & Sebenius, 1995, p. 103); "the deliberate interaction of two or more complete social units (including individuals) which are attempting to define or redefine the terms of their independence" (Walton & McKersie, 1965, p. 3); and Douglas's (1962) "magical" definition, which is set out in "The Magic of Negotiation." All of these definitions are consistent with the definitions of Gulliver and of Fisher, Ury, and Patton, who coined the term "principled negotiation."

The Magic of Negotiation

With no perceptible instrument but the human voice, and without stirring from their seats at the table, they move and change positions, to attain what they refer to as a meeting of the minds.

Source: Douglas (1962, p. 8).

In *Getting to Yes*, Fisher, Ury, and Patton (1991, p. 10) define principled negotiation as "a method that helps parties decide issues on their merits" while "behaving decently" themselves. As a method, principled negotiation is *prescriptive*. That is, it is a method that most negotiators do not use, but one that they should use, because it is more likely than other methods to produce a wise agreement.

In addition to being prescriptive, principled negotiation is also *formulaic*. The formula for achieving a wise agreement involves following the four principles that constitute the method. Also included in the formula is a rule requiring principled negotiators to focus on both substance (outcome) and procedure (method). Principled negotiation, then, is a prescriptive, formulaic, dual-focus method in which the merits of the case operate to bring about wise agreements. The merits of one party's case are greater than the merits of another party's case to the extent that the meritorious case is more logical, grounded in verified or verifiable facts, and more reasonable or fair.

The creation of a wise agreement is the goal of principled negotiation (Fisher, Ury, & Patton, 1991, p. 4). A wise agreement

- reconciles interests;
- does not damage and may improve relationships; and
- has relatively low transaction costs—costs that involve time, stress, and money, for example.

Fisher, Ury, and Patton maintain that negotiators can reach a wise agreement by implementing the following four principles:

1. Separate the person from the problem.
2. Reconcile interests, not positions.
3. Create options for mutual, not personal, gain.
4. Use objective standards.

We consider each of these principles in detail in the following sections.

Separate the Person from the Problem

Negotiators often become entwined with the problems they are attempting to settle. One of the chief difficulties lies in the use of ad hominem arguments. An ad hominem argument is one that evaluates a position, offer, or solution on the basis of the motivations or attributes of the person who proposed it, rather than on an assessment of whether the position, offer, or solution is logical, fair, or grounded in fact. Ad hominem answers and arguments are frequently used because it is easier to formulate one than to discover a solution to the problem (Engel, 1994). Ad hominem arguments integrate the person and the problem. In so doing, they divert attention from finding solutions that reconcile interests, and they inflict further damage on the relationship between the parties.

Another difficulty lies in the tendency of negotiators to confuse their egos with the positions they advocate. This confusion makes it easy for a negotiator to interpret a rejection of his stated position, or the statement of an opposing position, as a personal attack, an insult, or a demonstration of disrespect. The most successful negotiators are often those who remove their egos from the table.

At the start of many or most negotiations, the parties are often angry, frustrated, uncertain, and anxious. These heightened emotional states can undermine a negotiator's ability to discriminate between a problem and a person, and to facilitate a switch in attention from the person back to the problem, where it belongs. An example of these difficulties arose during negotiations between representatives of the police and representatives of a women's support group that were conducted to arrive at a joint decision on the steps required to protect women from a serial rapist in their neighbourhood. The women were angry because of the harm that other women had already suffered as a result of what they perceived to be ineffectual policing. They spent most of their negotiating time accusing the police representatives of being pawns of a patriarchal system, and therefore part of the problem. The police officers were angry because their efforts at protecting the community had been frustrated by bureaucratic territorialism and an elusive rapist. They spent an inordinate amount of time accusing the support group members of irrational "cop bashing." Needless to say, the meeting adjourned without the parties achieving their goals.

Separating the person from the problem is a precondition of a wise agreement. Negotiators can help to meet this precondition by dealing directly with relationship problems instead of attempting to settle conflicts by making substantive concessions. Fisher, Ury, and Patton (1991, p. 54) offer this advice: "Be soft on the people, hard on the problem, and the harder the problem is to settle, the softer you should be on the people."

Being "soft on people" involves perception skills, emotional skills, and communication skills. Negotiators who want to improve their perception skills should follow these rules:

- Be empathetic and facilitate empathy by imagining what it would be like to walk a mile in the other party's shoes.
- Avoid blaming others, and explicitly acknowledge that you may also be responsible for the problems at hand.
- Keep an open mind in interpreting the intentions. Avoid being led by your own fears in this regard; they are probably unrelated.

Negotiators can hone their emotional skills by considering the following suggestions:

- Acknowledge that emotional expressions are legitimate forms of communication.
- Refrain from responding in kind to hostile outbursts.
- Apologize in a timely manner and make other appropriate conciliatory gestures.

Negotiators can improve their communication skills by practising the following:

- Speak and write clearly.
- Listen respectfully with your mind and heart.

The authors of *Getting to Yes* reject "being nice" because it "makes you vulnerable" to exploitation by the other party (Fisher, Ury, & Patton, 1991, pp. 7-8). However, they offer no research findings in support of this assertion. Research findings reported by Nowak and Sigmund (1998) and Schneider (2002) indicate that niceness can improve relationships, and assist the person who chooses to be friendly and courteous in achieving the outcome he wants. In this regard, see the comments of National Basketball Association (NBA) commissioner David Stern, which are set out in "Niceness Works."

Principled negotiators prepare for negotiations by reminding themselves of two things:

1. They are about to negotiate with other human beings who, like them, have strong "emotions, deeply held values and different backgrounds" (Fisher, Ury, & Patton, 1991, p. 19).
2. They are wise to separate their desire to establish a working relationship with the other parties from their desire to reconcile substantive interests.

The second part of the advice offered by Fisher, Ury, and Patton is to be "hard on the problem." A negotiator can do so by following these guidelines:

- Clearly communicate your interests and your determination to achieve your goals.
- Let your strength and abilities serve the purpose of solving substantive problems.

A "hard on the problem" focus is evident in the negotiations described by Perkins (2003) concerning professional golfer Mike Weir and his caddy Butch Little. Weir and Little have been friends for over 20 years but maintain a professional relationship on the golf course. Golfer and caddy negotiate every hole in every tournament. According to Perkins, they share an interest in acquiring the money and fame that accompany a winning season. Their negotiations focus exclusively on settling differences about doing what it takes to win. Friendship plays no part in the golfing decisions that they make.

Reconcile Interests, Not Positions
In formulating their second principle for achieving a wise agreement, Fisher, Ury, and Patton define "interests" as "basic human needs [such as] security, economic well being, sense of belonging, autonomy" (1991, p. 28). Positions are often polarized statements about what the parties want, demand, reject, or offer. Interests are related to positions in that any interest may be served by a variety of positions. Interests are the secrets behind overtly stated positions.

A negotiator must be able to identify before she is capable of reconciling them. The questions "what" and "why" may assist her, as is evident in the conflict set out in "Identifying Interests and Positions: A Library Window."

Identifying Interests and Positions: A Library Window

Two university students, Padma and Patricia, are studying in a library room with a window. They start arguing about the window. The librarian overhears them and enters the room. In order to discover their positions, she asks each of them, "What do you want?" In order to discover their interests, she asks each of them, "Why do you want that?" Having discovered the interests that underlie their respective positions, she sets about reconciling them in the following way:

	Padma	*Patricia*
Position	Window open	Window closed
Interest	Health: fresh air	Health: avoiding a cold caused by a draft
Reconciliation	Provide fresh air without creating a draft by opening the window in the adjacent room	

Create Options for Mutual, Not Personal, Gain

Fisher, Ury, and Patton's third principle for achieving a wise agreement involves creating options for mutual, rather than personal, gain. This can be a highly creative exercise, as is demonstrated in "Creating Options for Mutual Gain: The Expansive Orange."

Creating Options for Mutual Gain: The Expansive Orange

Jim and John are arguing over the ownership of an orange. Jim's position is "it's mine." This is also John's position. Both Jim and John were determined to have "their own" orange. Their initial negotiation was power-based. As the argument got more heated, struggle—in the form of a fight—appeared to be a good winner-take-all solution for both of them. They continued talking, however, and soon became engaged in a rights-based (rights of finder/owner) negotiation. Eventually, they decided to compromise, and were about to cut the orange in half when Jim asked John why he wanted the orange. John told him, and asked Jim the same question. Suddenly, a better solution occurred them both: John got all the rind, which he needed to make chicken l'orange, his girlfriend's favourite dinner; Jim got all the pulp, which he wanted to eat right away because he was very thirsty. In this way, both John and Jim each got the whole orange.

Source: Fisher, Ury, and Patton (1991, p. 57).

Inventing options that expand an orange that is perceived to be fixed in size, and then dividing it can help bring about a negotiated end to a wide variety of international, labour-relations, environmental, community, and family conflicts (Zartman, 1975). The starting point for inventing mutual gain options in all of these conflicts is the generation of many options for consideration. We suggest that negotiators follow these four guidelines to help them with the task of generating options.

1. *Separate creation from evaluation.* Separate the creative process of generating options from the evaluative one of judging them. Insist on postponing evaluation until all options are on the table. The parties to a conflict are more likely to generate a large number of options if, at the start of the brainstorming session, the parties seek and receive assurances—in writing if necessary—that their ideas or suggestions will not be used against them in the future. The parties may be bolder in making creative suggestions if brainstorming sessions are conducted by means of email, rather than at face-to-face negotiations.

2. *Emphasize breadth of search.* Identify your task as a creative one that involves a search for more than one answer to the question, more than one solution to the problem.

3. *Focus on win–win options.* Focus on using your creative ability to search for win–win options while suspending any notion that a win–lose outcome is likely. In your quest, focus on *complementary* differences in values, interests, and attitudes. Not all differences are complementary. Two rhymes illustrate the difference between complementary and non-complementary differences, and the impact they have on outcomes.

Complementary	*Non-complementary*
Jack Sprat could eat no fat,	Jack Sprat ate lean and fat,
His wife could eat no lean;	His wife ate fat and lean.
And so betwixt them both, you see,	He and she would fight, you see,
They licked the platter clean.	To lick the platter clean.

Fisher, Ury, and Patton (1991) used the original Jack Sprat nursery rhyme to illustrate complementary differences, the basis of economic and social exchanges. We changed the rhyme to illustrate non-complementary differences, which can instigate impasses or struggle.

4. *Focus on all relevant problems.* Define your task as one that involves generating options to solve not just your own problems, but also those of the other party. All relevant problems merit focus.

Findings reported since the publication of *Getting to Yes* (Fisher, Ury, & Patton, 1991) indicate that "metacognitive processing," a process-oriented approach, can also increase the effectiveness of problem-oriented solutions aimed at creating value by enlarging the pie (Beradi-Coletta, Buyer, Dominowski, & Rellinger, 1995, p. 220). Metacognitive processing occurs when negotiators involved in attempting to create win–win options "explain aloud what they are doing and why." The "awareness of the particular steps being taken [by the parties during brainstorming] to solve the problem" facilitates the creation of options (Beradi-Coletta et al., 1995, pp. 217-218). Talking through the problem also helps negotiators "assess if the steps being taken are leading to an effective, mutually satisfying solution" (Beradi-Coletta et al., 1995, p. 218).

Kesterton (2004, p. A12) provides an example of metacognitive process-ing engaged in by chess players. When the players were asked to "speak their thoughts as they decided what moves to make," they took eight probable future moves by their opponents into account. The best players thought much more seriously about the probable moves of their opponents than good players did. The good players thought less seriously about their oppo-nent's probable moves, believing that if they themselves made a bad move, "things would eventually work out in their favour." Compared with the moves of the best players, a lower proportion of the moves of the good players were guided by rational calculation and logic, and a higher proportion were guided by a belief in good luck.

Use Objective Standards

Fisher, Ury, and Patton's fourth principle for achieving a wise agreement requires the use of objective standards. These are standards that exist in-dependently of the subjective feelings, thoughts, wishes, or willpower of the parties involved in negotiations. Laws are objective standards. Industry practice regarding safety fences, for example, is an objective standard. Terms defined in collective agreements are objective standards. DNA and other scientific evidence are generally considered to provide objective standards, although this matter is open to question. In principled negotiation, objec-tive standards can be used as a sword as well as a shield. As a shield, they protect negotiators from accepting agreements that violate them. As a sword, they persuade other parties to accept agreements because they conform with them. Fisher, Ury, and Patton (1991, p. 88) advise negotiators "not to yield to pressure [but] only to the principle of using objective standards to evalu-ate agreements."

Usually parties involved in negotiations present different standards for evaluating agreements. Fisher, Ury, and Patton identify criteria that can be used in persuading all parties of the wisdom of one's own standards. The first criterion is that the standard is "more widely accepted" than others. The second is that the standard is "more directly on point" than others. The third is that the standard is "more relevant in terms of time, place and circumstance" than others (1992, p. 48). These criteria do not eliminate positional bargaining in relation to the standard that will prevail in evaluating the outcome of an agreement. However, they do focus bargaining on a few standards that the parties have refined by discussing them in relation to specified criteria.

Consider the case of negotiating to purchase a house. A subjective standard, such as the vendor's assertion that "I have put a lot into this house, and it is worth every penny of the advertised purchase price," could be used to evaluate the proposed purchase agreement for the amount the vendor wants. An objective standard, such as the prices of similar houses that have recently sold in the neighbourhood, is likely to be more persuasive because it meets all three of the criteria described above. If a buyer used this standard and included the three criteria in the theory underlying his offer to purchase a house, the buyer would be following Fisher, Ury, and Patton's fourth principle of principled negotiation.

In some cases, the choice of specific objective criteria to be used by negotiating parties may need to be settled by bargaining, the services of an arbitrator, or the flip of a coin (Fisher, Ury, & Patton, 1991, p. 48). "Choosing Objective Criteria: The Nipping Dolphin" presents an instance in which the "widely accepted" criterion clashes with the "scientific evidence" criterion.

Choosing Objective Criteria: The Nipping Dolphin

Sarah, a visitor to Seaquarium, was bitten on the leg by a dolphin when she and other visitors were invited to swim with it. She claimed that Seaquarium was negligent, and demanded $15,000 to cover her medical expenses and "pain and suffering"; in addition, she claimed $100,000 in punitive damages (damages awarded to punish behaviour that falls well below acceptable norms). Negotiators for Seaquarium agreed to pay the $15,000, but refused to pay punitive damages because they claimed that Seaquarium was not negligent. They considered the terms of the agreement to be unacceptable because "over a period of three years, 1,600 visitors swam with ... the dolphin and not one of them reported being injured in any way," and because the dolphin was "playful, friendly and peaceful." Sarah thought that punitive damages were justified because recent findings reported by three oceanographic research institutes indicated that the dolphins killed porpoises, killed new-born dolphins, and assaulted and injured human swimmers with their beaks, teeth, and bulk.

Source: Broad (1999, p. A7).

In some cases, there is no widely accepted criterion that clashes with scientific evidence, but the scientific evidence itself is not objective. Thus, the average person is likely to accept the scientific evidence presented by officials working in police crime laboratories as independent and objective. Yet six forensic scientists who studied the evidence on blood type presented in court by a crime laboratory official concluded that it was tainted by ignorance and/or bias, and that it helped convict an innocent man. Moreover, the six forensic scientists suggested that results of tests on human bodily fluids in hundreds of other cases could have been unsound (*Toronto Star*, May 28, 2004, p. B1).

Problem-Solving Approach

In *Beyond Winning*, Mnookin, Peppet, and Tulumello (2000, p. xi) replace the terms "interest-based negotiation" and "principled negotiation" with "a problem-solving approach" characterized by

- a collaborative working relationship between negotiators,
- effective communication,
- creative options,
- minimizing transaction costs,
- treating distributive issues (for example, distributing slices of a pie that is fixed in size) as shared problems,
- improving or not damaging relationships, and
- defending parties against exploitation.

In our view, *Beyond Winning* does not offer a theory of negotiation that takes us much beyond *Getting to Yes*. It does attempt to persuade lawyers to adopt a problem-solving approach in dealing with their own clients and with the other client's lawyer. It also offers sound practical advice on how to establish a problem-solving negotiating process (p. 207).

The advice given by the authors of these two books is supported by findings reported by Schneider (2002), who surveyed 175 lawyer-negotiators. One of Schneider's major findings was that pleasant, courteous, well-prepared lawyers with superior problem-solving skills negotiated more effectively for their clients than antagonistic, deceptive lawyers with inferior problem-solving skills. Specifically, she found that 75 percent of ethical but adversarial negotiators were ineffective, and 75 percent of "true problem-solvers" were effective (Schneider, 2002, pp. 196-197).

Evaluation

STRENGTHS

The strengths of principled negotiation are that it

- is a humane, ethical, problem-solving, win–win approach to ending conflicts;
- has lower transaction costs than alternative ways of ending conflicts, such as struggle or positional bargaining;
- can bring balance to an imbalanced power relationship because it identifies the merits of the case as *the* basis of a fair agreement; and
- gives equal weight to relationship and substantive problems.

WEAKNESSES

Principled negotiation also has some weaknesses. It

- is not widely used by professional negotiators and its merits have not been supported by scientific research;
- is culturally biased in that it separates people from problems and favours individual over collective solutions, and therefore is not appropriate for settling conflicts involving parties who do not share the same culture as its creators, such as First Nations or South Asian peoples (Huber, 1993; Lajeunesse, 1990; Lund, Morris, & Duryea, 1994);
- is restricted to conflicts where the parties are willing to forsake the use of power tactics in favour of the merits of the case (McCarthy, 1995);
- offers a confusing theory of power by failing to differentiate between resources as potential power and use of resources, such as BATNA, as actual power;
- ignores trust, an important factor in producing negotiated agreements (McCarthy, 1995, p. 91);
- ignores principles that can be implemented during the positional bargaining phase of negotiations, even though positional bargaining takes place during the "evaluating and using criteria" phase of principled negotiation (Fisher, Ury & Patton, 1992, p. 48; White, 1992, pp. 45-47);
- assumes that people can be persuaded to be reasonable by the objective merits of a case, even when they can gain more by being persistently unreasonable (Gulliver, 1979, p. 17); and
- ignores the significant contribution of sincere, specific, and unqualified apologies in solving relationship problems (Gray, 2004).

Cyclical–Developmental Negotiation

Cyclical–developmental negotiation synthesizes positional bargaining and principled negotiation.

Gulliver (1979, p. 70), creator of the cyclical–developmental model, defines negotiation as a "process of interaction in which the parties give each other information directly and indirectly, each party attempting to discover relevant information about the preferences and preference rankings of the other, and [also] attempting to manipulate the opponent's understandings and preferences." Cyclical–developmental negotiation attempts to produce a "convergence on outcomes." Deals, agreements, memoranda of understandings, and terms of settlement, all represent a convergence on outcomes.

Gulliver's cyclical–developmental model of negotiation is cross-cultural and inductive. It is derived from observations of negotiations in a number of societies, including some in East Africa and North America. The model includes two universal cyclical and developmental processes that form its core and seven transitions across eight developmental phases.

Definition of Concepts

We have chosen to use a divorce-like negotiation that involves child support payments and access to children to illustrate the basic concepts of cyclical–developmental negotiation. The case, *Johnson-Steeves v. Lee*, was heard by the Alberta Court of Appeal in 1997.

Case Synopsis: Johnson-Steeves v. Lee

King Tak Lee and Virginia Johnson-Steeves were friends, but Lee wanted them to become lovers. During a trip to Las Vegas, Johnson-Steeves made the following proposal to Lee: "I want to become pregnant and bring up the child on my own as a single parent. So, I will agree to have sex with you, if you agree to pay child support in the amount of $300 a month and, apart from an occasional visit, not interfere in the child's life." After Johnson-Steeves became pregnant, her relationship with Lee deteriorated. After the child was born, Johnson-Steeves asked Lee to pay a larger amount of child support. Lee said he was willing to do this if he could visit the child often and participate more fully in his life. Johnson-Steeves refused to agree, and Lee refused to pay. The parties attempted to settle their conflict through negotiation. When they reached an impasse, they hired lawyers and took the case to court.

In Gulliver's terminology, a *preference set* refers to "an ordered list of interests you hope to satisfy by the positions you communicate" (1979, p. 88). Table 2.1 shows the preference sets of Lee and Johnson-Steeves. The numbers 1, 2, and 3 refer to the rankings of each of their preferences. In Lee's preference set, "establish and maintain father–child relationship" is ranked first. The preference ranked first in Johnson-Steeves's preference set is "increased child support."

By *positions*, Gulliver refers to stated wants or demands relating to preferences (1979, p. 88). Table 2.1 shows that Lee's position on his first preference is "greater access to child." "Increased child support" is Johnson-Steeves's position on her first preference. Table 2.1 also identifies the positions taken by the parties on each of their remaining two preferences.

Strategy refers to a plan chosen by the parties for achieving the objectives they seek (Gulliver, 1979, pp. 142-143). Pruitt (1995, p. 27) identifies problem solving, contending, yielding, and inaction as four strategies available to negotiators. Strategies guide tactics. Table 2.2 shows that contending—in which the parties treat each other as rivals—is the strategy chosen by both Lee and Johnson-Steeves.

Tactics refer to specific things said and done, or not said and done, to implement a strategy. Gulliver (1979, p. 104) defines tactics as "the kind of information offered and the response intended to be obtained." Table 2.2 shows that the tactics used by Lee and Johnson-Steeves include threats and attempts to engage each other's feelings of guilt.

Outcome refers to the results of negotiations. Gulliver (1979, p. 77) defines outcome as "the culmination of negotiation." An outcome can be distributive (win–lose) or integrative (win–win). Gulliver (1979, pp. 101-102) also classifies outcomes as maxima, minima, and target. Maxima outcomes are "high demands and offers that constitute the outer limits that a negotiator believes are realizable, and even if they are not fully realized, they will leave room for trading and making concessions later on." Minima outcomes (bottom lines) are "the lowest anticipated outcomes on issues that a negotiator hopes or expects not to go." Target outcomes are "anticipated outcomes that lie somewhere between the minima and maxima."

Outcomes can be produced by bargaining formulas. A *bargaining formula* is defined as an agreement in principle that "contains and justifies outcomes acceptable to both parties and provides a series of referents of the specific details of the agreement" (Zartman, 1975, p. 73).

Although Johnson-Steeves's initial feeling is that she wants no interference from Lee in the life of the child, she eventually moderates her stance. It becomes clear that a formula acceptable to both Lee and Johnson-Steeves would be one that increased Lee's involvement in the life of the child while preserving Johnson-Steeves's choice of family form. Specific details might include: joint legal custody, primary residence in Johnson-Steeves's home, residence with Lee during specified summer months and other holidays and birthdays, support payments to continue at the agreed-upon amount even when the child is with Lee, and the mediation of conflicts that arise in the event of alleged defaults.

TABLE 2.1 Preference Sets and Positions of Lee and Johnson-Steeves

Lee		Johnson-Steeves	
Preference set	Positions	Preference set	Positions
1. Establish and maintain father–child relationship	1. Greater access to his child	1. Maintain single-parent family	1. Increased child support
2. Autonomy: resist being blackmailed	2. Payment of current amount in child support	2. Economic well-being: maintain standard of living by increasing child support payments	2. No access
3. Economic well-being: maintain present standard of living	3. Trial if there is no agreement		3. Trial if there is no agreement

TABLE 2.2 Strategies and Tactics of Lee and Johnson-Steeves

Lee		Johnson-Steeves	
Strategy	Tactics	Strategy	Tactics
Contending	1. Threat of trial	Contending	1. Threat of trial
	2. No increase in child support until she provides greater access to his child		2. Threat she will withdraw all access to her child
	3. If she had best interest of the child at heart, she would want both parents involved in his life		3. If he had best interests of the child at heart, he would not be harming him by causing all this turmoil

Bargaining range refers to a range of values or outcomes "within which both parties are willing to accept any outcome rather than have no agreement at all" (Gulliver, 1979, p. 154). A similar but more specific definition is offered by Lewicki et al. (2004). Using but renaming Gulliver's (1979) classification of outcomes (maxima, target, and minima), they define a bargaining range as "the spread between the resistance points [minima or bottom lines]." If outcomes fall outside this spread, negotiations will usually fail because the parties would rather have no agreement at all than one that yields outcomes beyond their resistance points. For example, when a prospective house vendor's resistance point is $300,000 and a prospective purchaser's resistance point is $315,000, there exists a *positive bargaining range*, where "the buyer's resistance point is above the seller's" (p. 62). In this case, the parties would rather negotiate than have no agreement at all. In contrast, when a prospective house vendor's resistance point is $300,000 and a prospective house purchaser's resistance point is $285,000, there exists a *negative bargaining range*, where "the buyer's resistance point is below the seller's" (p. 62). In this case, the parties would rather walk away than negotiate an agreement *unless* the purchaser and/or the vendor can be persuaded to transform a negative bargaining range into a positive bargaining range by changing his, her, or their resistance points.

Table 2.3 describes the bargaining range for child support payments using concepts formulated by Gulliver (1979) and Lewicki et al. (2004). The table shows that the bargaining range is between the resistance points of Lee ($800) and Johnson-Steeves ($700). The spread or gap is $100.

An extended discussion of the bargaining range is warranted by the fact that highly regarded theorists and researchers such as Lewicki et al. regard "reaching a settlement within a positive bargaining range ... getting a settlement as close to the other party's resistance point as possible" as the fundamental objective of distributive negotiation (2004, p. 64). For a more detailed discussion of the bargaining range, see Gulliver (1979, pp. 154-156) and Lewicki et al. (2004, pp. 60-68).

Bargaining in good faith is defined as "a widespread norm, often protected in law, that requires the maker of an overt offer not to revoke it for a higher one later on" (Gulliver, 1979, p. 102).

The Cyclical–Developmental Dynamic

The cyclical and developmental processes we are about to describe are based on the assumption that coordination is fundamental to negotiation. Without it, the likelihood of reaching a negotiated agreement is relatively low. In this connection, Gulliver notes that "negotiators may never achieve amity, sympathy or trust but they have to attain sufficient coordination so as to work toward and ultimately achieve a joint decision on the issues in dispute" (Gulliver, 1979, p. 6). How is coordination attained by parties who are anxious, mistrustful, and antagonistic and who—especially during the early stages of negotiations—to talk and listen to each other?

The parties achieve *coordination* and reach agreements because negotiations are propelled toward these objectives by a dynamic inherent in the cyclical and developmental processes of all negotiations. *Contradiction* lies at the heart of this dynamic. The cyclical process depends on the operation of two linked contradictions. The source of the first contradiction is information exchange; the source of the second is alternation.

TABLE 2.3   Bargaining Range for Monthly Child Support Payments per Child, Lee and Johnson-Steeves

Lee			Johnson-Steeves		
Offers to pay	Expects to pay	Will not pay more than	Wants	Expects to get	Will not accept less than
$500 revealed maxima	$700 private target	$800 private minima/ resistance point	$900 revealed maxima	$800 private target	$700 private minima/ resistance point

The Cyclical Process

INFORMATION EXCHANGE

Negotiation depends on the repetitive exchange of information between the parties. Each party needs information about the other's preferences, priorities, interests, positions, overall strategy, expectations, alternatives, perceptions, feelings, and attitudes. In order to get information from each other, the parties, must give information to each other (Gouldner, 1960; Jensen, 1984; Mnookin, Peppet, & Tulumello, 2000; Weingart, Thompson, Bazerman, & Carroll, 1990). Reciprocity rules. Refusal to participate in a process of reciprocal disclosure creates an impasse. However, giving information in response to receiving information is invariably associated with a dilemma that can be resolved only by continuing to give and get information. Each party wants to overcome, and believes he can overcome, the liabilities associated with revealing more information than he wanted to reveal and being persuaded to make concessions he did not want to make. This process is described in table 2.4.

Lee and Johnson-Steeves's mutual efforts to recover from revealing information each would prefer to conceal, and from being persuaded by each other's revelations to make decisions they would prefer not to make, is a propulsive force that moves their negotiations in the direction of a mutually satisfactory solution.

ALTERNATION

Alternation serves the same purpose as information exchange in the process of negotiation. The negotiating parties are primarily interested in achieving the results that are important to them, regardless of the impact of this achievement on the quality and quantity of outcomes achieved by the other party. At the same time, each party knows that she is reliant on the other party to some degree—that is, she must take the preferences of the other party into account while working together to achieve a mutually satisfying convergence on outcomes. The "self" orientation is associated with antagonistic feelings.

TABLE 2.4   Information Exchange and Its Aftermath in Johnson-Steeves v. Lee

Lee	Johnson-Steeves
Says: I am willing to pay for the child's private school education.	Says: I am willing to share the travel expenses when the child comes to stay with you.
Reveals: He earns more money than he said he does.	Reveals: She is moving toward the idea of shared parenting.
Result: He continues talking in order to counteract the effects of the information he has revealed and pursue information she has revealed.	Result: She continues talking in order to counteract the effects of information she has revealed and pursue information he has revealed.

The "other" orientation facilitates coordination. Alternation in the dominance and suppression of self and other orientations is a dynamic that propels negotiations from one phase to the next until the parties reach a convergence on outcomes. In these transitions, the orientation that is dominant at the end of one phase is suppressed at the commencement of the next, and the orientation that is suppressed at the end of one phase becomes dominant at the beginning of the next.

The motivational and cognitive processes underlying the sequential dominance and suppression of antagonism and coordination is described in the following internal monologue. When both parties engage in such a monologue, alternation enters the negotiation process.

> Focusing on my own objectives helps me make some progress toward achieving them, but if I focus on them for too long, I get angry and so does the other party. Then we both spin our wheels and get nowhere. To get out of this rut, I'll shift my focus to the preferences and objectives of the other party. Maybe she'll do the same. If she does, I'll feel a bit better about cooperating with her, and maybe begin to trust her. We'll move our negotiations forward. But, if I spend too much of my time focusing on her preferences, I may not get what's important to me. So, I'll try to avoid that possibility by refocusing on getting what I need.

Fundamental contradictions that are, or appear to be, similar to those described by Gulliver have been identified by other scholars. For example, Carnevale and Pruitt (1992, p. 539) describe a "dual concern model" of motivation, in which self-concern (concern about a party's own outcomes) and other-concern (concern about the other party's outcomes) are regarded as independent sources of motivation. Lax and Sebenius (1995) and Mnookin (1993) describe similar self and other motivational models. Missing from these motivational models, however, is the idea of alternation as a mechanism for propelling negotiations toward convergence.

A *mechanism* is anything that explains why *x* causes *y* (Elster, 1991). In conflict resolution, compromise is one mechanism that helps bring about agreements and resolve dilemmas, in mundane and interesting ways. Information exchange and alternation are mechanisms inherent in cyclical and developmental processes that propel negotiations toward mutually agreeable solutions. They do not, however, guarantee convergence.

Developmental Process

Gulliver's developmental model is called a "stepping stones model" because it is "analogous to a series of well-designed stepping-stones across a stream each one solid and firm and a comfortable stride from the next" (Gulliver, 1979, p. 172). This eight-phase model possesses a number of distinguishing attributes. It describes phases through which the many negotiations Gulliver observed actually proceeded. The model is not a linear one in which negotiators move from the first distinct phase to the last in a straight line from which they cannot deviate. Instead, phases can overlap, negotiators may skip phases and/or return to earlier ones. Different phases focus attention on different matters. The cyclical process described earlier occurs within each phase; antagonism and coordination may be dominant or suppressed at the start and end of a given phase, as well as in different phases. The model is diagrammed in figure 2.2.

SEARCH FOR AN ARENA

Where social norms, such as "a neutral location," are institutionalized or generally accepted, and where available locations have the necessary attributes, such as a large meeting room, breakout rooms, and electronic communications facilities, the parties may find it easy to choose an arena for their negotiations. When more than one such location is available, the parties may weigh the benefits and burdens of each, rank their preferences, and if they differ, reach a joint decision through negotiation.

CREATING AN AGENDA

As this stage opens, the parties are not quite sure what their conflict is really about. They are uncertain, anxious, and angry, and they become increasingly emotional as underlying issues emerge, and add to the burden of the surface issues that instigated the conflict. Out of the parties' highly emotional exchanges of information, counterclaims, demands, and reactions, an

FIGURE 2.2   Developmental Stepping Stones Model of Negotiation

A   Disagreement in ongoing social life
A   Crisis precipitates conflict

A _____ **C**
1. Search for an arena

     A _____ **C**
     2. Creating an agenda

          A _____ **A**
          3. Exploring the field
            (Emphasis on differences)

               C _____ **A**
               4. Narrowing the differences
                 (Emphasis on tolerable agreement)

                    C _____ **A** _____ **C**
                    5. Preliminaries to final bargaining

                        A _____ **C**
                        6. Final bargaining

                            C _____
                            7. Ritualization of outcome

                              _____
                              8. Execution of the agreement

TIME ——————————▶

A   Predominance of antagonism
C   Predominance of coordination

Source: Adapted from Gulliver (1979, p. 122).

agenda gradually emerges. Sometimes the parties arrive with well-thought-out lists of issues ranked in their order of importance. Otherwise, they create them during the course of negotiations. Trading or bargaining may occur, and the tentative agenda will reflect this. As negotiations proceed, the parties may add or drop issues from the agenda. As the parties negotiate their agenda, the power structure of their relationship will emerge.

Taken together, the arena and the agenda phases make an important contribution to subsequent negotiations by

- identifying a place where negotiations can take place,
- demonstrating that adversaries can agree on something,

- clarifying what the conflict is about,
- establishing ground rules for negotiations,
- determining who the negotiating parties are,
- revealing relative personal and positional strengths and weaknesses, and
- indicating to the parties that trading is an alternative to struggle during the course of negotiations.

EXPLORING THE FIELD

During this limit-setting phase, the level of antagonism between the parties may be higher than it was before negotiations started. It is almost certainly higher than it is during any other phase of negotiations. The stone upon which negotiators step in this phase sinks in a morass of name-calling, blaming, accusing, yelling, and threatening. The parties express extreme positions, make unrealistic demands, and enunciate the inviolable principles and shared societal values that invariably underlie their positions and demands. The level of expressed antagonism may vary, as may the effort that the parties put into preserving themselves as confident, tough, and determined.

Motivated by stress, the parties engage in hostile exchanges that nonetheless make an important contribution to the progress of negotiations in the succeeding phases by

- helping to dissipate emotions that might otherwise get in the way of problem solving during later phases;
- identifying a wide range of more-or-less relevant issues and positions that facilitate bargaining in a later phase;
- communicating differences in positions, preferences, and the parties' varying degrees of emotional attachment to them;
- learning about the strength of opposition to the parties' demands; and
- revealing the parties' possession, control, and willingness to use resources that could influence the outcome of the negotiation.

NARROWING THE DIFFERENCES

This phase can begin quite abruptly. It is often triggered by one party's perception that the other party is "getting real," which prompts a key decision: make a real offer in return. The atmosphere is relatively cordial. Communication between the parties becomes more coordinated, and clear progress toward joint action is evident. More realistic positions and demands are stated and the outcomes associated with them are identified. Often there are many interconnected issues and criteria that apply to them. Negotiators then face the complex task of jointly deciding the order in which the issues will be negotiated and whether the issues will be dealt with individually or in clusters. Negotiators must also decide how they will use the decision-making criteria that are at their disposal.

There are several approaches commonly used by negotiators when confronting the challenges of interconnected issues:

- Start with one party's list of issues or have the parties take turns presenting one issue at a time. This may mean modifying the agenda.
- Have the parties jointly decide which issues are most important to them, and deal with these issues first.
- Reduce the number of issues by treating them as indicators of underlying values or interests. For example, unionized female employee demands for a higher wage rate, better opportunities for promotion, improved working conditions, and better pensions may be indicators of the underlying value of gender equality.
- Have the parties jointly decide which issues are least important, perhaps eliminate some of them, and deal with the remaining issues first.

This phase reorients negotiations toward a more conciliatory approach and simplifies the process by reducing the number of issues. It also serves to identify the more difficult-to-resolve issues, while at the same time achieving an integrative result in which each of the parties wins something.

Preliminaries to Final Bargaining

As the parties acquire more information about alternatives and preferences, and assess the relative strengths of their own and each other's cases, they are better able to calculate a viable bargaining range. This is the first step taken during this phase. The second step is to reduce the number of criteria applied to difficult-to-resolve issues. For example, if wage increases are a contentious issue in reaching a collective agreement, the parties might reduce the number of criteria governing this issue by substituting an across-the-board increase for a series of different increases for different categories of workers. The third step involves trading criteria or issues. The final preliminary step is finding a formula (Zartman, 1975). The formula includes outcomes, the values underlying them, and the principles justifying them. Details are left to be worked out later. For example, where outsourcing work—that is, diverting work done by unionized workers to non-unionized plants where workers are paid less—is an obdurate issue, a formula that describes an agreement in principle may state the following: "Money saved by outsourcing will be reinvested, workers will be given stock options, and the rate of worker attrition will be speeded up by improved early retirement packages funded partly by savings on outsourcing, the maximum value of outsourcing savings allocated to these uses being set at 60 percent of the total."

This phase of negotiation contributes to the succeeding one by focusing the parties' attention on the final bargaining to come in an atmosphere where the parties have demonstrated their ability to reach agreements in principle, even on thorny and complicated issues.

FINAL BARGAINING

Reaching an agreement through incremental concessions is the "predominant mode of behaviour and interaction" in this phase (Gulliver, 1979, p. 162). Here, parties who are wary of risk and those who have already made more concessions in the past are likely to make more concessions in the future. As a negotiator, if you want to make fewer concessions than the other party, manage the expressions you give and give off in such a way as to persuade the other party that the risks you face are relatively inconsequential, you are willing to face them, and you are unlikely to make many concessions. These tactics will not likely succeed if the other party is, or becomes, angry or if your stance violates one of the other party's strongly held principles. The result could be a lose–lose outcome.

Negotiators may also use concessions as a trading bluff. For example, in a divorce negotiation, you could demand the living room rug (which you don't really want) so that you can later concede it in return for the antique clock (which you do want, but which you believe your ex-spouse may have withheld). You could also concede it in an effort to convince your ex-spouse that you are more generous than, in fact, you are. Remember, the incremental concessions process is influenced by both rational and non-rational factors, and by both honest expressions of desire and stances crafted for strategic purposes.

This phase contributes to the succeeding one by producing results with which the parties concur.

RITUALIZATION OF OUTCOME

In this phase, the parties ritually affirm the end of negotiations by engaging in activities that vary from handshakes, hugs, and kisses to coffee, drinks, and dinner to international media events. The closing ritual will depend on the duration and level of the conflict, how well the parties know each other, whether or not their relationship is a continuing one, whether or not their relationship is a public one, and whether other conflicts between them still exist. Frequently, the agreement is publicly announced by third parties, such as civil, legal, or political authorities who can be called on to intervene if the parties fail to comply with it.

This phase celebrates the conclusion of negotiations through the joint efforts of the parties and may create good feelings, even if temporarily, between former adversaries. Mutual good feelings probably make a greater contribution toward the durability of agreements than the mutually hostile feelings held by the parties at the start of negotiations and expressed by them during negotiations.

Execution of the Agreement

Negotiators usually delegate the task of setting down the details of the agreement in writing to others with specialized knowledge, such as lawyers, judges, engineers, and administrative staff. They also delegate the task of monitoring the parties' compliance.

This phase contributes to the durability of agreement, and decreases the likelihood of costly interventions by third parties. The execution phase also assists in identifying steps that could be taken in the event of non-compliance.

Evaluation

Strengths

The cyclical model has a number of strengths. Its dynamics (information exchange and alternation)

- apply cross-culturally; and
- have been validated by the formulation of similar models by other influential scholars such as Carnevale and Pruitt (1992), Lax and Sebenius (1995), and Mnookin (1993).

Weaknesses

The cyclical model also has some weaknesses. It

- fails to differentiate between negotiations in which a formula is more likely to bring about a convergence than incremental concessions from negotiations in which incremental concessions are more likely to bring about a convergence than a formula; and
- fails to incorporate personality factors that are known to have an impact on information exchange and alternation.

The developmental model, which describes the eight phases of the negotiation process, also has a number of strengths and weaknesses.

Strengths

The strengths of the developmental model are that it

- validates the phases used by professional negotiators (Douglas, 1957, p. 80; Gulliver, 1979, p. 175; Moore, 1996, pp. 66-67);

- provides a detailed description of processes that are ignored in simpler, three-stage negotiation models, such as the one formulated by Douglas (1962); and
- provides flexibility, allowing negotiators to step on more than one stone simultaneously, or return to stones they have stepped on earlier.

WEAKNESSES

The developmental model fails to identify key results that facilitate transitions from one stepping stone to another. The cumulative achievements of the parties is one such result; struggle may be another.

WHY NEGOTIATIONS CAN FAIL

Despite their propulsive force, negotiations may fail to result in a satisfactory outcome for one or more of the following reasons:

1. *At least one party is negotiating to avoid an agreement.* This party has a better alternative to a negotiated agreement available to him, but laws, rules, third-party expectations, or public opinion make it legally or socially necessary to give the appearance of trying to reach a negotiated agreement. Wallihan (1998, p. 259) refers to this as "demand avoidance." Consider the following example.

   Following interviews with faculty, staff, administrators, and community representatives, an applicant for a university position emerges as the unanimous choice, save one demurrer. The program head responsible for hiring does not welcome competition for the deanship, which he believes the candidate represents. Unable to offer the position to another candidate, the program head opens negotiations with the candidate by offering an insultingly low salary, engages in cursory discussions, and claims inability to raise the offer because of budgetary difficulties. After a few exchanges, the program head achieves the desired effect: the candidate withdraws in disgust.

2. *At least one party is negotiating to achieve an unrelated outcome.* The party is not negotiating primarily to achieve an agreement, but to discover information that she can use in subsequent legal proceedings, or to buy time, for example. Wallihan (1998, p. 261) refers to this as "opportunistic avoidance." Consider the following example.

   The government of India entered into negotiations with the United States, which sought to persuade India not to implement its plan to test nuclear weapons. India succeeded in convincing US representatives that it did not intend to do this. India, however, used the time bought by the "negotiations" to prepare for and test its nuclear missiles (Werner & Risen, 1998, p. A23).

3. *A realizable alternative becomes more attractive than a negotiated agreement.* Parties may enter into negotiations in good faith, but during the course of negotiations, events may occur that make realizable alternatives more attractive. Consider the following example.

   During extended negotiations between ambulance personnel and the municipal government that employs them, the provincial government passes legislation that reclassifies the employees. Ambulance drivers, paramedics, and correctional staff become "essential service providers," which makes binding arbitration available in the event that negotiations falter or stall. These workers believe that they will receive a higher annual pay increase through arbitration than they expect to receive through a negotiated agreement.

4. *Levels of hostility prevent shift to other orientation.* The parties' mutual level of hostility and mistrust may be so high as to inhibit, if not prevent, them from shifting from a self to an other orientation. Consider the following example.

   During the Camp David negotiations, high levels of hostility between Israelis and Palestinians were maintained by the fact that the Israelis saw themselves as victims of Palestinian violence and the Palestinians saw themselves as victims of Israeli oppression (Ross, 2004, pp. 274-276). Perceived victimization promotes a self orientation and undermines a self-and-other orientation.

5. *Deviations from the standard process cannot be absorbed.* Gulliver (1979, p. 75) posits the existence of a "more or less well recognized regular pattern of expectations and behavior" in the negotiation process. Deviations from this process that occur because of ignorance, inexperience, or attempts by negotiators to impose undue haste on the parties may result in failed bargaining. Consider the following example.

   During collective bargaining between the Canadian Autoworkers Union and General Motors in 1984, workers staged a wildcat strike at a General Motors plant. The strike turned out to be "the kiss of death at the negotiation table" (Hargrove, 1998, p. 109).

6. *The time is not ripe for negotiation.* For a variety of reasons internal and external to a conflict, it may not be the right time for a negotiated settlement by the parties, or by a third party called in to facilitate negotiations (Haas, 1990, p. 27; Zartman, 1983, p. 6). Consider the following example.

   During a conflict between mine owners and unionized workers at the Caney Creek coal mine (Ury, Brett, & Goldberg, 1993, p. 102), it was only after the parties reached a stalemate that hurt both sides, and the closure of the mine seemed imminent, that the parties agreed to call in a third party to set up a less costly means of resolving their conflict.

Goldberg, Sander, and Rogers (1992, pp. 84-85) identify the following reasons for the failure of negotiations:

- *Poor preparation.* The parties fail to collect relevant information, or if they do collect it, they analyze it poorly. If they collect and analyze it, they do not use it wisely in developing a plan.
- *Poor communication.* Communication is poor and ineffective.
- *Emotionalism.* The parties' emotions are so intense as to prevent the coordinated exchange of information.
- *Constituency pressures.* For example, in union–management conflicts, union members and shareholders may exert pressure on negotiators by identifying very different bottom lines.
- *Compromise impossible.* The stakes involved in negotiation may not be suited to compromise if they involve intensely held values, economic or group survival, or a threat or perceived threat to identify.
- *Risk.* The parties may have irreconcilably different attitudes toward risk.
- *Time.* The parties may have irreconcilably different attitudes toward the desirability of a prompt settlement.
- *No common ground.* There may be no common ground or zone of agreement.
- *Extrinsic factors.* Extrinsic factors may include linkages with other conflicts or pre-existing commitments.
- *Lack of trust.* Despite the best efforts of the parties, a fundamental lack of trust may fatally undermine their negotiations.

Beyond Failure: Conflict Escalation

Sometimes conflicts brought to the negotiating table do not merely remain unsettled; they may actually escalate in breadth and intensity (Rubin & Zartman, 1995). Pruitt and Rubin (1986, pp. 64-65) identify five stages of conflict escalation. These are

1. ignoring an incident or event that violates a party's sense of entitlement, or social or legal norms, or that offers an inadequate response to such real or perceived violations;
2. proliferation of issues;
3. generalization from issues to personal character attacks;
4. threats of sanctions; and
5. obtaining support from allies.

An extreme example of escalation arose in the road toll conflict between the government of Ontario and 407 ETR. The conflict spread from negotiations over the unilateral decision of 407 ETR to raise road toll rates to arbitration, to an appeal of the arbitrator's decision, to a threat from the Spanish government to veto a trade deal between Canada and the European free trade area (EFTA). A Spanish company is a part owner of ETR 407, and as a member of the EFTA, Spain has veto power. The threatened use of a veto helped persuade the Ontario government to reconsider its decision not to proceed with its annual purchase of 1.6 million litres of Spanish wine (Ibbitson, 2004). Stages 1, 2, 4, and 5 are evident in Ibbitson's description of this conflict.

CHAPTER SUMMARY

This chapter began with an introduction to several approaches to conflict resolution. We presented struggle and negotiation as two approaches in which the parties themselves attempt to settle a conflict. We defined struggle as the use of any means, including force, to settle conflict and drew attention to the costly nature of struggle. We then focused on negotiation, defining it as a process that involves verbal and non-verbal communication and joint decision making. We demonstrated that negotiation has lower transaction costs than struggle, and that negotiators experience less difficulty in achieving win–win outcomes than parties who use struggle to settle their differences.

Following our description of two general types or phases of negotiation—distributive and integrative—we focused on three negotiation models: positional bargaining, principled negotiation, and cyclical–developmental negotiation. In examining the major strengths and weaknesses of the three models, we found that positional bargaining is simple but ignores underlying values or interests. Principled negotiation focuses on underlying interests or values but is of limited applicability. Cyclical–developmental has cross-cultural applicability but neglects to consider personality, a factor that can influence the cyclical processes of information exchange and alternation.

RECOMMENDED READING

Delman, A.V. (1998). *Talking to the enemy*. Toronto: Oberon Press. This book, written by an Israeli soldier, describes a number of deadly struggles and concludes by identifying a mechanism for changing struggle to dialogue and negotiation.

Hargrove, B. (1998). *Labour of love*. Toronto: Macfarlane, Walter, and Ross. First-hand accounts of union–management struggles and negotiations are described by a union leader.

Ross, D. (2004). *The missing peace: The inside story of the fight for middle east peace*. New York: Farrar, Straus & Giroux. This book describes the strategies and tactics used by the Israeli, Syrian, and Palestinian negotiators who participated in negotiations aimed at settling conflicts in the Middle East.

Tannen, D. (1998). *The argument culture: Moving from debate to dialogue*. New York: Random House. This book describes how North Americans can reinvent their adversarial culture as one that embraces dialogue and aims at enlightenment, rather than winning.

Ury, W., Brett, J.M., & Goldberg, S.B. (1998). *Getting disputes resolved: Designing systems to cut the costs of conflict* (2nd ed.). San Francisco: Jossey-Bass. This book describes the impact of implementing a dispute resolution system based on interest-based negotiation on the context of a recurrent coal-mining conflict.

FILMS, VIDEOS, AND DVDS

Struggle

American dream. Documentary film directed by Barbara Kopple concerning union–management conflict in a meat-packing plant (180 minutes).

Matewan. Feature film directed by John Sayles concerning union–management conflict in a coal mine (180 minutes).

Thunderheart. Feature film directed by Michael Apted describing events leading to an armed conflict between native Americans and law enforcement agents (185 minutes).

Negotiation

Final offer. Film describing contract negotiations in the automobile industry that led to conflict within the union. Available from the National Film Board of Canada, Montreal, Canada, 1-800-267-7710 or http://www.nfb.ca (79 minutes).

Getting to yes. Eight tapes by R. Fisher, W. Ury, and B. Patton. Available from Program on Negotiation, 500 Pound Hall, Harvard Law School, Cambridge, MA 02138 (30-40 minutes each).

Resolving school conflict creatively in the school community. Available from triune@triune.ca or http://www.triune.ca (22 minutes).

WEBSITES

Japan Center for Conflict Prevention. http://www.jccp.gr.jp. The JCCP website monitors conflicts in different parts of the world and regularly offers dialogues and email symposia on conflict and its prevention.

CHAPTER THREE

Mediation, Arbitration, and Adjudication

{

Chapter Objectives

Define mediation, and describe criteria for assessing the usefulness of definitions.

Describe rights-based mediation, and identify its strengths and weaknesses.

Describe interest-based mediation, and identify its strengths and weaknesses.

Describe transformative mediation, and identify its strengths and weaknesses.

Describe narrative mediation, and identify its strengths and weaknesses.

Describe co-mediation, and identify its strengths and weaknesses.

Describe arbitration, and identify its strengths and weaknesses.

Describe mediation–arbitration, and identify its strengths and weaknesses.

Describe adjudication, and identify its strengths and weaknesses.

Identify criteria that are useful in selecting the conflict resolution procedure most suited to the needs of the parties.

MEDIATION

What Is Mediation?

A valid definition of "mediation" is a definition that captures the essence of the procedure. A useful definition is one that offers clear guidelines to theorists, researchers, and practitioners.

Moore (1996, p. 5) defines mediation as "the intervention of an acceptable third party who has limited or no authoritative decision-making power, but who assists the involved parties in voluntarily reaching an agreement." One problem with this definition is that it excludes mediations in which mediators influence the decisions made by the parties, even though they have no "authoritative decision-making power." Many of the mediators observed by Ellis (2003) influenced the decisions made by the parties by stating that the proposed terms of settlement were as good as, if not better, than the parties could obtain by choosing more costly and less certain options, such as arbitration or adjudication. These mediators, as well as others studied by Kolb and Associates (1994), adopted a style of mediation referred to as "evaluative" by Riskin (1996).

Mediators who adopt an evaluative style use techniques such as "urging, pushing parties to adopt settlements" and "predicting [the] impact of not settling" (Riskin, 1996). Moore's definition covers mediations in which mediators adopt a non-intrusive, "facilitative style," which "helps parties evaluate proposals" and "helps parties develop options" (Riskin, 1996). It excludes mediations in which mediators adopt an intrusive, evaluative style. A definition that more accurately captures the reality of mediation practice would be more valid and useful. It is important to bear in mind that some mediators are predominantly evaluative and others are predominantly facilitative; some are more evaluative in certain cases and more facilitative in others.

Kressel (1989, p. 522) defines mediation as "a process in which disputants attempt to resolve their differences with the assistance of an acceptable third party." If mediation is defined in terms of the parties' acceptance of the mediator, then mandatory mediation—including California's mandatory divorce mediation procedures and Ontario's government-funded mediation services that are connected to family court—is not mediation because the acceptability of mediators to litigants is not the criterion used in assigning mediators to cases.

Folberg and Taylor (1984, p. 7) define mediation as "the process by which participants together with the assistance of a neutral person or persons systematically isolate disputed issues in order to develop options, consider alternatives, and reach a consensual settlement that will accommodate their needs." This definition does not exclude mandatory mediation, but its validity is diminished by its exclusivity. For example, narrative mediation would be excluded because the third party is not neutral, and the methods adopted by narrative mediators are different from those included in Folberg and Taylor's definition (see below, under the heading "Narrative Mediation").

Lang and Taylor (2000, p. 157) define mediation as a triadic (three-party) interaction, and state that "interaction in mediation is the combination of communications, thoughts, feelings, intentions, interpretations and behavior of each person, which can and do affect the experiences and reactions of the other participants. It includes the internal and hidden processes as well as the external, observable communications and behaviors. Interaction includes all that is directly and indirectly communicated." This definition does not distinguish mediation from human social interaction as it is defined by sociologists, such as Goffman (1959) and Mead (1934). Fisher's review (1972, pp. 67-94) of "third-party interventions" suggests that the triadic social interaction referred to by Lang and Taylor is goal-oriented, guided by non-adversarial norms or rules, and by the presence of a third party who helps the parties involved in the conflict communicate with each other and solve their problems.

According to Wilmot and Hocker (2001, p. 43), communication "is the central element in all interpersonal conflict" and also "the vehicle for the productive or destructive management of conflict." Mediators Bennett and Hermann (1996, pp. 73-96) agree. At the same time, they state that "constructive communication," rather than communication as such, is the vehicle for the effective management of conflict through mediation (p. 730). Constructive communication is a skill learned and used by mediators to increase understanding through clear speech, attentive listening, paraphrasing, and summarizing (Bennett & Hermann, 1996, pp. 73-93). "Neutralizing" is a constructive communication skill that can be used to "de-escalate unproductive conduct that interferes with negotiation and problem solving [and to] help the parties communicate and hear each other better by neutralizing highly charged statements and antagonistic behaviors" (Bennett & Hermann, 1996, p. 19). For example, when one party says, "Before I make a public apology, I'll see you rot in hell," and the other party is about to respond in kind, a mediator can help to de-escalate the situation by saying, "So, how outsiders view this is extremely important to you" (p. 19). Bennett and Hermann (1996, pp. 19-23, 73-93) identify a number of constructive communication and basic mediation skills. For Bennett and Hermann, increasing understanding between the parties is not an end in itself; rather, it is a means to the end of mutual problem solving through negotiation.

Our review of the definitions presented here (and in other writing about mediation) suggests that an inclusive, useful, and valid definition of mediation is one that

- refers to the process as informal,
- identifies third parties as the facilitators of mutual decision making and understanding between the parties, and
- states that the parties themselves make decisions about outcomes.

With these criteria in mind, we define mediation as *a relatively informal process in which a third party facilitates understanding and/or mutual decision making by the parties to a conflict, who make decisions about outcomes.*

Most parties who participate in mediation are unfamiliar with this or any other definition of mediation. Because most of them do not know what mediation is, mediators invariably describe the process to them, inform them about their roles and the role of the mediator, and suggest ground rules for interactions between them.

An Overview of Principles and Procedures

Most mediators include all or some of the following points in their descriptions of the mediation process:

- *Agency.* The parties make decisions about the results of the process.
- *Mutual decision making.* The parties mutually decide the outcomes.
- *Full disclosure.* Mediation works best when the parties fully disclose relevant information to each other.
- *Fairness.* The parties have equal opportunities to present the merits of their cases.
- *Caucusing.* The mediator may ask to speak privately with the parties, and the parties may ask to speak privately with the mediator.
- *Qualified confidentiality.* Confidentiality is absolute unless the parties explicitly waive it. However, mediators must breach confidentiality in the event of a legal obligation to report child abuse or neglect, to prevent a crime, or to respond to a request by police who are investigating a crime that involves a party as suspect, victim, or witness.
- *Voluntary participation.* The decision to participate in mediation is voluntary, and the parties' continued participation is also voluntary in the sense that they can decide to conclude their participation at any time. This point is excluded where mediation is mandatory.
- *Alternative procedures.* By participating in mediation, the parties do not give up their rights to participate in other procedures such as negotiation, arbitration, or adjudication.
- *Unique outcomes.* Mediation is not governed by legal precedent or prejudice. Decisions made by parties in one mediation have no bearing on decisions made by parties in other mediations. Moreover, decisions made by parties in mediation have no bearing on decisions made by arbitrators or judges should the case proceed to arbitration or adjudication.
- *No adverse legal consequences.* No adverse legal consequences can arise from participating in mediation.

Roles

Mediators

- do not have the authority to make decisions about outcomes;
- help the parties fully communicate with each other to negotiate fair and mutually satisfactory results;
- establish or collaborate with the parties in establishing ground rules;
- manage the process of mediation;
- manage the content of mediation;
- help establish and maintain a productive working relationship between the parties;
- create a setting that makes the parties feel safe, physically and emotionally;
- determine that the parties have the capacity to mediate—for example, they understand the language in which the mediation is conducted and have adequate mental faculties to participate in the process—and that mediation is appropriate to the parties' needs; and
- communicate the power rule, "the harder you make it for the other party to say 'no'; the harder you make it for [the other party] to say 'yes.' " (Ury, 1991, p. 140).

Parties

- comply with the ground rules established by the mediator and/or each other;
- fully disclose information to each other;
- mutually participate in the negotiation process; and
- mutually make decisions as to outcomes.

General Ground Rule

A mediator may communicate the general ground rule of mediation to the parties in the following way:

> As parties, you are expected to treat each other with respect, not only because it is the right way to treat each other, but also because mutual respect helps establish and maintain a good working relationship between you. A good working relationship will help us solve problems quickly and effectively. What does mutual respect mean to you? If you agree that mutual respect excludes name-calling, yelling, threatening, insulting, interrupting, not listening, not responding, and making sarcastic remarks, then none of these things should happen during the course of this mediation. Do you agree?

MODELS OF MEDIATION

The mediation literature identifies four major models of mediation:

1. rights-based mediation,
2. interest-based mediation,
3. transformative mediation, and
4. narrative mediation.

The models differ from each other as a result of the objectives they seek to achieve. Rights-based mediation aims at reconciling positions on claims for restitution that arise from alleged violations of human rights codes and collective agreements. Interest-based mediation aims at reconciling the interests that underlie the parties' positions. Transformative mediation aims at changing individuals and relationships. Narrative mediation aims at changing relationships.

Rights-Based Mediation

The "rights" referred to in rights-based mediation are human rights. In 1948, the *Universal Declaration of Human Rights* was proclaimed and adopted by the General Assembly of the United Nations. The declaration includes a preamble and 30 articles that describe different rights and freedoms. Article 3 states, "Everyone has the right to life, liberty and security of person." Article 5 states, "No one shall be subjected to torture or to cruel, inhuman or degrading treatment or punishment." Article 12 states, "No one shall be subjected to arbitrary interference with his privacy, family, home or correspondence, nor to attacks upon his honor and reputation. Everyone has the right to the protection of the law against such interference or attacks." Article 18 states, "Everyone has the right to freedom of thought, conscience and religion." Article 23 states, "Everyone has the right to work, to free choice of employment, to just and favourable conditions of work and to protection against unemployment" and "Everyone, without any discrimination, has the right to equal pay for equal work." Article 26 states, "Everyone has the right to education."

The declaration applies globally. It has influenced human rights codes that apply locally. For example, Ontario's *Human Rights Code* cites the declaration in its preamble (Ontario Human Rights Commission, 1999, p. 10) and protects residents against discrimination in 5 "social areas" on 15 "grounds." The 5 social areas are services, housing, contracts, employment, and membership in trade unions and vocational associations. The 15 grounds are race, ancestry, place of origin, colour, ethnic origin, citizenship, creed (religion), sex (including pregnancy), sexual orientation, age, marital status, family status, disability, receipt of public assistance (in housing only), and record of offences (in employment only).

Human rights and freedoms are also protected in collective agreements between unions and management in government, business, and educational institutions. For example, York University's *Procedure for Dealing with Complaints of Harassment or Discrimination* (Sexual Harassment, Education and Complaints Centre, 2003, p. 1) allows complaints about human rights violations to be filed only by an "individual who believes she/he is being harassed or discriminated against on a prohibited ground set out in the Collective Agreement." Prohibited grounds include sex, religion, disability, and race or ethnicity.

The rights referred to in codes and agreements are written in formal language. Other rights—or generally accepted values that are involved in mediation, such as honesty or privacy—are unwritten. Rights are protected by both formal and informal, written and unwritten standards or values. For example, in Ontario, a pregnant 18-year-old who is denied housing because of her pregnancy can file a complaint with the Ontario Human Rights Commission, alleging sex discrimination in housing. (Complaints procedures included in formal human rights codes and agreements usually include mediation as an option for attempting to resolve alleged infractions.) If the pregnant teenager is living with her parents, she can complain about invasions of her privacy if her parents open and read her email messages and walk into her room without warning. She may attempt to negotiate a settlement with her parents. If negotiations fail, she and her parents may ask a respected relative, such as a grandmother, to mediate their rights conflict. If mediation by friends or relatives failed to produce a settlement, this teenager would not be able to take her case to the Ontario Human Rights Commission because it does not meet either "social areas" or "grounds" criteria.

In *Getting Disputes Resolved*, Ury, Brett, and Goldberg (1993, pp. 6-7) define rights-based mediation as a procedure in which a mediator relies "on some independent standard with perceived legitimacy or fairness to determine who is right." This definition is more appropriately applied to adjudication and arbitration than to mediation because, unlike judges and arbitrators, mediators are more interested in facilitating resolutions through mutual problem solving, increasing understanding, changing people, and mending relationships than they are in determining who is "right." In this connection, Sander and Goldberg (1994, p. 56) state that a mediator "can persuade the parties to put aside their factual dispute while at the same time agreeing on a mutually acceptable resolution of the dispute." Consider, for example, a case in which an employer and a disabled employee disagree about the facts relating to the employer's decision to dismiss the employee.

The employer states that the employee lacks the computer skills necessary for the job and that she is harassing him by taking the case to a human rights commission. The employee alleges that the employer has discriminated against her because of her disability. The case is referred to mediation, and is settled without reference to an independent investigator's report about the facts of the case. In most cases, mediation is an early, speedy, and relatively inexpensive first step. A time-consuming investigation of the facts of the case by an independent investigator takes place only if the parties fail to reach an agreement (Ellis, 2003).

A more useful definition of rights-based mediation is one that substitutes third-party facilitation of mutual decision making and understanding for a third-party determination of who is right. The substitution is evident in our definition of rights-based mediation: *a process in which a third party facilitates understanding and/or mutual decision making by parties involved in conflicts over alleged violations of human rights.*

Our definition covers mediators who facilitate understanding as an end in itself, as well as those—such as Bennett and Hermann (1996)—who facilitate understanding as a means to the end of mutual decision making. According to Kolb and Kressel (1994, p. 469), differences in the objectives of rights-based mediators reflect differences in the mediation frames they adopt. Kolb and Kressel (p. 469) define "frames" as "interpretative schemes mediators use to make sense of and organize their activities while at work on a dispute." Observations of mediators at work indicate that their practice is influenced by one of two mediation frames: communications or settlement.

Rights-based mediators who adopt a communications frame believe that

- misunderstanding is a major cause of conflict,
- the goal of mediation is understanding, and
- changing the ways in which the parties communicate with each other is the means to this end.

Rights-based mediators who adopt a pure communications frame view a successful mediation as one in which the parties are unlikely to become involved in future human rights conflicts caused by misunderstanding, because they now understand each other better.

Rights-based mediators who adopt a settlement frame believe that

- rights are violated because the violation brings benefits to the violator and/or helps the violator avoid costs,
- the goal of mediation is to settle the conflict that exists between the parties, and
- the means to this end is the reconciliation of the polarized positions taken by the parties with respect to how the conflict should be settled.

Observations of mediators at work suggest that a majority of mediators—including some who claim to use a communications frame—in fact adopt a settlement frame. For example, Kolb and Kressel (1994, p. 476) report that mediators who adopt a communications frame "influence how issues are framed, the ways problems are understood, and the flow of information between and among the disputants [and] the influence over conversations is one of the primary ways that mediators can foster agreements even when they claim that it is not a major aim they pursue."

Ellis (2003) has observed over 90 rights-based mediations of conflicts concerning alleged violations of Ontario's *Human Rights Code*. He has also mediated conflicts over alleged violations of a university's human rights code by employees and students. His observations indicate that the vast majority of parties involved in human rights conflicts want settlement more than they want understanding. Specifically, claimants want results that include monetary compensation, a job, transfers to a new job, reference letters, postings of human rights codes in places of work, funding for speakers on sexual harassment in high schools, and human rights training for managers and other employees. Respondents want outcomes that include payment of the smallest possible monetary compensation, avoidance of actions or documents that suggest they are guilty, and avoidance of publicity. Reconciliation of these positions is reflected in the terms of settlement agreed to by the parties.

Mediations conducted by mediators who adopt a communications frame require face-to-face communication and tend to take longer to complete than mediations conducted by mediators who adopt a settlement frame. Rights-based mediators who adopt a settlement frame complete mediations more speedily and increase settlement rates by engaging in shuttle mediation. *Shuttle mediation* is a process in which the mediator acts as a go-between, communicating with each party privately and conveying information from one party to the other. Control over this information helps the mediator present it in a manner that is objective and most likely to yield a mutually satisfactory settlement. Arguments, emotional outbursts, irrelevant discourse, and other communications that tend to prolong mediation and jeopardize settlement are avoided. In some cases where a significant power imbalance exists between the parties—for example, where an employer has retained a lawyer to act for her and an employee has no legal representation—one or both parties may prefer shuttle mediation to face-to-face contact. This may also be the case if the mediation involves allegations of sexual harassment.

Mediation services offered by bureaucracies, such as governments and established human rights organizations, encourage the use of a settlement frame and shuttle mediation to prevent backlogs and produce higher settlement rates. For all of these reasons, mediators employed by these organizations tend to adopt a settlement frame and use shuttle mediation (Ellis, 2003).

The rights-based mediation process is illustrated by two cases described in "The Rights-Based Mediation Process: Case Studies."

The Rights-Based Mediation Process: Case Studies

An Aborted Mediation

A student who was employed by a university during the summer filed a complaint based on sexual harassment against her supervisor after he transferred her from an interesting indoor job to a boring outdoor job. The student asserted that the supervisor was biased against women. The supervisor filed a rebuttal, stating that his decision to have the student work outside was based solely on her poor work performance and his belief that her level of motivation and skill was better suited to the outdoor job.

Neither party wanted to meet the other in face-to-face mediation. The mediator used shuttle mediation to meet privately with each of the parties on three occasions, and carried information acquired during the private sessions from one party to the other. The student stated that she was angry at the supervisor because of what he had done, but was willing to participate in mediation to resolve the conflict. She also wanted the matter settled as quickly as possible. The supervisor, who vehemently denied the student's allegation, was unwilling to participate in mediation because he felt that mediation would not reveal who was telling the truth. However, he was willing to participate in arbitration because he believed that the arbitration process would vindicate him. On receiving this information, the student stated that she would file a complaint with the Ontario Human Rights Commission.

Because only one of the two parties was willing to participate in mediation, the process was terminated.

A Completed Mediation

An employee filed a complaint with the Ontario Human Rights Commission in which she claimed that her employer had sexually harassed her over a period of approximately four years. She alleged that the employer's behaviour had resulted in her experiencing anxiety attacks, low self-esteem, and feelings of having been violated. The employee appeared to regard the mediation process as a means by which she could recover her strength and dignity—her ability to "feel whole again." Toward this end, she asked for compensation in the amount of $25,000. The employer made a counteroffer of $10,000.

The mediator told the parties that if the case went to a human rights tribunal, the tribunal would probably award the employee more than $10,000 because past awards had been significantly higher than $10,000. In a private session, the mediator told the employer that he could pay the employee a larger sum but recover most of the funds exceeding $10,000 by means of a tax refund. The employee responded to the employer's $10,000 offer by asking for $20,000. The employer then increased his offer to $17,500, and the employee accepted it.

The parties also agreed that the employer would write a "letter of regret" (not an apology) to the employee and a "letter of assurance" to the Ontario Human Rights Commission, stating that in the future his firm would comply with the Ontario *Human Rights Code*. In return, the employee would sign a letter releasing the employer and his firm from liability, and would undertake not to disclose any information pertaining to the case to any clients in the course of her employment in another firm.

Evaluation

STRENGTHS

Rights-based mediation has a number of strengths. It

- aims at achieving equality between the parties;
- produces a relatively high rate of settlements; and
- can simultaneously serve the private interests of the parties, the interests of organizations that create and enforce human rights codes, and the public interest generally.

WEAKNESSES

Rights-based mediation also has some weaknesses. It

- is useful only in cases where the parties are not primarily interested in public vindication or punishment;
- sometimes is unable to reconcile the significant gap that may exist between the public interest objectives identified in human rights codes and the private interests of the parties;
- deals with narratives (partisan accounts) brought to the table by the parties, but interventions such as "constructing alternative stories" and "dialogic practices" used by narrative mediators (Winslade & Monk, 2001) are not used by rights-based mediators facilitating positional bargaining; and

- favours shuttle mediation, which tends to produce less durable settlements that require monitoring and enforcement by agents of the state, over face-to-face mediation, which produces more durable, self-regulated settlements.

Interest-Based Mediation

Interest-based mediation is *a process in which a third party facilitates understanding and mutual decision making on outcomes by parties involved in conflicts of interest.* Interests can be manifest or latent. Manifest interests are interests that parties communicate to each other. Latent interests are interests that underlie the interests that the parties communicate. For example, in the Eastern Airlines union–management conflict (McKersie, 1995), the manifest interests of the union were higher wages and better working conditions, and the manifest interest of management was increased profit. The latent interest of their chief negotiators, Bryant and Lorenzo, was control over the airline (p. 215).

Manifest and latent interests can be shared, complementary, or non-complementary (opposing). Shared interests are evident when separating parents place the best interests of their children above their own individual interests. Complementary interests are those illustrated in the rhyme about Jack Sprat and his wife in chapter 2 under the heading "Create Options for Mutual, Not Personal, Gain." Non-complementary (or opposing) interests are evident in the alternative rhyme. In the original version of the rhyme, Jack and his wife share the roast in a complementary fashion; in the alternative version, Jack and his wife are opponents at the dinner table since each wants to eat everything in sight.

Mainstream interest-based models of mediation, such as those created by Bennett and Hermann (1996), are aimed at reconciling latent interests by facilitating principled negotiation. Bennett and Hermann's interest-based mediation model has seven stages, which are set out below.

Stages of Bennett and Hermann's Model

STAGE 1: INTAKE

At intake, mediators focus on conflict analysis (see "Conflict Analysis" in chapter 1) and screening for the appropriateness of mediation (see "Guidelines for Selecting Procedures" below). They also screen the parties for their capacity to mediate—for example, their ability to understand the language in which the mediation is conducted and their ability to articulate the merits of their case. Finally, mediators assess the parties' readiness and motivation to resolve their conflict through mediation. With a view to ensuring fair outcomes and a fair process, mediators also access power imbalances between the parties. Skills used by mediators during this stage include attentive listening and questioning, and accurate paraphrasing and summarizing.

A paraphrase is a shortened version of a statement made by one of the parties that includes the essential elements of the party's message. Thus, a mediator may paraphrase a long statement made by a party that identifies a number of concerns and reasons for them by saying, immediately after listening to the statement, "I understand that you have three major concerns, and that the last one you mentioned—your neighbour's dog attacking your children when it roams unleashed all over your property—is the most important one. Is that correct?"

Summarizing occurs when a mediator succinctly states the major points covered in a longer series of communications between the parties—at the conclusion of negotiations for the day or the morning, for example. Accurate paraphrasing and summarizing demonstrate to the parties that the mediator has been listening attentively to their messages and understands what is important to them.

STAGE 2: CONTRACTING

During this stage, mediators describe the mediation process in enough detail to enable the parties to make a fully informed decision about signing a contract to participate in mediation. They also collaborate with the parties in establishing guidelines for negotiation and communication between the parties, and describe the roles of the mediator and the parties.

STAGE 3: GATHERING INFORMATION

During this stage, mediators attempt to create a safe setting for the full disclosure of relevant information by the parties. A safe setting is one in which the parties feel free to communicate, negotiate, and problem-solve without fear of being harmed psychologically or physically. The mediator's job is to make the parties sufficiently comfortable so as to disclose information about the facts of the case, current issues, positions, interests, feelings, relationships between them, and areas of agreement and disagreement. Skills used by mediators include effective questioning using open- and closed-ended questions. Open-ended questions such as "Can you tell me what brought you to mediation?" invite a subjective opinion response, often in narrative form. Closed-ended questions such as "Do you prefer mediation sessions to be held on Tuesdays or Wednesdays?" often seek factual information. Other skills employed by mediators include attentive listening (which involves looking directly at the speaker and concentrating on the content and manner of the communication), careful observation and interpretation of non-verbal communications, paraphrasing, summarizing, and reframing.

Reframing is defined by Bennett and Hermann (1996, p. 87) as "a response to a message being sent from one party to another that intends to redirect, limit or shape the perception of the message being sent ... so that the message and its response become more constructive." The following is an example of reframing that changes a non-productive accusatory focus to a productive problem-solving focus. Party A says to Party B, "You are a liar. You don't deserve my trust. All I get from you is broken promises." The mediator reframes this by saying, "I understand, Party A, that you feel strongly about this and that you will need safeguards to be built into the agreement in order to feel confident that it will be carried out" (Bennett & Hermann, 1996, p. 88).

In another example of reframing, Kate and Max were participating in a separation mediation. Kate earned considerably more than Max did and resented having to conform with a family law that requires the higher-earning partner to pay spousal support to the lower-earning partner. Her resentment was partly based on the fact that Max, who earned a modest salary working for a non-profit organization, had often criticized Kate for earning a far greater salary working for a business corporation. Kate perceived the payment she would be making as Max "plundering" her savings. The mediator helped bring about a "mental shift" in Kate by reframing her payments as an "income supplement for a specified length of time" (Thernstrom, 2003, p. 43).

STAGE 4: IDENTIFYING ISSUES

In this stage, mediators focus on identifying all of the issues that the parties are concerned about and the strength of their feelings about each of them. Mediators identify issues and rank their importance to the parties by asking the parties open- and closed-ended questions. This information is used by mediators to "accurately frame the problems to be addressed" during the mediation and to frame them in such a way as to permit or invite different kinds of solutions (Bennett & Hermann, 1996, pp. 48-49).

Parties involved in identifying issues and ranking their relative importance tend to make blaming or partisan statements that may offend the other party and undermine progress toward the development of a collaborative, problem-solving relationship. Mediators attempt to prevent this from happening by using the mediation skill called "neutralizing." *Neutralizing* is a form of intervention by a mediator that "help[s] the parties communicate better with each other by neutralizing highly charged statements and antagonistic behaviors" (Bennett & Hermann, 1996, p. 19). For example, if Party A says, "My supervisor is an idiot. I want to be assigned to a work team with a different supervisor," the mediator can neutralize or reframe the supervision issue by saying, "Future supervision arrangements is a problem we need to address because it is of some concern to you."

STAGE 5: SETTING THE AGENDA

In this stage, mediators help the parties place issues on an agenda according to one or other of the following principles:

- Issues that both parties define as most important (or least important) are dealt with before (or after) issues that both parties define as less important (or more important).
- Issues that the parties mutually define as more urgent are dealt with before issues that the parties mutually define as less urgent.
- Where the parties differ as to the relative importance of issues, issues that one party defines as important are always followed by issues that the other party defines as important.

In some cases, logic dictates the ordering of issues on the agenda. For example, in a divorce mediation, the issue of custody usually precedes the issue of child support because child support payments usually depend on where the children live and for how long.

STAGE 6: RESOLVING EACH ISSUE

Bennett and Hermann refer to this stage as "the heart of mediation" (1996, p. 54). In this stage, mediators identify, classify, and list the interests and needs of the parties. Interests that underlie positions taken by the parties can be uncovered by asking the parties to answer questions such as "Why is this important to you?" or "How will this meet your needs?" (Bennett & Hermann, 1996, p. 58).

Classifying Interests

Bennett and Hermann (1996, p. 193) classify interest (or needs) as substantive, procedural, and psychological. Substantive interests are those that can be satisfied by such things as money, land, goods, or other material resources. More generally, substantive interests are those that are satisfied by the terms included in agreements and minutes of settlements. Procedural interests are those that are satisfied by implementing fair, democratic, timely, and respectful problem-solving procedures aimed at reconciling interests. Psychological interests are those that are satisfied by acknowledging, validating, and respecting the values, thoughts, feelings, and self-images of the parties. Values include equality, freedom, safety, education, health, harmony, peace, cooperation, winning, sharing, and exchanging (Bennett & Hermann, 1996, p. 94). Interests that underlie positions are usually psychological in nature.

Determining the Relationship Between Interests

After listing the interests of the parties, mediators compare them to determine their relationship. The parties may share certain interests, and other interests may be complementary or non-complementary (opposing) (Bennett & Hermann, 1996, p. 193). The revelation and identification of interests as shared or complementary significantly contributes to their reconciliation. *Mutualizing* is the mediation skill used in identifying interests as shared or complementary. Mutualizing occurs when mediators "help parties recognize areas of shared [or complementary] concerns, interests or benefits" (Bennett & Hermann, 1996, p. 190). For example, during a separation mediation, one parent may say, "I want our son Zhou to live with me so that he can continue his treatment for his liver problems with our family doctor, and if she thinks it's necessary, who will refer Zhou to a specialist." The other parent may say, "I want Zhou to live with me so that he can get an appointment with a local well-known specialist fairly quickly because my doctor is a personal friend of his." The mediator mutualizes the parties' interests by saying, "It is clear that the health of your child is very important to both of you."

Brainstorming, Bargaining, and Compromise

Non-complementary or opposing interests may be reconciled through brainstorming that reveals win–win options that were not immediately obvious. An example is provided in "Brainstorming at Summer Camp."

Brainstorming at Summer Camp

The owners of a summer camp were engaged in negotiations with cleaners who worked at the camp. The cleaners objected to the amount of time and effort they were putting into cleaning the campers' washrooms. The campers had been applying green lipstick and pressing their lipstick-covered lips on the large mirrors there. The owners of the camp claimed that they were unable to offer the cleaners more money to compensate them for their increased workload because the camp's budget was stretched to its limit. They attempted to solve the problem by appealing to the campers, threatening to write letters to their parents, asking counsellors to make random visits to the washrooms, forbidding campers from possessing green lipstick, and supplying anonymous "snitch" opportunities. The lipstick problem got worse.

Finally, the owners of the camp met with the cleaners with a view to collaborating with them to find a solution. During a brainstorming session, a number of new solutions were suggested. One of them was rated "best in camp" by everyone. The next day, the owners randomly selected one camper from each division and asked them to meet in the washroom. At the meeting, the owners asked a cleaner to demonstrate not only how she always attempted to remove lipstick marks from the mirror, but also how difficult and time-consuming the process was. The cleaner responded by dipping her long-handled mop in the toilet bowl and using it to clean the mirror. The lipstick problem disappeared immediately.

Non-complementary interests can also be reconciled through bargaining and compromise, as is illustrated in "Compromise for Ceasefire in the Middle East."

Compromise for Ceasefire in the Middle East

Palestinians seek the return of the West Bank and Gaza, land that formerly belonged to them. Israelis believe that their security from bombings, shootings, and other violent attacks will be jeopardized if Palestinians control land adjacent to Israel. Israelis and Palestinians want peace but militant Palestinian groups—such as Hamas—use violence as a means of attempting to drive Israelis from Gaza and the West Bank, and Israeli military forces use violence to achieve security from attacks by Palestinian militants.

In February 2005, Palestinian leader Mahmoud Abbas and Israeli Prime Minister Ariel Sharon agreed to take the first step toward peace by agreeing to a ceasefire. In return for Abbas's agreement to take effective steps to prevent militants from attacking Israelis, Sharon agreed to gradually release Palestinians held in Israeli prisons, transfer control over security to Palestinians in a number of West Bank cities, and stop assassinating Hamas leaders. Each side would probably prefer to obtain what they want without giving or doing anything to complicate relations with their constituents, but the Palestinian and Israeli leaders compromised, accepting some degree of difficulty with their respective constituencies, in return for a ceasefire.

Source: Kalman (2005, p. A1).

Using Objective Standards

Bennett and Hermann (1996, p. 58) advocate the use of objective standards in evaluating options or proposals put forward by the parties. Frequently, the parties bring different standards with them to mediation. Mediators can help settle these differences by identifying criteria that legitimate standards, such as relevance to the parties' case or general acceptance throughout an industry. Where the standards are equally legitimate, the parties can use bargaining and compromise to settle their differences.

Caucusing

During the face-to-face mediation process, the parties may say or do things that make it more difficult to resolve issues. Mediators attempt to prevent or deal with relationship-damaging conduct that undermines collaboration by caucusing. Bennett and Hermann (1996, p. 123) define a *caucus* as "a private meeting between the mediators and one of the parties" (p. 123). Unlike shuttle mediation, where the parties either never meet face to face or only do so at the start and end of mediation, caucusing involves relatively brief "interruptions" in the face-to-face mediation process.

In caucuses, mediators may attempt to balance imbalanced power relations by pointing out to the more powerful party that the less powerful party is less likely to comply with the terms of any agreement if he feels coerced or forced to agree. In addition, a mediator may provide both parties with information that is more useful to the less powerful party. For example, consider a mediator's decision to impart information about family court judgments that require ex-partners who earn high incomes to pay approximately $1,000 a month to ex-partners who earn lower incomes in situations similar to that of the parties. The effect of this information may be considerably more profound for a high-earning ex-partner who wants to pay no support than for a low-earning ex-partner who seeks only $750 monthly. Offering the information in caucus may also help the high-earning partner save face by conceding the matter to the mediator, rather than to the ex-partner.

Similarly, if one parent is angry with the other, because of "emotional manipulation, using the children as a weapon," the mediator may privately invite, validate, and thereby defuse the expression of strongly felt emotions that could jeopardize a collaborative working relationship if they were expressed in a face-to-face session. Later, in caucus with the manipulative parent, the mediator may point out that family law supports shared parenting, and that the parent's insistence on "sole custody" may result in the other parent's withdrawal from mediation in favour of taking the case to court.

Summary of Stage 6

In sum, resolving issues involves five steps:

1. identifying, classifying, and ranking the interests of the parties;
2. determining the relationship between the parties' interests;
3. brainstorming to discover win–win options and/or bargaining and compromise;
4. using objective standards to evaluate options and agreements; and
5. caucusing.

STAGE 7: REVIEW AND DRAFT FINAL AGREEMENT

In this stage, mediators work with the parties to draft an agreement that is "clear, concrete, easily understood and responsive to the interests of the parties" (Bennett & Hermann, 1996, p. 64). Mediators also advise each party to hire a lawyer to review the agreement.

Facilitating Negotiations in Interest-Based Mediation

In the interest-based model formulated by Bennett and Hermann (1996), mediators attempt to reconcile interests through facilitating principled negotiation. They also attempt to reconcile positions by facilitating positional bargaining to narrow the parties' bargaining range and settle the issues before the public reach their bottom lines (p. 103). In chapter 2, we noted that the bargaining range for positions on any issue is the gap between the bottom lines of the parties. Thus, if Party A would rather take a case to court than accept less than $4,000 in compensation for damages to her home and Party B would rather defend the case in court than pay more than $3,000 in compensation, the bargaining range between Party A's position and Party B's position is between $3,000 and $4,000. The mediator would therefore attempt to facilitate bargaining that resulted in the acceptance of an offer that fell somewhere between these two amounts.

Sometimes mediators attempt to change the bottom lines of one or both parties if they believe that the consequences of not reaching a settlement are very serious and that a change in bottom lines will facilitate the achievement of an agreement. For example, Dennis Ross, US President Bill Clinton's chief peace negotiator for the Middle East, acted as a mediator in shuttle mediation sessions between Binyamin Netanyahu and Yassir Arafat and members of their negotiation teams. During the private sessions held with each of the parties, Ross (2004, pp. 306, 324-335) pressured Arafat into accepting less than his bottom line, which was "nearly all of the West Bank" and then "13 percent of the West Bank." In private meetings, Ross also pressured Netanyahu into offering more land to the Palestinians than his bottom line of 3 percent. In fact, Ross presented a formula to Netanyahu in which 9 percent of the land was transferred to the Palestinians from different zones in the West Bank; the transfer was effected so as to transfer only 2 percent from a particular zone that was very important to both parties.

Evaluation

STRENGTHS

Interest-based mediation, which is designed to reconcile interests and positions, has all the advantages of principled negotiation and positional bargaining—that is, it does not damage and may improve relationships and has relatively low transaction costs. In addition, interest-based mediation

- is the model adopted by most practising mediators;
- facilitates a democratic process of mutual decision making; and
- facilitates positional bargaining, a conflict resolution procedure that is used in societies all over the world.

Weaknesses

Interest-based mediation that seeks to facilitate principled negotiation has four weaknesses associated with principled negotiation. It

- is culturally biased (LeBaron Duryea & Grundison, 1993; Kochman, 1981) and male gender biased (Kolb & Coolidge, 1995);
- offers little or no guidance to mediators who facilitate negotiations that include both distributive and integrative phases;
- offers mediators no coherent theory to inform power-balancing interventions; and
- has limited applicability because it may be inappropriate for large-scale conflicts involving negotiators who represent large constituencies—such as nations, unions, and shareholders—who expect to see their relative power positions reflected in agreements (McCarthy, 1995).

Transformative Mediation

Transformative mediation is *a process in which a minimally intrusive third party facilitates moral change in people through empowerment and recognition.*

Bush and Folger (1994) created the transformative mediation model as an alternative to interest-based mediators' conceptions of conflict. Interest-based mediators conceive of conflict as a state or condition, but Bush and Folger conceive of it as and ever-growing onion, whose layers represent conflicts. As one conflict ends (or layer is peeled away), a new conflict (or new layer) emerges. Interest-based mediators also view conflict as presenting a problem to be solved, or a matter to be managed, whereas Bush and Folger view conflict as "an opportunity for moral growth toward both strength and compassion" (1994, pp. 28, 81-82).

Unlike interest-based mediators—who are exclusively or primarily interested in satisfying the parties needs, solving problems, and settling conflicts—transformative mediators are primarily interested in transforming the parties. They believe that "mediation can be worthwhile even if settlement is not reached, because of new insights parties gain about their own situation and about the other party" (Bush & Folger, 1994, p. 142).

Concepts

Bush and Folger (1994) identify three major concepts: transformation, empowerment, and recognition. They define *transformation* as "change in the consciousness and character [of individuals] in the direction of moral growth."

Empowerment refers to "the restoration to individuals of a sense of their own value and strength and their own capacity to handle life's problems." The authors insist that empowerment does not mean giving advice to, or advocating on behalf of, weaker parties. In fact, transformative mediators empower the parties by avoiding advice giving, advocacy, counselling, and other interventions that undermine the ability of the parties to make decisions for themselves (p. 96). Empowerment is achieved when the parties believe that they are the authors of their own fate, and that they have the capacity and the ability to solve their own problems and make decisions that affect their lives.

Bush and Folger (1994) define *recognition* as "the evocation in individuals of acknowledgment and empathy for the situation and problems of others" (p. 2). Recognition is not conceived of as reconciliation, but rather as a non-contingent gift that one party gives to another with no expectation of a return (p. 96). Transformative mediators attempt to evoke recognition by encouraging "dual perspective taking" (p. 97). Dual perspective taking refers to a process in which each party views the conflict from the perspective of the other. Recognition is achieved when each party takes the situation of the other into account in making decisions.

Approach

A transformative approach is grounded in the following assumptions:

- people are inherently good,
- people are fully capable of making decisions,
- people look out for themselves, and
- people seek connection with others (Antes & Saul, 2001, p. 313).

Other distinguishing attributes of this approach include the following:

- commitment to the larger, more distant objective of changing society as a whole by changing individual members of society who are involved in conflicts with each other;
- dialogue, sometimes in the form of mutual story telling;
- minimally intrusive facilitation by the mediator;
- a focus on changing people, not settling the conflicts that participants bring with them to mediation;

- a conviction that restoring power and evoking recognition are the mechanisms that underlie transformation; and
- seizing all opportunities for transformation.

Process

Seizing all opportunities for empowerment and recognition requires careful and detailed observation of verbal and non-verbal communication between the parties. When transformative mediators observe opportunities, they intervene in non-intrusive or minimally intrusive ways, using established mediation skills such as attentive listening, effective questioning, and inviting each participant to take the perspective of the other.

Antes and Saul (2001, p. 318) provide an example of how a transformative mediator would respond to an opportunity for facilitating empowerment and recognition.

> The mediator is mediating a conflict between a husband and wife. During an early stage of the mediation process, the husband says, "I don't have a clue as to why she thinks I've been mistreating her." The mediator who has been carefully observing and the listener, his wife and also attentively listening to the speaker, perceives an opportunity for empowerment— the husband seeks clarification, he wants to know why his wife believes he is mistreating her—and she also perceives an opportunity for recognition— the husband is really interested in understanding his wife's perspective on this specific matter and perhaps on their relationship.
>
> The transformative mediator responds in the following way: *Says nothing and continues to look at the husband. The wife may choose to respond. Depending upon how she responds she may provide some clarity to her husband (empowerment). She may also provide her husband with insight about her thinking (empowerment and recognition). It may provide the wife with an opportunity to say things she has been wanting to say for a long time (empowerment).*
>
> An interest-based mediator responds in a different way: *Looks at the wife and asks her if she would like to respond. This puts pressure on her to respond (dis-empowerment). She responds by becoming defensive or by saying something the husband perceives to be non-genuine. In either case, empowerment and recognition opportunities are diminished.* [Emphasis added.]

In *The Promise of Mediation* (1994, p. 140), Bush and Folger refer to the mediator's use of communication and mediation skills as "mediator moves." The authors describe the process of transformative mediation, as it is practised in a case study, in terms of 27 mediator moves. Move 1 is "defining mediation in transformative terms." Mediators foster empowerment by "allowing parties to decide on commitment to ground rules" (move 3), "helping parties clarify their goals and options without direction from the mediator" (move 10), "allowing parties to control discussion of options" (move 13), "keeping evaluation/choices of options in parties' hands" (move 16), "asking questions to help parties clarify their options and make choices" (move 21), and "preserving recognition in the face of impasse" (move 25).

Mediators foster recognition by "probing past events to elicit a party's views of the other" (move 4), "probing in caucus to elicit a party's view of self and other and surface opportunities for recognition" (move 11), "offering possible reinterpretations of the other's behavior to evoke recognition" (move 12), "helping the parties respond to the opportunities for recognition surfaced in caucus" (move 18), "translating between the parties to evoke recognition" (move 19), "reframing parties' differences on substantive issues to maintain recognition" (move 20), and "preserving empowerment in the face of impasse" (move 26).

Model and Theory

The transformative–therapeutic model of mediation is presented in figure 3.1.

The model described in figure 3.1 is grounded in an explicitly formulated theory of society and its ills, which is described in figure 3.2.

FIGURE 3.1 Model of Transformative Mediation Practice

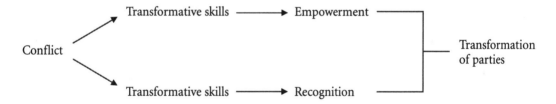

FIGURE 3.2 Transformative Theory of Societal Change

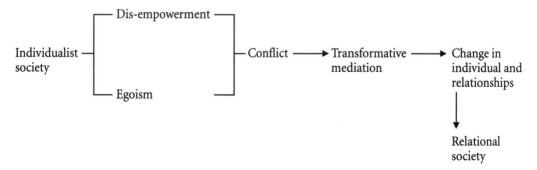

Evaluation

STRENGTHS

The transformative mediation model has a number of strengths. It

- identifies mechanisms—empowerment and recognition—that are thought to bring about desired changes in individuals;
- advocates the careful and direct observation of the minute details of interaction and communication between participants as the basis for mediator moves; and
- offers an innovative approach to practising mediators.

WEAKNESSES

Menkel-Meadow (1995) has identified a number of problems associated with the transformative approach. The following are among the more salient:

- Practitioners are asked to adopt a vague, but also a rigid, conceptualization of a transformation process that is indifferent to whether or not an agreement, which the parties may want, is reached (p. 231).
- Transformative mediation is based on the assumption that it is easier to change people than to change their situation, but no research evidence is presented to support this assumption, with which most psychologists (and sociologists) would disagree (p. 235).
- Transformational mediators criticize mainstream practising interest-based mediators for having their own agendas and interests, apart from those of the participants, yet the same thing is true of transformative mediators (p. 237).
- Two additional weaknesses with transformational mediation come to mind. Nothing inherent in the transformative approach hinders the integration of empowerment and recognition with the parties' desire to settle conflicts; however, this approach is presented in such a way as to divert attention from this possibility.
- The relative power of most parties involved in mediation, including transformative mediation, differs, yet transformational mediation ignores power balancing, leaving us with the impression that agreements or understandings achieved by the parties will reflect the power imbalances between them.

Narrative Mediation

Narrative mediation is *a process in which a third party facilitates the mending of relationships between parties by discovering and revealing positive, relationship-building content in their conflict-saturated narratives and assists the parties in creating new narratives.*

In Le Baron's (2002) relational approach to conflict, differences in meanings and identities—rather than differences in interests—underlie all conflicts. Resolving conflicts requires tools for "bridging meanings and identities." Mediators who adopt Le Baron's approach attempt to build bridges by using three types of tools: metaphors (p. 183), rituals (p. 25), and (the one narrative mediators use) narratives (p. 218). Narratives reveal values, identities, and feelings, and they build connections. Conflicts are transformed when the stories originally narrated by participants change. Changes in narratives are associated with changes in values, perspectives, attitudes, and relationships because narratives are paths to transformation (pp. 218-249).

Like Le Baron, Winslade and Monk (2001) adopt a relational approach to mediation in which building or rebuilding the relationship is either an end in itself or a precondition for achieving negotiated agreements about material results. Unlike Le Baron, Winslade and Monk explicitly ground their approach in postmodernism. Postmodernism is a theory of present-day societies that defines reality in terms of language, symbols, and images. For example, postmodernists emphasize the influence of clothing on how people think, feel, and act rather than the influence of peoples' thoughts, feelings, and actions on the clothes they wear. Postmodernist theory celebrates cultural diversity, and holds no specific perspective, account, or theory to be more valid than any other (Nicholson, 1990).

Winslade and Monk (2001, p. 70) characterize the postmodernist perspective by the following three attributes.

1. *Ethic of curiosity.* The narrative mediator's curiosity is unlike the non-narrative mediator's curiosity. The narrative mediator is genuinely curious about the stories that the parties tell and the meanings or interpretations that they offer spontaneously and/or in response to the mediator's questions. Non-narrative mediators are curious about whether information elicited from the parties through questioning confirms their hypotheses or reveals relevant facts.

2. *Diversity of perspectives.* Narrative mediators listen to and respect the diverse perspectives that the parties bring to mediation. They consider no perspective privileged, including perspectives grounded in science, objectivity, or neutrality. Thus, they reject the "objective standards" of Fisher, Ury, and Patton (1991) in evaluating agreements because these standards elevate the objective perspective of others. While non-narrative mediators emphasize empathy, neglect curiosity, and venerate the mediator's position and perspective, narrative mediators emphasize curiosity as much as, if not more than, empathy and the perspective and position of the mediator enjoys no particular privilege.

3. *Deconstruction of conflict-saturated stories.* Unlike non-narrative mediators, who believe that knowledge communicated by the parties represents reality or "the facts of the case" to a greater or lesser degree, narrative mediators believe that all forms of knowledge brought to mediation by the parties and the mediator are cultural products— that is, they are versions of reality created during conversations and discourses. Since all forms of knowledge, including knowledge presented in the form of conflict-saturated stories, are created by people within a social context, they can be deconstructed by narrative mediators and the parties working together as partners.

Narrative mediators Winslade and Monk (2001, p. 70) conceive of stories as "the backbone of experience" and "constitutive of the conflict" that brings the parties to mediation. Stories narrated at mediation are always selective in the sense that they include some elements of experience and exclude others. Conflict-saturated stories are selective in that they emphasize experiences, meanings, attributions, and motivations that support the continuation of the conflict. They ignore or downplay material that might end the conflict, such as positive relational experiences with the other party outside of or predating the present conflict.

Narratives filled with conflict originate in perceived violations of the parties' sense of entitlement (Monk & Winslade, 2001, p. 94). *Senses of entitlement* arise in specific socio-political contexts and are associated with "intentions and desires that have been socially constructed" (p. 96). For example, a society characterized by a long-standing race, class, and gender hierarchy creates different senses of entitlement in different citizens. Those who most amply embody society's most valued attributes are generally supported in their claim to greater entitlement than those who embody fewer of the attributes that society most values. Conflict is rooted in the "clash of entitlements that occurs between individuals and groups in overt or covert ways on a day-to-day basis" (p. 95). Clashes of entitlement, then, are viewed as not merely one cause, but as *the* cause of conflict. Consequently, narrative mediation is defined as a process that "addresses the conflict over differing notions of entitlement, rather than as a process that sets out to meet [or reconcile] people's needs [or interests]" (p. 96).

To address the conflict over differing notions of entitlement, the narrative mediator seeks to find the subjunctive spirit within each disputant and assist in the establishment of collaborative relationships between disputants. Unlike the disjunctive spirit, which is inflexible and closed-minded, the *subjunctive spirit* is flexible and open to change. Attaining substantive outcomes through solving problems is not a primary goal. Rather, it is an objective that is most likely to be achieved when negotiations aimed at solving problems follow conversations that facilitate the emergence of relational harmony and the subjunctive spirit.

As described by Winslade and Monk, the narrative mediation process that facilitates the attainment of these goals has three phases: engagement, deconstruction of conflict-saturated stories, and construction of alternative stories (pp. 57-93).

Engagement

Engagement is defined in terms of a relationship. Promoting engagement means helping to establish a relationship between the parties (Winslade & Monk, 2001, p. 62). During the engagement phase, narrative mediators attempt to achieve the following three objectives:

1. *Establish a trusting, respectful relationship with the parties.* To this end, the narrative mediator pays attention to the physical setting, cultural differences, and non-verbal behaviour of the parties. The mediator uses active listening, accurate paraphrasing, and timely summarizing to demonstrate that she understands the feelings, thoughts, and concerns that the parties express.
2. *Validate the perspectives revealed in the parties' stories.* In addition to demonstrating an understanding of the parties' concerns, the narrative mediator must avoid assuming an authoritative position. The assumption of such a position would undermine the process by simultaneously elevating the mediator's perspective and diminishing the parties' perspectives.
3. *Liberate the parties' subjunctive spirit.* The narrative mediator attempts to motivate the parties to work together as partners fully engaged in liberating the subjunctive spirit from domination by the disjunctive spirit, and "rescuing the spirit of understanding and cooperation from the jaws of conflict" (Winslade & Monk, 2001, p. 71).

Deconstructing the Conflict-Saturated Story

During this phase, the narrative mediator attempts to maintain the positive relationship established in the preceding phase and works to elicit from the parties "moments of agreement, cooperation, [and] mutual respect [that are] left out of the stories [that the parties] tell" (Winslade & Monk, 2001, p. 71). These moments are called *unstoried elements* precisely because they are excluded from the narrowly focused conflict-saturated stories.

These stories are narrowly focused because they communicate only the elements that support conflict. They include *position calls*, which "call the hearer into a position from which to respond" (Winslade & Monk, 2001, p. 72). For example, a historically dominant partner's story may call his historically submissive partner into a position of submission, and a historically submissive partner's story may call his historically dominant partner into a position of domination. Either or both of the partners can now choose to accept or refuse to accept the position they were called into. Mediator interventions focus on revealing the relative positions of the partners. Revealing relative positions sets the stage for engagement in dialogic practices (Winslade & Monk, 2001, p. 78).

A mediator uses *dialogic practices* when he "asks questions that will open up space for reconsideration of the conflict-saturated story" (Winslade & Monk, 2001, p. 78). For Monk and Winslade, dialogic practices are the "heart of the deconstructive phase" (p. 78). The narrative mediator's aim is to change the relative positions of the parties by revealing positive unstoried experiences. Unstoried experiences encourage the parties to accept positions that are inconsistent with the continuation of the conflict. The mediator asks questions that reveal the origin and progress of the conflict, and dialogic practices help the parties to separate themselves from their conflict-saturated stories and from the positions that these stories called them into.

The separation, however, is only partial. Dialogic practices do not help the parties identify their tactics—such as name-calling, accusing, arguing, and threatening—as the cause of problems in their relationship. Each party still believes that the conflict was caused by the other or by problems in their relationship.

For example, consider a situation in which domestic partners are arguing and calling each other names because each of them believes that it is the other's turn to take out the garbage, and neither wants to do it because both are habitually running late for work. Each blames the other and the pressure of work for their recurring arguments over taking out the garbage. Neither considers the possibility that the arguing and name-calling are themselves the cause of their relationship problems. Yet, this behaviour must be acknowledged and separated from the other alleged causes if their relationship problems are to be settled.

To facilitate this separation, narrative mediators develop externalizing conversations (Winslade & Monk, 2001, p. 79). *Externalizing conversations* identify the conflict itself and the tactics used by the parties as the cause of relational difficulties. They also identify the parties as victims of the conflict. In the words of Winslade and Monk, "argument is the cause of relational difficulties, rather than relational difficulties causing the argument" (p. 79). To the extent that parties view themselves as victims of the conflict, they adopt a new perspective on their relationship problems.

Dialogic practices and externalizing conversations help the parties separate from their conflict-saturated narratives. However, the separation is not yet complete because the narratives, which are based on assumptions that create and enlarge senses of entitlement, remain intact. Often, these assumptions are part of *dominant cultural discourses*, such as discourses that assume the superiority of men over women, Christians over Muslims, whites over non-whites, the employed over the unemployed, homeowners over the homeless, and so on. The parties separate themselves from conflict-saturated I-win–you-lose stories completely when they deconstruct the assumptions that underlie dominant discourses.

Narrative mediators assist the parties in deconstructing assumptions by asking them questions about what they are taking for granted when they say they are entitled to whatever they are claiming from the other party. Winslade and Monk view the mediator's "curious exploration" of linkages between assumptions, entitlements, and claims "as a step towards the creation of an alternative story, one that may be more inclusive of both persons' concerns" (p. 80).

Constructing an Alternative Story

During this phase, the narrative mediator focuses on unstoried positive experiences that contradict or refine the parties' conflict-saturated stories. For example, a spouse may exclude from a conflict-saturated narrative the evening that the couple joyously shared their daughter's concert performance, the strong emotional support they gave each other when their parents died, and the marvelous weekend they spent together at a cottage in Muskoka. This unstoried material is referred to a unique outcome. *Unique outcomes* are outcomes that "would not be predicted by" preceding events or communications (Winslade & Monk, 2001, p. 161). In the above example, the parties' shared joy would not be predicted by the conflict-saturated stories they tell about their relationship. With narrative mediators as partners, the parties construct alternative stories out of unique outcomes.

The parties' separation from the conflict-saturated story is now complete. The subjunctive spirit has been internalized by parties who respect each other, and relate to each other in a positive, conflict-free way.

The stage is now set for the narrative mediator to facilitate negotiations aimed at solving problems that relate to substantive outcomes. To this end, narrative mediators attempt to elicit reciprocal compromises from the parties. Compromise, then, is the mechanism that produces agreement on substantive outcomes in narrative mediation.

Narrative mediations conclude with a written account of the change that occurred in the course of mediation. The parties and the mediator collaborate in writing this account. The document is not a record of the narrative mediation process, but a part of it. The mediator may identify other positive unique outcomes and suggest that they be included in the written account. When reading the account, the parties are reminded about the good experiences they enjoyed and are motivated not to engage in conduct that might jeopardize their relationship (Winslade & Monk, 2001, p. 90).

Narrative mediation created by Winslade and Monk differs from nonnarrative mediation in three significant ways:

1. It is grounded in postmodernist ideas about social construction and deconstruction. The parties construct conflict-saturated stories and tell them to narrative mediators, who deconstruct them and help the parties create a different story to mend their relationship.
2. It identifies entitlement as the cause of conflict.
3. It rejects the notion of mediator neutrality and replaces it with the view that mediators "select ... some perspectives over others, or ... attune themselves to some people more than others" (Winslade & Monk, 2001, p. 36).

Evaluation

STRENGTHS

Narrative mediation has a number of strengths. It

- offers a relatively new model for practising mediators to reflect on;
- is cross-cultural in that it does not elevate individuals over the collective, as interest-based mediation does; and
- offers a theoretically grounded mediation model.

WEAKNESSES

Narrative mediation also has a number of weaknesses, which are set out below.

- An almost exclusive focus on relationships limits the applicability of the model to parties who want to maintain a relationship with the other party.
- There is no evidence to indicate that narrative mediation's single focus on relationships is more effective in helping parties settle clashing entitlement claims than a dual focus on relationships and results.
- It presents an inadequate account of facilitating problem-solving negotiation, and identifies only one agreement-producing mechanism: compromise.
- Narrative mediation practice, which favours some perspectives over others (Winslade & Monk, 2001, p. 36), appears to contradict the postmodernist directive against doing so.

- Narrative mediators ignore the issues of power and power imbalance, which characterize most relationships.

Co-mediation

Co-mediation is *a relatively informal process in which two or more mediators work together to facilitate negotiations and storytelling between contending parties, who make decisions about outcomes.* Mediations facilitated by two or more mediators are either ignored or neglected in the literature on mediation. For example, two major books on conflict resolution, *The Handbook of Conflict Resolution* (2000), edited by Deutsch and Coleman, and *Dispute Resolution* (1992), edited by Goldberg, Sander, and Rogers, do not include chapters on co-mediation, and co-mediation is not referred to in the index of either book. The same can be said of *The Mediation Process: Practical Strategies for Resolving Conflict* (Moore, 1996), one of the most frequently cited textbooks on mediation.

The neglect of co-mediation is surprising because of its usefulness to many societies. North American society, for example, is characterized by cultural differences and inequality among members of different gender, class, and racial or ethnic categories. Co-mediation provides a means of bridging cultural differences, balancing imbalanced power relationships, and producing settlements (Bennett & Hermann, 1996, pp. 115-116). Bennett and Hermann's findings indicate that in small claims court mediations involving whites and Hispanics, Hispanic claimants received "15% less than white claimants," and Hispanic respondents paid "18% more than white respondents" in the presence of a single mediator. The disparity was eliminated when the same case was co-mediated by two mediators of colour. Moreover, female co-mediators were more likely to achieve agreements than a single female mediator, and female co-mediators were more likely to achieve agreements than male co-mediators or a male and female co-mediating team. These findings suggest that the presence of two mediators, as well as the mediators' gender and ethnicity, influence the outcome of mediations.

Evaluation

ADVANTAGES
Co-mediation has a number of advantages, some of which are set out below.

- Conflicts can be multi-dimensional, involving emotional, financial, legal, and psychological aspects. By coordinating the expertise of specialists in these areas, co-mediation can provide a more effective service than mediation conducted by a single mediator.

- Negotiations facilitated by mediators require a dual focus on relationship and problem-solving aspects of a case. Well prepared co-mediators can implement a dual-focus approach more effectively than can a single mediator.
- Respectful, collaborative, focused interaction between co-mediators can serve as a conflict resolution model for contending parties (Folberg & Taylor, 1984, p. 143).
- Inter-cultural conflicts may be more effectively mediated where the ethnic, class, and gender composition of the mediating team reflects that of the contending parties.

DISADVANTAGES
Co-mediation also has disadvantages. It

- is more expensive for the parties to pay two mediators than one;
- is subject to delays associated with accommodating the schedules of two or more mediators; and
- involves a greater time investment on the part of mediators, who must know the history of the conflict and the "facts" of the case, as well as coordinate their interventions in an appropriate and timely way.

MEDIATION ETHICS

The term "ethics" refers to "principles/rules of right conduct" (*New Oxford Thesaurus of English*, 2000). The term "right mediator conduct" refers to "decisions, choices and actions ... that reflect/enact [professional] values" (Bagnell, 2004). The term "values" refers to actions, interactions and outcomes that society believes to be good or bad, right or wrong, desirable or undesirable. For example, whenever we find ourselves saying that lying is wrong and honesty is right (action), bullying is bad and helping another person is good (interaction), and one agreement is fair and another is unfair (outcome), we are making judgments about values.

Ethical standards (rules of right conduct) for mediators are formulated by professional mediation and conflict resolution associations such as the Association for Conflict Resolution (ACR), the Alternative Dispute Resolution Institute of Canada (ADRIC), and Family Mediation Canada (FMC). Appendix 3A sets out the ACR's *Uniform Mediation Act* principles. In addition, many scholars and practitioners have defined and discussed mediation ethics in books, reports, and journal articles. A review of these sources reveals that at least six ethical standards are consistently identified by most writers on the topic:

1. *Self-determination.* The parties' decision to participate in mediation is fully informed and voluntary. The parties themselves make decisions as to the outcome of mediation. The parties are free to decide to withdraw from mediation.
2. *Impartiality.* Mediators should not engage in conduct that is likely to create the perception that they are aligned with one of the contending parties.
3. *Fairness.* If evident power imbalances are likely to lead to unfair, and consequently unstable, outcomes, mediators should intervene to increase the negotiating power of the weaker party.
4. *Safety.* Mediators should create and maintain a safe environment during mediation, and manage the risk of coercion, violence, and abuse after mediation.
5. *Confidentiality.* At intake, mediators should inform the parties that the information they disclose in caucus and joint sessions will be treated as confidential, subject to these conditions:
   a) If the law, professional standards, and/or the possibility that others will suffer harm requires disclosure of information given in confidence, the information will be disclosed; and
   b) if the mediator believes that the information disclosed will be helpful in achieving outcomes that are desired by both parties and not harmful to others who are absent from the table, confidential information conveyed during caucuses may be disclosed in subsequent joint sessions.
6. *Conflict of interest.* Mediators should always declare interests or obligations that may interfere with judgments and decisions that serve the interests of the parties and others who are absent from the table.

The ethical standards described here are intended to "protect the public as well as members [of professional associations] from practices that might harm those they have chosen to serve" (Bagnell, 2004, p. 12). The protection offered by non-licensed professional conflict resolution associations, such as the ACR and ADRIC, is not as great as the protection offered by government-licensed associations, such as the Canadian Bar Association and Ontario's College of Physicians and Surgeons. The latter organizations create legal standards and rules of liability for lawyers and doctors, respectively. Lawyers and doctors found guilty of illegal or unethical conduct by complaint committees composed of their peers can be denied a licence to practise in a specific province, and the enforcement apparatus of the provincial government enforces the prohibition. The ethical standards created by the ACR and ADRIC, on the other hand, are not enforceable by the state, and the sanctions for deviating from them are much less severe (Bagnell, 2004,

p. 13). If they are not legally enforceable, what is the purpose of the ethical standards of the mediation profession? The answer is that they are standards that mediators should aspire toward, even if they sometimes fall short of fully achieving them in practice (Bagnell, 2004, p. 12).

When parties to a mediation file formal complaints about the allegedly unethical conduct of mediators, complaints committees have a tendency to identify "misunderstandings" as the cause of the impugned conduct (Bagnell, 2004, p. 130). Consequently, the committee's attention is diverted from an examination of violations of ethical standards, such as conflicts of interest, to an examination of the mediator's communication skills. Committees may suggest that a mediator attend training workshops that focus on communications skills. The identification of misunderstandings as the cause of all, or most, complaints filed against mediators may explain why education, rather than the imposition of sanctions, is the most frequent response of complaint committees. In some cases, however, education plus the imposition of sanctions may offer greater protection to the public from unethical or incompetent mediators.

A mediator against whom an unethical conduct complaint is filed may argue that the profession invites unethical conduct by publishing contradictory ethical standards—such as the need for client self-determination as well as the need for power balancing—but no guidelines for resolving the ethical dilemmas that result. Powers and Lipschutz (2004, p. 24) define an ethical dilemma as "a situation in which a practitioner is confronted with two conflicting duties that both have merit." Mediators also face an ethical dilemma when they are confronted with the duty of ensuring power-balancing, power balancing and impartiality, or confidentiality and trust. Another difficulty is that mediators may belong to other professional associations, such as the Canadian Bar Association or the National Association of Social Workers, whose ethical standards may contradict the standards included in the ethics codes of professional mediation associations. It seems that deviation from ethical standards is built into mediation practice, but guidelines promoting conformity with them are conspicuous by their absence (Powers & Lipschutz, 2004).

Regardless of whether a mediator practises narrative, transformative, or interest-based mediation, and regardless of the setting in which a mediator chooses to practise, the six ethical standards set out above are applicable. Some scholars, such as Moore (1996), state that "ethical standards developed for independent [practice] mediators are not always applicable to—and often do not fit—the roles and activities of many authoritative mediators (e.g. court based mediators doing mandatory mediation)" (p. 352). Scholar practitioners Kolb and Kressel (1994) agree with Moore. Based on observations of 12 "top professional mediators" at work, Kolb and Kressel (p. 46) conclude that a "new perspective on ethical standards is needed, one that recognizes ... the practical realities of the work" (p. 461). The mediators that Kolb and Kressel describe (p. 491) frequently violated ethical standards relating to conflict of interest and client self-determination.

On the other side are mediators such as Bagnell (2004), Bennett and Hermann (1996), and Picard, Bishop, Ramkay, and Sargent (2004), who contend that all mediators should aspire to conform to ethical standards.

Ellis's observations of human rights and divorce mediations indicate that bureaucratic objectives—such as achieving a high settlement (clearance) rate—trump self-determination and a mediator's obligation to declare potential conflicts of interest as guidelines for decision making. We are not convinced that the practical realities of conducting mediations in these settings justify the adoption of lower ethical aspirations; nevertheless, situational difficulties may stimulate thinking about practice-specific ethical standards.

ARBITRATION

Ury, Brett, and Goldberg (1993, p. 56) define arbitration as "a rights procedure in which the parties (or their representatives) present evidence and arguments to a neutral third party who makes a binding decision." More specifically, they regard arbitration as a "procedure for determining who is right" (p. 7) in the event of an alleged violation of rights. When a claim based on an alleged violation is rejected and the case is referred to private arbitration, the parties participate in a procedure that

- offers objective standards—such as fairness, legitimacy, or conformity—on which arbitrators must base their decisions;
- gives the parties an opportunity to select a mutually acceptable arbitrator who has the requisite expertise in the relevant subject matter, and to formulate the procedural rules the arbitrator must apply; and
- requires the parties to pay the arbitrator.

The Arbitration Practice Handbook, published by the Arbitration and Mediation Institute of Canada (1996), defines arbitration as "a legal procedure for resolving disputes using one to three neutral, private persons called 'arbitrators.' " The arbitrator is a decision maker appointed by or on behalf of the parties to a conflict to resolve the issues in dispute by applying the rules of law and fairness. The decision of the arbitrator is final and binding, unless the parties agree otherwise (p. 30). *The Arbitration Practice Handbook* was written with the Ontario *Arbitration Act* in mind. A brief summary of this act is included as appendix 3B.

Conscious that arbitration systems vary greatly because arbitration is "a private dispute resolution procedure designed by the parties to serve their particular needs," Goldberg, Sander, and Rogers (1992, p. 199) do not offer a definition of arbitration. Instead, they identify "essential elements" of the arbitration procedure as "proofs and arguments submitted to a neutral third party who has the power to issue a binding decision."

Binding and Non-Binding Arbitration

The Arbitration Practice Handbook identifies binding and non-binding arbitration as different forms of arbitration. *Binding arbitration* is "arbitration in which the arbitrator's decision is final, with finality being grounded in the parties' agreement, a statute or a court decision." *Non-binding arbitration* is arbitration in which the parties are not bound to accept the decision of the arbitrator (1996, p. 2). The authors of *The Arbitration Practice Handbook* state that binding arbitration is the most frequently used form of arbitration; non-binding arbitration is mainly used in conflicts involving organized labour and is "not recommended for commercial disputes" (1996, p. 2).

Judges and Arbitrators

Like judges, most arbitrators make binding decisions. Unlike judges, who are bound by certain significant decisions of other judges, arbitrators are not bound by any decisions of other arbitrators. However, observers of the National Hockey League's arbitration process have noted a "domino effect," in which salary awards made by some arbitrators to specific players in specific markets under specific circumstances are used by other arbitrators in other markets to award salary increases to other players in different circumstances (Naylor, 2004).

The parties themselves select an arbitrator, but they cannot remove or replace him. While arbitrators' decisions can be reviewed by courts in a process known as "judicial review," courts are very reluctant to interfere with the decisions of arbitrators. In fact, in some jurisdictions, courts support the parties' decision to replace an arbitrator they have selected only if the parties can show that the arbitrator is biased or lacks the requisite qualifications. Committing a fraudulent or corrupt act or unduly delaying the proceedings also are grounds for judicial review.

There are other noteworthy differences between arbitrators and judges. The following are some examples:

- Judges strictly enforce the rules of evidence; arbitrators do not.

- Judges conduct a formal process; arbitrators conduct a relatively informal process.
- Judges participate in a process that can be observed by the public; arbitrators participate in a private process.
- Judges are paid by governments; arbitrators are paid by the parties who hire them.
- There are penalties, such as fines or imprisonment, for failing to comply with a judge's order; there are no penalties for failing to comply with an arbitrator's decision, unless the arbitrator's decision is supported by a judicial order following a judicial review.
- Judges can review arbitrators' decisions; arbitrators cannot review judges' decisions.

The case of *Horton v. Jones*, in "Arbitration Case Study: Horton v. Jones," illustrates how arbitration works and how it compares with adjudication in a court.

Arbitration Case Study: Horton v. Jones

Synopsis

Professors Arthur Horton and Ruth Jones (pseudonyms) collaborated over a period of about three years on a lengthy article. The article was twice rejected by academic journals, and both rejections were accompanied by extensive criticism. Each time, the authors substantially revised the paper to respond to the criticisms. When they were ready to resubmit it for publication, a conflict arose over whose name should appear first. Originally, they had agreed that Jones would do most of the writing, and that her name would appear before Horton's. According to Horton, however, the numerous drafts followed by the two rejections and the extensive rewriting had resulted in his doing most of the work. Thus, he claimed he was entitled to have his name appear before Jones's. Jones denied Horton's claim, contending that the bulk of the writing in the current version was hers, and insisted that their original agreement about writing credits prevail.

Both authors wanted a prompt, inexpensive resolution of the conflict, and they agreed that arbitration would be preferable to litigation. The journal's editor informed both authors that their article would not appear until they resolved the authorship credit conflict.

Horton's Position

I am a full professor, the highest academic rank a professor can achieve. For the past three years, I have been working on a paper with Ruth Jones, a former student of mine. Jones is now an assistant professor at another university. (In fact, I helped her get the job by writing a strong letter of reference.) Jones wrote most of the original manuscript, but I offered suggestions. Because my full professorship outranks her assistant professorship, I believe my name should go first. Besides, the original idea for the article was mine. Each of the journals rejected the article and the reviewers suggested a number of revisions, which I wrote. There's another reason my name should go before hers when the article is published. I did agree to Jones's request that her name be listed before mine, but this was before I wrote the revisions. The article is an important one, and I would like to be credited as the lead author because my chances of getting a research grant will improve significantly. Jones rejected my suggestion about placing my name before hers. This surprised me because I am well known in the field, and Jones would gain a lot by having her name linked with mine on a major article. All her talk about the injustice of an alphabetical listing with my name first was really beside the point. Moreover, I offered her second authorship on two other papers—not of the same quality—that I was writing. She would, of course, have to contribute to the work. Negotiations between the two of us have gone nowhere. Jones and I agree that arbitration is preferable to taking the case to court.

Jones's Position
I am an assistant professor and a former student of Arthur Horton. When Horton and I decided to collaborate on a paper, we agreed that I would do most of the writing and that my name would be listed before his. In accordance with our agreement, I wrote most of the original article. Horton did revise the article, but revising an article is not as great a contribution as writing it. I felt that Horton's suggestion that our names be listed alphabetically (Horton and Jones) would not reflect this fact, and therefore I rejected his suggestion. Instead, I proposed that we adhere to our original agreement and list my name first. I am coming up for promotion to associate professor with tenure, and I believe that a published article with me credited as the lead author would enhance my chances. If Horton's name is listed first, the promotion and tenure committee will assume that Horton was the lead author and my colleagues will refer to our article as "Horton's." This is not fair. I am entitled to have my work recognized. Crediting Horton first might result in a delayed decision on my promotion and tenure. Horton's offer of second authorship on two other papers will have no impact on the promotion and tenure decision, which will be made before these articles are published—if they are published. Besides, I am not at all certain that I ever wish to collaborate with Horton in the future. Negotiations between us have

gone nowhere. Horton and I agree that we should try arbitration before getting lawyers involved and taking the matter to court.

Outcome and Analysis
Both parties wanted to avoid a trial. By participating in arbitration, they achieved some—but not all—of arbitration's "theoretical advantages" over court adjudication (Goldberg, Sander, & Rogers, 1992, p. 200). Specifically, arbitration gave the parties greater privacy and control over the process. It also saved them time and money. On the other hand, the relationship costs were probably as high as they would have been had they gone to trial.

Neither Jones nor Horton wished to have anything to do with the other in 21 of 27 role-playing simulations that were arbitrated by students in a number of conflict resolution classes held at York University. In almost all cases, the mock arbitrators decided that Jones's name should be credited first. They also decided that Jones should write a footnote acknowledging the significant contribution made by Horton. The most frequently cited reason for their decision was the verbal agreement between Horton and Jones in which the parties agreed that Jones's name would be listed first.

Source: Goldberg (1990).

Arbitration and Mediation

Like mediation, arbitration is a procedure for ending conflicts. It is structurally similar to mediation in that it involves a minimum of three people (a triad). However, in arbitration—but not mediation—one person is to make decisions about outcomes. The roles are also different in the two procedures. Mediators assume either a collaborative role, in which they work with the parties, or a facilitative role, in which they assist the parties. Arbitrators assume either partisan roles or non-partisan roles in which they make decisions about outcomes.

Arbitration and mediation take different approaches to the application of rules. In arbitration, rules exist to authorize a third party to make decisions about outcomes; no such rules exist in mediation. In mediation, the parties are expected to conform with rules that require them to communicate with each other during the process; no such rules exist in arbitration. In arbitration, rules created by professional associations, such as the Arbitration and Mediation Institute of Ontario and the American Arbitration Association, differ from rules formulated by professional mediation associations, such as Family Mediation Canada. For example, the former creates rules for binding arbitration, but Family Mediation Canada does not distinguish between "binding" and "non-binding" mediation.

Mediation and arbitration involve triadic interaction, but the approach, content, and patterns of communication that characterize the two procedures are different. Figure 3.3 shows that mediation is characterized by a non-adversarial approach and content that relies on the full disclosure of information. Arbitration, on the other hand, is characterized by an adversarial approach and the partial and strategic disclosure of information.

Patterns of communication are indicated by the arrows in figure 3.3. They show that there is direct communication between the parties in mediation and no direct communication between them in arbitration. In arbitration, the parties communicate with each other indirectly, either through their lawyers or through the arbitrator. Arbitrations are commonly settled by informal negotiations between lawyers for both sides, which take place under the "shadow" of an arbitration hearing. Because the parties generally want to avoid a hearing, sometimes cases are settled minutes or hours before the hearing is scheduled to begin.

Most arbitrations result in the arbitrators "splitting the difference" between the parties, which can result in win–win outcomes. For example, a teacher's association and a school board may realistically expect a 7.5 percent salary increase, but the union's opening offer may be 10 percent, and the board's opening offer may be 5 percent. The arbitrator splits the difference between them by awarding the predictable salary increase of 7.5 percent.

Baseball Arbitration

Baseball arbitration is an exception to the arbitration norm because in baseball arbitration win–win outcomes are not possible. The relationship costs can be as high as they are in court-based adjudication.

Mort Mitchnick is a private arbitrator whose work involves making a number of win–lose decisions about salaries for which there are "no replays and no explanations" (Millson, 1997, p. 55). Because there is no right of appeal, and no requirement for an arbitrator to give reasons for his decision, management–player relationships tend to be harmed by baseball arbitration. The process also exposes both management and players to unflattering and inflammatory comments and the use of statistics as weapons. In addition, the failure of salary negotiations results in frustration and anger, and means that players must take their original (unreasonably high) demands, and management must take its original (unreasonably low) counteroffer with them to an arbitrator, who will decide for one and against the other (Millson, 1997).

In non-baseball arbitrations involving unions and management, research findings indicate that arbitrators' awards tend to favour unions on the

FIGURE 3.3   Mediation and Arbitration: Approach, Content, and Patterns of Communication

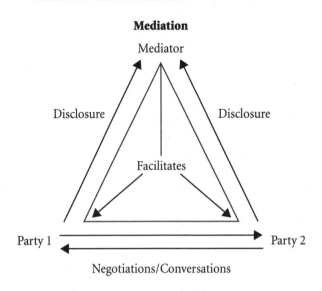

Mediation

Mediator

Disclosure   Disclosure

Facilitates

Party 1 —————————————▶ Party 2

Negotiations/Conversations

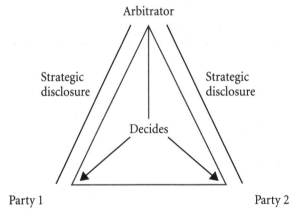

Arbitration

Arbitrator

Strategic   Strategic
disclosure   disclosure

Decides

Party 1   Party 2

subject of wage settlements and employers on non-financial subjects, such as restructuring (Cavalluzzo, 1999).

Evaluation

Strengths

Arbitration has been used since at least the 13th century. In England, merchant traders preferred to settle their conflicts by participating in a procedure that enabled them to apply their own trading customs, to appoint people familiar with these customs as arbiters, and to have a voice in determining the procedural rules. Today, arbitration is fully institutionalized. Goldberg, Sander, and Rogers (1992, p. 199) report that final and binding arbitration is included in "95 per cent of all collective bargaining contracts" and that it is used in a wide variety of conflicts.

As long as the arbitration system resists pressures to make it more like adjudication—with its extensive pre-trial procedure, strict rules of evidence, greater formality, and increased time and cost—arbitration has some distinct advantages over adjudication. Chief among these is the parties' ability to control the process used to settle their conflict. Arbitration also

- offers the parties control over the selection of arbitrators;
- permits arbitrators to apply the parties' own standards or norms in making their decisions;
- permits arbitrators to make decisions that are final;
- has lower transaction costs than adjudication; and
- facilitates negotiations between parties who know that if they do not reach an agreement, an arbitrator will make a decision that could go against them.

Weaknesses
Arbitration also has weaknesses, some of which are set out below.

- Relationship costs can be as high as those associated with adjudication and higher than those associated with mediation.
- The increasing formality of arbitration procedures can result in financial and time costs that are similar to those experienced by parties who participate in adjudication.
- Public confidence in the process is undermined by the selection or appointment of arbitrators on grounds other than their expertise in the subject matter.

MEDIATION–ARBITRATION

Goldberg, Sander, and Rogers (1992, p. 126) define mediation–arbitration as a process in which a third party "functions first as a mediator, helping the parties arrive at a mutually acceptable outcome. If mediation fails, the [mediator] then serves as an arbitrator, issuing a final and binding decision."

Mediator–arbitrator Adams (2003, p. 2) has described the Ontario English Catholic Teachers' Association case in which he acted as the mediator–arbitrator in the following terms:

Mediation–arbitration is a very informal process where the mediator–arbitrator is entitled to meet with each party separately or with all parties together. The parties executed a protocol of ground rules aimed at supporting the effectiveness of the process. Substantial written briefs were exchanged by the parties and filed with the mediator–arbitrator well before the facilitated hearing [took place]. The briefs were supplemented by extensive oral representations during plenary and closed sessions.

In this case, the parties failed to reach a mediated agreement. Acting as arbitrator, Adams issued an award, the terms of which are described in chapter 2 in "Punishing Struggle Tactics: Fallout from a Strike and Lockout."

The mediation–arbitration process is more complex than mediation or arbitration alone. Mediation aims at reaching an agreement; arbitration aims at rendering an award. Information relevant to reaching an agreement—such as information about the parties' underlying interests and the relationship between the parties' interests—is not relevant to rendering an award. On the other hand, whether the established facts support the position of one party over that of the other, is relevant to rendering an award but not to reaching an agreement. If the mediation portion of mediation–arbitration reaches an impasse, the mediator–arbitrator must then set about fulfilling her role as arbitrator (Fuller, 1962, p. 30).

The parties must also prepare for both procedures, and they are aware as they participate in mediation that they may reveal information that can be used against them if the matter evolves from mediation to arbitration.

In *Horton v. Jones*, role simulations conducted at York University revealed that strategic disclosure—motivated by fear of losing at an eventual arbitration—trumped full disclosure—motivated by the possibility of a win–win outcome at mediation.

It should be noted that Ontario's *Arbitration Act, 1991* prohibits arbitrators from participating in arbitration–mediation because acting in the role of mediator may taint the parties' impressions of the arbitrator's impartiality. The statutory rationale for equating mediation with perceptions of partiality is not provided.

Mediation–arbitration frequently follows mediations that reach an impasse for two reasons:

1. On the basis of past experience and/or the merits of their case, both parties believe that mediation–arbitration will yield the results they want.
2. If the parties do not reach a mediated agreement, only one third party is involved, and this third party can make a decision more quickly than a new arbitrator who is unfamiliar with the circumstances of the case.

Evaluation

Strengths

Mediation–arbitration has a number of strengths. It

- is more efficient than either mediation or arbitration alone because it takes less time to complete and yields a final binding decision (Goldberg, Sander, & Rogers, 1992, p. 226); and
- has a high settlement rate (of the 1,500 cases studied by Goldberg (1989, p. 9), 85 percent were settled through mediation–arbitration and only 15 percent proceeded to arbitration.

Weaknesses

Mediation–arbitration also has the following weaknesses:

- The integrity of the process may be undermined when the third party acting as mediator receives information from the parties that they would not give to an arbitrator—for example, their bottom line or BATNA—and then uses this information when acting as an arbitrator to make an award (Fuller, 1962).
- The integrity of the process may also be undermined by the tendency of the parties to disclose and exchange information during mediation with an arbitrated decision in mind.
- Arbitration is less likely than mediation to yield win–win outcomes.
- Settlements imposed on the parties by a mediator–arbitrator when acting in the capacity of an arbitrator are likely to have lower compliance rates than settlements produced by the parties themselves with the assistance of a mediator.

ADJUDICATION

Adjudication is *a process in which a third-party judge, authorized by the state and backed by its coercive power, compares partisan information presented to him by the parties in court in accordance with the law of the land and then renders a binding judgment that favours one party over the other.* The partisan presentations made in court by lawyers representing clients is part of the litigation process. Recorded judgments are the source of legal precedents followed by other judges. The report of a case cited by Hovius (1992, pp. 753-756), which was adjudicated in the trial division of the Newfoundland Supreme Court, appears in "Adjudication Case Study: Dean v. Dean." It may be helpful in understanding the process of adjudication as we have defined it.

Adjudication Case Study: Dean v. Dean

When a couple separated after three years of marriage, their child was a few months old. The mother was awarded custody. The father, Wayne, visited the child three or four times a year. The child enjoyed the visits and named a road that led to his father's cabin "Wayne's Road."

The child's mother applied for an order denying the father access to the child. In court, her lawyer presented evidence that indicated that the father was an alcoholic and that continued contact with him would harm the child. The lawyer also stated that the child would not miss his father, who was virtually a stranger to the child. The father, who wanted to continue visiting the child, testified that he no longer consumed alcohol. His evidence and demeanour made a favourable impression on the judge. The judge also noted that the mother presented no evidence to indicate that the father was uninterested in visiting the child, that his visits disturbed the child emotionally, that his lifestyle would adversely influence the child, or that he was undermining the upbringing of the child.

Legal precedents cited by the judge revealed a common pattern: access should be awarded to the parent who does not have custody of the child unless there is a clear reason for not awarding it. The mother failed to present this sort of evidence. The judge was also moved by the idea that a continuing relationship with both parents was desirable for the child's healthy development, and in the event that one of the parents should be rendered incapable of fulfilling parental duties as a result of illness, death, or accident.

After warning both parents about the consequences of engaging in conduct that may harm the child, the judge ruled that the father was entitled to reasonable access to the child at specified times, would be denied access on any day that he consumed alcohol, and must pay the mother's costs for bringing the case to court. He also ruled that the mother was entitled to have custody of the child and must notify the father promptly of any change of address.

Source: Hovius (1992, pp. 753-756).

Note that this case was adjudicated by a judge appointed by the state (the federal government), partisan evidence was presented to him by lawyers representing the parties, and the judge's decision was legitimated by family law and enforced by agents of the state (the provincial government).

Dean v. Dean is a relatively simple case. Most cases that proceed to trial are more complex. Many cases—for example, product liability cases—can involve costly and time-consuming procedures, such as examinations for discovery (where relevant documents are produced or individuals involved are medically examined), adjournments, interviews of witnesses and efforts to ensure that they appear in court, the cross-examination of witnesses, and the collection and organization of evidence.

Mini-Trial

Adjudication that takes place in a court is a public process. A mini-trial, on the other hand, is a private process in which the parties

- voluntarily agree to participate;
- sign an agreement on the procedure and timing of the mini-trial;
- participate in an informal and speedy disclosure process that involves exchanging briefs containing relevant information, such as the names of witnesses;
- mutually select a neutral adviser, often a former judge, who evaluates the strengths and weaknesses of each party's case and advises them about the likely outcome of the case should it go to trial;
- agree that the rules of evidence do not apply; and
- agree that information exchanged and agreements reached are confidential and cannot be used in any subsequent legal proceeding (Goldberg, Sander, & Rogers, 1992, pp. 230-233).

Mini-trials are "real-time" trials—that is, they deal with conflicts where serious consequences are either imminent or actually being experienced. Crosariol's (2005, p. B14) description of such a mini-trial appears in "Mini-Trial Case Study: Air Canada v. WestJet Airlines."

Mini-Trial Case Study: Air Canada v. WestJet Airlines

Air Canada and Deutsche Bank AG had an agreement in which the latter would provide recapitalization funds to the former. In the agreement, funding was contingent on Air Canada's occupying 14 gates at Pearson International Airport. In the meantime, the Greater Toronto Airport Authority, which operates Pearson, decided to award 6 of the 14 gates to WestJet Airlines. This decision jeopardized Air Canada's recovery from bankruptcy because the agreement it signed with Deutsche Bank AG made the receipt of $858 million contingent on the occupancy of 14 gates.

The parties, WestJet and Air Canada, agreed to participate in a mini-trial presided over by Mr. Justice Farley of the Ontario Superior Court of Justice. Lawyers for the parties presented their cases. Rules governing the parties' discovery of each other's cases were suspended, and witnesses were called on short or no notice and allowed to give evidence over the telephone. Within three weeks, the case was settled, with Air Canada retaining occupancy of the 14 gates.

Source: Crosariol (2005, p. B14).

Compared with adjudication as we defined it, real-time litigation is a speedier and less costly procedure for settling conflicts that involve serious imminent or ongoing consequences for the parties. Real-time litigation is most appropriate in business contexts where the life or death of a company hangs on speedy settlement of ongoing conflicts. Adjudication is most appropriate for settling conflicts that require the establishment of judicial precedents, profoundly change society, or require public acknowledgment of innocence or public denunciation and punishment of serious crimes against people and the environment (Sander & Goldberg, 1994).

Evaluation

Strengths

According to Fiss (1992, p. 247), adjudication has a number of advantages over negotiated and mediated settlements. One of the most important is that it alone "explicates and gives force to the values embodied in authoritative texts [such as the *Canadian Charter of Rights and Freedoms*] and interprets those values and helps bring reality into accord with them" (p. 247). Freedom of expression and security of the person are the kinds of values that Fiss has in mind.

Adjudication also has a number of other strengths. It

- results in final decisions, in the sense that there is no higher forum to which the parties can take their conflict;
- is transparent because trials are open to the public; and
- can be enforced by the power of the state.

Weaknesses

Fiss (1992, p. 244) criticizes settlements that lawyers negotiate before cases come to trial and mediation as an alternative to trial because these procedures represent a "capitulation" to the overwhelming workload of the judicial system. As alternatives to trials, negotiations and mediation may reduce court caseloads and speed up the rate at which conflicts are settled, but Fiss argues that "justice may not be done." Evidence cited by Glaberson (2000, p. 4) indicates that judges respond to increasing caseloads by taking shortcuts that "keep the courts functioning" but "undermine the fairness of the justice system."

One such shortcut is the failure to publish judges' decisions in case reports. The consequence of the failure to publish decisions is that new cases cannot be cited by lawyers and judges as precedents. In some of the jurisdictions examined by Glaberson (2000, p. 4), 90 percent of 2,500 rulings made by judges went unpublished. The absence of precedents "encourages inconsistent rulings that seem to be based on whim or bias." As a result, justice may neither be done nor be seen to be done. Another shortcut that contributes to the same result is "deciding thousand of appeals with one-word rulings like Affirmed instead of giving reasoned explanations for … decisions."

Adjudication has other weaknesses. It

- has significantly higher transaction costs than mediation and arbitration;
- yields far fewer satisfied participants than non-adversarial procedures (77 percent of mediation participants were satisfied compared with 40 percent of litigants (Ver Steeg, 2003));
- has lower compliance rates than mediation (Ver Steeg, 2003);
- is more likely to produce win–lose or lose–lose outcomes than mediation and arbitration; and
- offers participants minimal control over process and outcomes.

Guidelines for Selecting Procedures

We have identified struggle, negotiation, mediation, arbitration, and adjudication as five conflict resolution procedures. In this and earlier chapters, advocates for ending conflicts through struggle, negotiation, mediation, arbitration, and adjudication advanced reasons for preferring one procedure over the others, or preferring one procedure as a supplement or a precondition for others. For example, Luttwak (1999) prefers struggle over negotiation for ending some conflicts because the former was more likely to produce stability. Fisher, Ury, and Patton (1991) prefer principled negotiation over struggle or positional bargaining because it is more likely to produce a wise agreement. Rothman (1997) prefers dialogue over positional bargaining and regards it as an essential precondition for principled or other forms of negotiation. Bush and Folger (1994) prefer transformative mediation because it helps individuals change themselves, while interest-based models of mediation do not. Houck (1992) prefers arbitration over adjudication because it is less costly in terms of time and money. Fiss (1992) prefers adjudication over all other procedures because it proclaims and reinforces significant societal values.

Practitioners may use the selection criteria identified by scholars in choosing procedures for resolving particular conflicts, provided that they acknowledge that these may not be the same criteria that the parties prefer, *and* they offer good effectiveness and ethical reasons for ignoring the parties' preferred criteria.

The part played by party objectives in the selection of conflict resolution procedures included in a system designed to reduce the frequency of wildcat strikes is illustrated in the Ury, Brett, and Goldberg's study (1993) of union–management conflict in the Caney Creek coal mine. In 1980, Caney Creek was one of the most strike-ridden coal mines in the coal industry, "averaging more than one wildcat strike a month ... hundreds of thousands of dollars in lost wages and production, a high degree of dissatisfaction with the outcomes of disputes, a strained relationship on the verge of total breakdown and frequently recurring disputes" (p. 23). In February, Goldberg received a telephone call from "the president of the union district in which Caney Creek was located and the industrial relations manager for the coal company" (p. 102), informing him that the situation had reached the point where the mine might need to be closed, and asking him if he could help it survive by resolving the wildcat strike problem. Ury and Brett were called in as consultants.

In Ury, Brett, and Goldberg's "dispute resolution ladder" (pp. 62-63), prevention is the first and least costly step. It is followed by interest-based negotiation, mediation, and rights-based procedures, such as advisory and expedited arbitration and mediation–arbitration. Expedited arbitration is a relatively quick and streamlined procedure that excludes the presentation of a great deal of evidence and detailed arguments. Expedited arbitration is advocated for cases where "the stakes are low" or similar disputes are less likely to recur (Ury, Brett, & Goldberg, 1993, p. 56). Advisory arbitration refers to a procedure where an experienced arbitrator examines evidence and arguments and predicts the likely outcome of the case if it went to arbitration. The arbitrator's non-binding advice is delivered orally to the parties (p. 137). The last step in the dispute resolution ladder involves the most costly power-based procedures, such as strikes and lockouts.

Following its implementation, this sequence of procedures achieved a number of cost and relationship outcomes described in Ury, Brett, and Goldberg (1993). A reduction in the frequency of wildcat strikes was not one such achievement, however. Why not? Part of the answer is that the procedures ignored objectives that were important to the coal miners. These objectives included the opportunities for venting emotions and building comradeship that wildcat strikes provided. If alternative opportunities for achieving these objectives been included in the conflict-resolving procedures that Ury, Brett, and Goldberg implemented, the rate of wildcat strikes may well have decreased.

Engagement of the parties is an important factor in Sander and Goldberg's (1994) guidelines for selecting procedures designed to resolve conflicts. Sander and Goldberg advise practitioners to

- identify the parties' goals (by asking the parties what they want and how much they want it);
- identify barriers (by asking the parties why they have not yet been able to achieve their goals); and
- select a conflict resolution procedure that research indicates is most likely to overcome the barriers identified by the parties.

The identification of goals and barriers helps the parties select a private or a public procedure that is appropriate for them. Mediation, negotiation, and arbitration are private procedures that serve the interests of the parties. Adjudication in court is a public procedure that serves the interests of the public, as well as those of the parties. An example of a case in which a public forum is appropriate appears in "Adjudication: A Public Focus."

Adjudication: A Public Focus

Nicole Dussault (pseudonym) is approaching the age at which university policy requires her to retire. She wants to continue working full time as a full professor because she enjoys her work, wants to set a precedent that will affect other professors in other universities, and wants to affirm the value of the contribution she can make to society as an older citizen. She rejected the university's offer to continue teaching eight full-time courses over six years after her retirement.

The public interest is clearly involved in this case. It is best served by court adjudication because no other procedure can give Dussault a decision on mandatory retirement that will allow her to keep her full-time job, change the composition of the work force in other universities as well as her own, and reinforce the value of her seniority. Had Dussault been willing to accept the university's offer if it offered her 12 rather than 8 courses, negotiation would have been the most appropriate conflict resolution procedure.

We have cross-tabulated procedures designed to resolve conflicts with the parties' objectives in a table originally devised by Sander and Goldberg (1994, p. 59). The numbers in table 3.1 indicate the degree to which, in our estimation, each procedure achieves the listed objective. As long as our readers interpret the numbers as guidelines, and not precise indicators of ranking, table 3.1 will serve its purpose. Another purpose of table 3.1 is to elicit suggestions for improving it, or replacing it with something else.

TABLE 3.1 Selection Guidelines for Conflict Resolution Procedures

Client objectives[a]	Conflict resolution procedure				
	Struggle	Negotiation	Mediation	Arbitration	Adjudication
Client control over process	5[b]	5	4	5	0
Client control over outcomes	5	5	5	0	0
Minimizing costs	0	5	4	4	0
Speed	3	5	3	2	1
Privacy	0	4	5	5	0
Improvement or no deterioration in relationship	0	3	4	0	0
Vindication	5	0	0	3	5
Setting precedent	5	0	0	2	5
Reinforcing societal values	5	0	0	0	5
Recurrence of conflicts	5	3	1	4	5
Voluntary compliance	0	3	4	3	1
Maximizing recovery	5	0	0	0	5

[a] Clients are likely to have more than one objective; these objectives and their order of importance to clients are usually taken into account in selecting a procedure(s).

[b] Scoring assigns a number from 0 to 5 to each conflict resolution procedure, with 5 indicating the greatest likelihood of clients meeting their objectives and 0 indicating the least likelihood of their doing so.

Source: Adapted from Sander and Goldberg (1994, p. 59).

The information presented in table 3.1 suggests the following guidelines:

- Negotiation is the preferred procedure for parties who want to control both process and outcome, minimize transaction costs, and ensure voluntary compliance with the terms of settlement.
- Struggle is the preferred procedure for parties who want to control both process and outcome, seek to avenge themselves, set a precedent, or reinforce societal values.
- Mediation is the preferred procedure for parties who want to control both outcome and privacy, and who want to minimize costs, improve or at least not worsen their relationship, reduce the likelihood of future conflicts, and ensure voluntary compliance with the terms set out in the agreement.
- Arbitration is the preferred procedure for parties who want both control over the process and privacy and who want to minimize costs.
- Adjudication is the preferred procedure for parties who want to be vindicated, set a precedent, obtain large sums of money, or have their values reinforced in a public forum.

Sander and Goldberg (1994, p. 52) concluded that "it is only when the party's primary interests consist of establishing a precedent, being vindicated or maximizing (or minimizing) recovery that procedures other than mediation are more likely to be satisfactory." This conclusion, plus another stating that mediation is more likely than other procedures to overcome most barriers to settlement, and one more stating that "most clients in most business disputes" want what mediation delivers—speed, lack of expense, and no relationship damage—led Sander and Goldberg to formulate a rule of presumptive mediation (p. 44).

The rule of presumptive mediation states that "if ... mediation, satisfies the party's goal [it] should, absent of [*sic*] compelling indications to the contrary, be the first procedure used" (Sander & Goldberg, 1994, p. 59). Note that the authors state that mediation is not the only, but the first, procedure used. In cases where the parties want final decisions, orders enforceable by the state, large sums of money, winning outcomes, and public vindication or punishment, adjudication is the most suitable procedure.

The rule of presumptive mediation is a prescriptive rule. Most collective bargaining agreements follow the rule of presumptive negotiation when employers and unions are involved in conflicts. If negotiations reach an impasse, collective agreements usually call for mediation, which is commonly referred to as "conciliation." If conciliation fails, the parties proceed to arbitration. Frequently, the parties view conciliation as a stage through which they must pass quickly in order to get to the preferred procedures of arbitration or mediation–arbitration. In the labour relations field, the real contest is between negotiation and arbitration, and the criterion that the parties use in selecting one or the other procedure is the relative likelihood of obtaining the deal that they want (Hargrove, 1998, p. 71). If struggle tactics—such as threats of closures, lockouts, strikes, intimidation, or violence—will help the parties in obtaining a desirable deal, the parties tend to use them in conjunction with negotiation and arbitration (Goldberg, Sander, & Rogers, 1992, p. 435).

CHAPTER SUMMARY

This chapter began by defining mediation as a process in which a third party facilitates understanding and mutual decision making by parties who make decisions about outcomes. We then described four types of mediation: (1) rights-based mediation, in which mediators facilitate understanding and/or mutual decision making in situations that involve alleged violations of human rights; (2) interest-based mediation, a seven-stage model with a central problem-solving stage; (3) transformative mediation, a process designed to change people and relationships; and (4) narrative mediation, a process designed to replace people's conflict-saturated narratives with relationship-enhancing narratives. Rights-based, interest-based, transformative, and narrative mediators can mediate cases on their own, or with one or more other mediators. The chapter next designed and evaluated co-mediation. We then analyzed arbitration and mediation–arbitration, drawing comparisons among arbitrators, judges, and mediators. Court-based adjudication was the last procedure we described in the chapter. The weaknesses account for the great decline in the use of this procedure since the late 1970s. We devoted the final part of the chapter to the identification of criteria that can be used in selecting the appropriate resolution procedure for various types of conflicts.

APPENDIX 3A: UNIFORM MEDIATION ACT PRINCIPLES

These principles were developed by the Association for Conflict Resolution (ACR) as the basis of its response to the *Uniform Mediation Act* (UMA), and presented to the UMA drafters in spring 2001.

1. address only those areas (such as confidentiality) where uniformity is required;
2. preserve party empowerment and self-determination;
3. provide adequate, clear and specific confidentiality protections and, where necessary, limited and clearly defined exceptions that would maintain mediation as an effective confidential process in which people are free to discuss issues without fear of disclosure in legal or investigatory procedures;
4. reflect an understanding of the diversity of mediation styles and range of disputes mediated;
5. ensure that ground rules, and the role of mediators, parties, the mediation process, are easily understandable to mediation participants;
6. preserve mediation as a process that is separate and distinct from the practice of law, arbitration, and judicial proceedings;
7. provide that mediators may come from a variety of professional and non-professional backgrounds;
8. provide procedural protections for the disputants, the mediator, and the process when exceptions to confidentiality are raised;
9. adequately address how mediators, parties and representatives are to comply, if at all, with mandatory reporting requirements that may be required by law or professional ethical standards;

10. preserve the impartiality of the mediator; and
11. take into consideration the special concerns raised when the threat of violence is present.

Source: Association for Conflict Resolution, http://www.ACRnet.org/uma/principles.htm.

APPENDIX 3B: A SUMMARY OF THE ONTARIO ARBITRATION ACT, 1991

Arbitrations are conducted pursuant to "arbitration agreements," which can take any form. They can stand alone, or be part of another agreement. Such agreements need not be in writing. They can be revoked only under the standard principles that govern contract law.

Arbitrations are meant to be relatively informal. If "mistakes" are made and no one complains about them promptly, courts do not allow the parties to set the process aside on a "technicality."

The Act applies to all arbitrations in Ontario, unless another statute prevents it from applying or the *International Commercial Arbitration Act* applies.

Parties can agree that the provisions of the *Arbitration Act* do not apply to their situation. However, they cannot agree to an arbitration that does not provide "equality and fairness" and they cannot agree to limit the power of a court to extend time limits, set aside arbitration awards, or enforce arbitration awards.

The Act instructs courts not to intervene in an arbitration except to assist the process, ensure that arbitrators follow the procedure set out in the arbitration agreement, prevent unfair or unequal treatment of the parties, or enforce an arbitration award.

If one of the parties requests a court to adjudicate a matter that is already in arbitration, the court must stay (halt) the proceedings before it if a party asks it to do so. However, a court may refuse to stay the proceedings if it believes that a party signed an arbitration agreement while incompetent, the agreement is legally invalid, the subject matter cannot be arbitrated under Ontario law, the party waited too long to ask for a stay of proceedings, or the matter is a summary or a default proceeding.

Arbitrators have full power to decide questions of law that arise during an arbitration; however, judges can be asked to make decisions if all parties and the arbitrators agree.

Unless otherwise specified, an arbitration is conducted by one arbitrator. If the parties cannot agree on who should arbitrate or refuse to follow their own agreement, the court may be asked to appoint an arbitrator. If there are three or more arbitrators, the arbitrators must elect a chair. If there are two arbitrators, they may appoint a chair. A panel of arbitrators is called a "tribunal."

Arbitrators are under the general duty to act fairly and impartially. If an arbitrator comes to realize that she has or develops a "reasonable apprehension of bias," she must report that to the parties. Because arbitrator appointments cannot be revoked by the parties, it is a serious step to appoint an arbitrator.

The parties can challenge an arbitrator only on the grounds of bias or failure to possess the agreed upon qualifications. A party who knew that either of these grounds existed before he agreed to the arbitrator's appointment cannot use these grounds to challenge the appointment later.

A party who wants to challenge an arbitrator must first notify the other parties, who may agree to remove the arbitrator, or the arbitrator may resign because of the challenge. If not, the arbitrator must rule on the challenge herself. If the party is unsatisfied with the decision, he can apply to have a court decide the issue. The arbitration can continue while all this is being done.

A court can remove an arbitrator if the arbitrator is unable to do the job, commits a fraudulent or corrupt act, unduly delays the proceedings, or does not ensure equality and fairness in the process. If the grounds for removal are fraud or corruption, the arbitrator has a right to present a case to the court before it makes a decision. If a court orders the removal of the arbitrator on the grounds of fraud or corruption, it can order that the parties not pay the arbitrator for any work done and/or that the arbitrator compensate the parties for their costs.

The parties' arbitration agreement may provide a method for substituting a new arbitrator in the event that an arbitrator is removed. Alternatively, the parties may ask the court to provide such a method.

Each party must be given the opportunity to "present a case." The arbitrator or arbitration tribunal determines the procedure to be followed. If there is a chair, the tribunal can delegate power to make procedural rulings to the chair. The arbitrator of the tribunal determines such matters as the date, time, and place of hearings, whether the hearing will be oral or in writing, and whether lawyers will be present.

The arbitration process begins when "notice to arbitrate" is served in accordance with the arbitration agreement. Sometimes the agreement describes how and by whom an arbitrator is appointed. The authority to act begins at the moment that all of the arbitrators accept their appointments. Unless the appointment document specifies otherwise, the tribunal is empowered to decide all issues that the parties bring before it.

Arbitrators can compel people to be examined in separate procedures known as "discovery" or to produce documentary evidence. They can also administer oaths. Courts must enforce arbitration awards in the same manner that they enforce their own judgments.

Arbitrators can deal with "default" situations in the same way that courts can. They can, for example, issue subpoenas to compel witnesses to attend and give evidence under oath. They can also appoint experts to assist them if necessary.

In the event that an arbitration tribunal is not unanimous in its decision, the opinion of the majority prevails. Arbitrators can order any remedy that a court can—including specific performance. They can also grant injunctions. Arbitrators can, of their own accord, ask a court for assistance on any matter.

Arbitrators are not authorized to act as mediators or conciliators, or to engage in any process that may create the impressions that they are not impartial. If the parties settle their conflict during an arbitration, the arbitration ends.

Arbitrators make their awards in writing, and communicate them to the parties. They may or may not give reasons for their decisions. If an arbitrator does not give reasons for making an award, the parties or the court can demand that the arbitrator provide them. Arbitrators can also make interim awards. An arbitration ends once an arbitrator hands down an award, although the costs of the procedure are determined later. However, within 30 days, an arbitrator can correct her award if she discovers mathematical errors or if an amendment is needed to "correct an injustice."

If the parties' arbitration agreement does not cover the matter of appeals, an appeal can be made to the courts by convincing a judge that the relevant matter is of general public importance. An appeal can succeed on such grounds as party incompetence or lack of equality between the parties. The parties can eliminate the possibility of an appeal by agreeing to do so in their arbitration agreement.

Limitation periods apply to arbitrations.

Arbitrators can require the losing party to pay the winning party's costs. Without such an order, each party pays his own costs. Arbitrators' fees and expenses may be assessed by the courts, in the same manner as lawyers' fees and expenses.

RECOMMENDED READING

Delman, A.V. (1998). *Talking to the enemy.* Toronto: Oberon Press. This book, written by an Israeli soldier, describes a number of deadly struggles and concludes by identifying a mechanism for changing struggle to dialogue and negotiation.

Kolb, D.M. (1994). *When talk works.* San Francisco: Jossey-Bass. This book provides first-hand accounts of mediators at work, attempts to explain the gap between myth and reality, and includes an insightful discussion about mediator power and ethics in the final chapter.

Menkel-Meadow, C. (1995). The many ways of mediation: The transformation of traditions, ideologies and paradigms. *Negotiation Journal*, 217-242. This article provides an insightful discussion and analysis of mediation and mediation models.

Sherif, M. (1996). *In common predicament: The social psychology of intergroup cooperation and conflict.* Boston: Houghton Mifflin. This book presents theory-guided field experiments, which identify mechanisms that bring about cooperative changes in intergroup relations.

Stone, D., Patton, B., & Heen, S. (1999). *Difficult conversations.* New York: Viking. This book offers useful advice about difficult conversations during negotiations and in life away from the bargaining table.

Ury, W., Brett, J.M., & Goldberg, S.B. (1993). *Getting disputes resolved: Designing systems to cut the costs of conflict* (2nd ed.). San Francisco: Jossey-Bass. This book describes the impact on labour relations of implementing a conflict resolution system based on the rule of presumptive interest-based negotiation in a coal-mining context.

FILMS, VIDEOS, AND DVDS

Environmental mediation. Available from Stitt Feld Handy Houston http://www.adr.ca (35 minutes).

Facilitation and collaborative problem solving: Dispute resolution techniques. Directed by David Straus. Available from the Program on Negotiation (PON) at Harvard Law School.

Mediation—Is it for you? Available from the American Bar Association, 541 N Fairbanks Court, Chicago, Illinois, 60611-3314 (18 minutes).

School mediation. Available from triune@triune.ca or http://www.triune.ca (29 minutes).

The neighbourhood spat. Directed by Nancy Rogers. Video describing a mediated neighbour conflict involving age, lifestyle, and noise. Available from Rogers Salem Video Library. (36 minutes).

WEBSITES

Japanese Center for Conflict Prevention. http://www.jccp.gr.jp. This website offers opportunities for participating in Internet conferences about international conflicts.

National Film Board of Canada. http://www.nfb.ca/showpeace/. This website offers excellent videos about healing circles and peacemaking in a variety of social contexts.

Triune Arts. http://www.triune.ca. This website offers a wide variety of videos and booklets that demonstrate the effectiveness of negotiation and mediation in resolving conflicts in schools and communities.

CHAPTER FOUR

Power

{ **Chapter Objectives**

Define "power" according to resource and process theory.

Compare the usefulness of resource and process definitions to negotiators and mediators.

Describe resource and process theories of power and their practical implications for mediators and negotiators.

Apply the process theory of power to the Cree–Hydro-Quebec conflict.

DEFINITIONS OF POWER

Definitions of power vary, but many of those most relevant to the conflict resolution procedures discussed in chapter 2 fall into two major groupings: unidimensional and multidimensional.

Unidimensional Definitions

Unidimensional definitions equate power with resources (Blood & Wolfe, 1960; Scanzoni, 1970). Power varies with the possession or control of resources; the party who possesses or controls the greater resources has the greater power. For example, according to Blood and Wolfe (1960, p. 12), in domestic conflicts, "The balance of power [is] on the side of that partner who contributes greater resources to the marriage." Blood and Wolfe define power resources as "anything that one [party] can make available to the other [party] to satisfy his/her needs or attain his/her goals." Following Blood and Wolfe, Allen and Straus (1980, p. 196) and Scanzoni (1982, p. 69) define power in terms of the possession or control of resources. For both, the greater power of husbands is due to their possession or control of greater resources.

In international conflicts, the balance of power favours the nation with greater military and economic resources. For example, US-led forces won the most recent war against Iraq because "the weight of firepower and high-tech [instruments of war]" produced by a military budget that was "over 250 times bigger than Iraq's" greatly favoured the US-led forces (Dyer, 2003, p. A29). In the Middle East, the balance of power is allegedly shifting from Persian Gulf countries that control oil to Turkey, which controls water (Kaplan, 1994, p. 68).

Multidimensional Definitions

Various authors have proposed multidimensional definitions of power. Cromwell and Olson (1975, pp. 5-6) define power as having three dimensions: resources, how resources are used, and outcomes that result from having resources and/or using them. In the multidimensional definition formulated by Giddens (1993, p. 227), power means "the use of resources, of whatever kind, to secure outcomes." Rubin and Zartman (1995, p. 350) define power as "the perceived capacity of one side to produce an intended effect on another through a move involving the use of resources." In Coleman's (2000, p. 113) definition, power is "usefully conceptualized as mutual interaction between the characteristics of a person and the characteristics of a situation, where the person has access to valued resources and uses them to achieve personal, relational or environmental goals."

Distinguishing Unidimensional (Resources) from Multidimensional (Process) Definitions

Multidimensional definitions that include resources and the use of resources are called "process definitions." Unidimensional definitions that define power in terms of resources are called "resource definitions." Differences between resource and process definitions of power are illustrated in "Weight, Use of Weight, and Outcomes."

Weight, Use of Weight, and Outcomes

In sumo wrestling, weight is a resource. In a recent championship match one wrestler weighed 400 pounds; the other weighed 600 pounds. In a resource definition, the balance of power favours the heavier wrestler. Yet, the lighter wrestler, the one with fewer "weight resources," won the contest because he used his other resources—balance, speed, and agility—more effectively than the heavier wrestler used his weight and strength resources. Of course, if the weight difference was more extreme—for example, 600 pounds versus 140 pounds—size and strength alone would probably have resulted in a victory for the heavier wrestler.

Because resource differentials between parties involved in actual conflicts can be extreme, scholars formulating multidimensional definitions include resources as a dimension of power.

The Parties' Use of Resources

Sometimes, the resources possessed by parties involved in a conflict are roughly equal, and yet one party achieves a desired outcome because she uses her power more effectively than the other party by taking a risk and making a credible "irrevocable commitment" (Schelling, 1960, p. 24). Schelling does not define commitment. Lax and Sebenius (1995, p. 105), however, define commitment as taking "a position from which one cannot recede [without] exposing yourself to large costs if you accept settlement less than the specified cost."

Schelling's example of the power of commitment is instructive. Consider the case of Sam and Sally, two truck drivers. They are driving 18-wheeler trucks at 100 kilometres an hour approaching a narrow one-lane bridge from opposite directions. Each driver is equally determined to cross the bridge first. When both drivers are about 50 metres from the bridge, Sally—in full view of Sam—hurls her detachable steering wheel out of the window. She is now fully committed to crossing the bridge without veering off or stopping. Sam responds by driving onto the shoulder of the road and stopping, leaving the bridge clear for Sally (Schelling, 1960, pp. 35-36).

One of the major advantages of making irrevocable commitments for parties with few power resources is that they can use them to achieve desired ends in conflicts with more powerful parties. In this connection, Pruitt and Rubin (1986, p. 58) note that Mahatma Gandhi used "commitment of his frail body to a fast he could not endure for very long as a powerful lever to force the mighty British [government] to yield." Gandhi, a man possessed of powerful spiritual and political resources but few material ones, led India in achieving independence from the British in 1947.

Credible irrevocable commitments can be a risky, but effective, way of achieving desired ends under certain conditions (Pruitt & Rubin, 1986, pp. 58-61). For example, when Sally threw her steering wheel out the window, she relinquished control over her truck, forcing Sam to give way or collide with her. The effectiveness of her risky commitment depended on Sam's "understanding and acknowledging the consequences of the commitment that has been made." Suppose Sam had been glancing at a map at the moment when Sally threw the steering wheel out of the window. Or suppose Sam had become panic-stricken and unable to do anything but grip his own steering wheel more tightly. Sam might also have assumed that Sally was merely divesting herself of a spare steering wheel that she customarily carried with her. He might have thought that Sally was playing a trick and kept driving until it was too late to avoid a collision.

Finally, if Sally knew Sam well, she might be reasonably certain that he would prefer to drive onto the shoulder of the road than to collide with her truck. If she did not know him well (or know him at all), she might be unaware that he was deeply depressed over the untimely death of his wife and had decided to commit suicide. Playing "Chicken" with strangers or relative strangers is a very risky business. According to Pruitt and Rubin (1986, p. 59), irrevocable commitments should be made only when the parties have a "thorough knowledge of [their] opponent's perceptions and values."

Not infrequently, resources provide leverage—that is, resources can be regarded as levers that can be moved or depressed in order to get people to do things they do not want to do (Freund, 1992, p. 45). For example, in 2002, Andrew Fastow, Enron's former chief financial officer, was charged with 78 counts of fraudulent conduct that resulted in his gaining millions of dollars at the expense of shareholders and taxpayers (Mclean & Elkind, 2003, p. 409). In 2003, his wife, Lea Fastow, former assistant treasurer at Enron, was charged with wire fraud, money laundering, and filing false tax returns. According to Lea Fastow's lawyer, prosecutors were using the charges against her as leverage to get her husband to plead guilty to all charges in return for dropping or reducing the gravity of the charges filed against his wife (Smith, 2003, p. 6).

In the context of relations among nations, Nye (2002) distinguishes between "hard" and "soft" US power. Hard power refers to the US's power to coerce other nations by threatening to use or using military resources. Soft power refers to its power to co-opt or persuade other nations by using cultural resources, such as "the American way of life," an amorphous notion that includes films, songs, clothing, food, religion, values, and medical, educational, and economic assistance. Recent criticisms of Nye's dichotomy of power types draw attention to the fact that hard power resources—such as battleships, helicopters, and military cargo—are being used to provide medical and other kinds of humanitarian assistance (soft power) to nations experiencing catastrophic natural events, such as the tsunamis that devastated several countries in Southeast Asia in 2004 (Traub, 2005).

Relational Definitions

A review of the definitions of power indicates that an integrated multi-dimensional definition—one that includes both resources and their use—functions better for theorists, researchers, and practitioners than a uni-dimensional definition. Accordingly, we define power as *a relationship in which differences in the parties' resources and in their willingness and ability to use them are reflected in the reliability of achieving the outcomes they desire.* This definition covers both cases in which parties with more potent resources prevail over parties with less potent resources in reaching their objectives, as well as cases in which parties with less potent resources prevail over ostensibly more powerful parties.

A relational definition of power is also formulated by Deutsch (1973, pp. 84-85) and adopted by Lewicki, Saunders, Barry, and Minton (2001, p. 148). The definition we offer differs from theirs in two ways. Our definition

1. distinguishes between resources and the use of resources, and
2. involves two personal resources—willingness and ability—which determine whether the parties use their resources in ways that reliably yield desired outcomes.

The resources we refer to in our relational definition include material, cultural, and personal resources. Material resources include property, oil, water, money, food, and shelter. Cultural resources include values, ideals, norms, rules, expectations, stereotypes, and senses of entitlement. Personal resources include intelligence, willpower, size, physical strength, and personality.

RESOURCE THEORIES OF POWER

Chapters 2 and 3 have illustrated that struggle, negotiation, mediation, arbitration, and adjudication are all processes aimed at ending conflicts. The conclusion of a conflict can result in three different outcomes: win–win, when both parties gain; win–lose, when one party wins and the other loses; and lose–lose, when both parties lose. Resource theories of power link the variety of outcomes with differences in the quantity and quality of resources possessed or controlled by the parties. The link between resources and outcomes is expressed in the following proposition: the greater the resources possessed or controlled by an individual or group, the greater the power of the individual or group. This proposition is central to resource theories of power that have been applied to struggle (Hobbes, 1651; Luttwak, 1999; Dyer, 2003); negotiation (Blumberg & Coleman, 1989; Fisher, Ury, & Patton, 1991; Lax & Sebenius, 1995; Scanzoni, 1982; Straus, 1980); mediation (Bottomley, 1984; Grillo, 1991; Fischer, Vidmar, & Ellis, 1993); and adjudication (Erlanger, Chambliss, & Melli, 1987).

Scope of Power Resources
In the widely cited resource theory of negotiating power formulated by Fisher, Ury, and Patton (1991), the primary negotiating power resource is

the BATNA (best alternative to a negotiated agreement). According to these authors, "The better your BATNA, the greater your power [and] ... the relative negotiating power of two parties depends primarily on how attractive to each is the option [alternative] of not reaching an agreement" (p. 102).

Lax and Sebenius (1995, p. 105) focus on alternatives available to negotiating parties. According to their resource theory, the "improvement in a [negotiator's] alternatives improves the distribution of his or her negotiated outcomes." Why? Because more or better alternatives change the bargaining range by changing "the standard of acceptability to which possible settlements are compared" (p. 107). This theory is illustrated in "Better Alternatives Change the Bargaining Range."

Better Alternatives Change the Bargaining Range

The successful candidate for a position of assistant professor is negotiating his starting salary with the dean. The department that submitted the candidate's name to the dean wants this candidate and no other because he is uniquely suited to and qualified for it. The dean offers him a starting salary of $50,000 plus a one-course reduction in teaching load during his first year. The successful candidate, who is an excellent teacher, has a better BATNA than the dean because the dean has no alternative candidate to whom she can offer the position.

The candidate's BATNA is an offer from another university of a starting annual salary of $60,000, with an additional $15,000 for research, a one-course reduction in teaching load in his first year, and the services of a research assistant during his first year. When the candidate tells the dean the details of the rival offer, the dean revises her offer, matching the starting salary, research money, and research assistant offered by the other university and offering an additional half-course reduction during the first year. The candidate accepts the dean's revised offer.

The resource and process theories described above identify BATNA, alternatives, education, income, emotional independence, love, and gender as power resources, but power resources themselves have not been defined. What, then, is a power resource? For Blood and Wolfe (1960, p. 12), as we have already seen, it is "anything that one [party] can make available to the other [party] to satisfy his/her needs or attain his/her goals." In order to help the other party achieve his or her objectives, the party with the resources must guess, assume, or know the motivations of the other party.

French and Raven (1959) use the assumed or known motivation of the party over whom power is exercised to derive their widely cited classification of power resources. They define power resources as "bases of power," and identify six bases (types) of power: information, expertise, legitimacy, rewards, punishment, and reference power. Reference power refers to a heightened concern for the opinions, judgments, and welfare of others.

Dependency and dominance are implicit in French and Raven's definition of power resources. Party A is dependent on Party B to the extent to which Party A is the sole, most reliable, or least costly source of outcomes desired by Party B. In relational theories of power—formulated by Blau (1964), Emerson (1962), Scanzoni (1982), and Wilmot and Hocker (2001)—power exists only in the context of a relationship between two or more persons, groups, or nations. One person, group, or nation is dependent; the other is dominant. Following Emerson (1962), Wilmot and Hocker (2001) offer a relational theory of power in which power is "based on one's dependence on resources or currencies that another person controls" (p. 105). In any two-party relationship, Party B's dependence on Party A is directly proportional to Party B's motivational investment in goals mediated by Party A, and inversely proportional to the availability of these goals to Party B outside of the Party A–Party B relationship (Emerson, 1962, p. 31). For example, if Party A currently possesses the last desirable gizmo in the toyshop, and Party B needs it for his son's birthday tomorrow, Party A has greater negotiating power than Party B because he controls something that Party B is highly motivated to possess. Of course, if Party A does not exploit Party B's dependency, then his negotiating power may not be greater than Party B's. Party A's use of resources is central to the process theory of power, which we explain below.

PROCESS THEORIES OF POWER

In a process theory of power, "process" refers to values, norms, perceptions, meanings, and interest-guided patterns of interaction that help to explain why parties involved in a conflict use their resources differently in attempting to achieve the outcomes they desire. Unlike static resource theories, which equate outcomes with power, dynamic process theories link outcomes with the parties' use of resources. Scholars such as Blalock (1989), DeDreu (1995), Giddens (1993), and Gulliver (1979) have all propounded dynamic process theories. The difference between static and dynamic theories is illustrated in "Akemi Returns to University: A Resource and Process Analysis."

> ### *Akemi Returns to University: A Resource and Process Analysis*
>
> Akemi wants to return to university to obtain a master of laws degree in the autumn. Her partner, Rachel, does not want her to do this. Akemi nevertheless pursues her plans and returns to university despite Rachel's objections.
>
> A static resource theory would describe the situation as follows: Akemi has greater power because she achieved the outcome she wanted. And she was able to achieve the outcome because she has greater power than Rachel within the couple's relationship. This is tautological (circular) reasoning because power is equated with the outcome, and the outcome is equated with power.
>
> Dynamic process theories are more useful than static resource theories because they separate ways of attempting to achieve outcomes from the outcomes themselves. Thus, a process theory focuses attention on the strategy and tactics used by Akemi in her negotiations with Rachel. For example, Akemi may have anticipated some of Rachel's more serious objections by stating that she would be attending class only one evening a week and that her firm would be paying the tuition fees. In addition, Akemi may have pointed out benefits for Rachel, such as using the extra income she would receive as a lawyer to pay for Rachel's return to university to obtain the fine arts degree she has always wanted.

Gulliver's Process Theory of Power

Four factors are interrelated in the process theory of power formulated by Gulliver (1979), an anthropologist: resources, the use of resources, external factors, and outcomes.

Resources

Resources are *potential* power. According to Gulliver (1979), resources refer to "anything that, in context, offers potential power in negotiations" (p. 202). "Anything" refers to the six bases of power identified by French and Raven (1959). The "in context" qualification is included as a reminder that the resource must be relevant to the negotiation. For example, consider the case of a professional basketball player negotiating a salary increase with the general manager of his team, while at the same time also negotiating with the school principal not to suspend his eight-year-old son for persistently violating the school's dress code. The player's field goal percentage and number of blocked shots, steals, and assists are relevant resources in the first context and irrelevant in the second one. On the other hand, his story about his young son's identification with his recently deceased grandfather, who often wore a black beret, is a relevant resource in the second context and irrelevant in the first.

Not all contextually relevant resources are equally potent. Highly potent resources are associated with the following six matters, each of which we consider below: dependency, quantity and quality, legitimacy, information, reputation, and support.

1. *Dependency.* If one party is dependent on a resource possessed or controlled by another, the other party's resource is highly potent. Consider Syria's dependency on Turkey for its supply of water. Turkey, an upstream country, controls the headwaters of the Euphrates River, which runs through Syria, a downstream country (Slim, 1993).

2. *Quantity and quality.* The United States possesses nuclear weapons that can destroy entire countries and kill millions of people. It also possesses wealth in sufficient quantity to feed, clothe, and shelter the population of many countries. These resources give the United States greater potential power than any other country in the world. Furthermore, the United States can use these resources to thwart the United Nations and other international third parties from empowering adjudicators to use their authority (a resource) to make decisions that run counter to US interests.

   The possession or control of resources that influence the lives and livelihoods of people give governments and employers potential power in conflicts with citizens and employees, respectively. When governments are also employers, their potential power increases. The same thing is true of multinational corporations, which can influence governments by virtue of their control over such resources as foreign investment and employment levels. Globalization further increases the potential power of multinational corporations relative to that of governments (Kane, 1995).

3. *Legitimacy.* Consider, for example, the legitimacy of the authority of judges, which is traceable to the public will, as expressed by statutes passed by elected governments. In certain cases, the authority of judges is also traceable to the agreement of the parties to a conflict, who mutually cede decision-making power to a third party.

4. *Information.* Discovering the preferences, priorities, alternatives, and bottom lines of an opponent can contribute significantly toward achieving the outcomes desired by the party in possession of the information. Mediators who acquire information from parties in conflict also possess a potentially powerful resource that they can use to persuade the parties to reach an agreement.

5. *Reputation.* Air Canada has acquired a reputation for its espousal of self-interested policies regardless of government transportation policy. The former Canadian Airlines had a reputation for attempting to work with the government. When both airlines and their US partners were locked in takeover struggles, Canadian Airlines' better reputation was a potential power resource. This resource did not prevail, however.

6. *Support.* During divorce negotiations, for example, material and emotional support by new partners, children, relatives, and friends represents a significant potential power resource. Conversely, the lack of support by allies or other third parties can hasten to the "ripeness" of negotiations. Rubin (1992, p. 10) defines "ripeness" as a stage of conflict in which all parties are ready to take the conflict seriously, and are willing to bring the conflict to a close.

Use of Resources

Gulliver (1979, p. 202) equates the use of resources with *actual* power or "persuasive strength." "Persuasive strength" refers to the degree to which the resources used by one party moves the other party toward agreement. The distinction between possessing or controlling resources and actually using them, or using them effectively, is based on evidence that indicates that some parties do not use the resources they possess.

External Factors

Gulliver (1979, p. 202) also identifies external factors within a community or society as relevant to the process theory of power. These factors influence the conduct and outcome of negotiations "by augmenting, depleting, and modifying the resources available to the disputing parties—that is, their potential power."

For example, the power of one party may be depleted by conforming to a social norm that favours hierarchies, when the other party circumvents this thinking and establishes a broader base of support from a larger community. Recall "Brainstorming at Summer Camp" from chapter 3 in this regard. The camp owners were stymied in their conflict with the campers until they pooled their intelligence with that of the cleaners. Conformity to the social norm of honesty can also deplete a party's bargaining power if the other party is skilled in the art of deceit, and willing to apply his skills. By contrast, parties' resources increase when they receive financial and/or emotional support from friends, relatives, or other members of the community (England & Kilbourne, 1990).

Gulliver (1979, p. 204) refers to external factors as "the totality of resources available to negotiators." By "totality," Gulliver means all resources, material, cultural, or personal.

In Gulliver's process theory, external factors are not only potential power resources, they can also influence the process of negotiations (pp. 202-203). Process includes the expectations, preferences, and objectives of the parties, as well as the strategies and tactics they use. For example, Mnookin (1979, p. 966) conceives of external factors, such as family laws, as "bargaining chips or endowments" that separating parties can use in negotiations. He states that bargaining endowments "are created by legal rules that indicate the particular allocation that a court will impose if the parties fail to reach agreement." So, if family law indicates that courts usually grant fathers custody of willing male children aged 13 and older, such a father could use the law as a resource in proposing that his female ex-partner have greater access to her son in return for accepting lower spousal or child support payments.

Outcomes

The final variable in Gulliver's (1979) process theory of power is outcomes. Outcomes refer to the general or specific objectives of the contending parties that are more or less fully realized at the conclusion of any process aimed at ending conflicts. Gulliver (1979, p. 78) refers to outcomes as the results of struggle, negotiation, mediation, arbitration, and adjudication. Outcomes may involve shorter- or longer-term goals and objectives. An outcome also has a qualitative aspect to it, in that some outcomes are "settlements" involving changes in conduct; others are "resolutions" involving changes in attitudes, values, norms, and conduct (Rubin, 1992).

Fisher, Ury, and Patton (1991) categorize outcomes as "positional" or "interest." Positional outcomes reconcile the stated positions of the parties during positional bargaining. Interest outcomes reconcile the deeper interests, values, or needs of the parties that are revealed during the process of principled negotiation (pp. 1-14). Outcomes can also be clear or ambiguous. Sometimes both parties involved in a conflict prefer ambiguous outcomes because they allow both sides to claim victory or to minimize unavoidable losses (Gulliver, 1979, p. 78). "The Negotiator's Toast" testifies to the illusory power of outcomes. Finally, as we stated earlier in this chapter, outcomes can be win–win, win–lose, or lose–lose.

The Negotiator's Toast

Here's to our new collective agreement. It allows the union to proclaim victory publicly, the company to count its gains privately, and the consumer to assume that someone else is paying for it.

Source: Kesterton (February 8, 1998, p. A16).

Modifications to Gulliver's Process Theory of Power

Gulliver's (1979) process theory is, in our view, a major contribution to academic literature about power. However, we feel that two modifications increase its usefulness in explaining the outcomes of conflicts.

1. *Linking resources with outcomes.* In Gulliver's theory, resources are not directly linked with outcomes, but they should be. We cited evidence supporting this link above, under the heading "Definitions of Power."

2. *Linking external factors with outcomes.* Gulliver does not link external factors with outcomes, yet external factors can influence outcomes independently of resources or the use of resources. For example, consider a city and a construction company that are in the midst of negotiations involving a bridge that links the city to a small offshore island. The city wants construction stopped and the half-completed bridge dismantled because an environmental impact assessment was never completed. The construction company claims that the existing impact assessment is valid, and it intends to complete the bridge link to the island. While the parties are negotiating, there is a violent thunderstorm, and a barge runs into one of the two pylons holding up the bridge. The bridge collapses into the lake. Here, the thunderstorm, an external factor, determines the outcome of the negotiation.

Evidence cited by Mnookin, Peppet, and Tulumello (2000), as well as findings cited by Bahr (1972), Blood and Wolfe (1960), Blumstein and Schwartz (1983), Canan and Pring (1996), Luttwak (1999), Mnookin (1979), and Scanzoni (1982), also suggest that the explanatory power of Gulliver's theory can be increased by revising it to connect resources with outcomes and to link external factors with the use of resources and outcomes. The revised model is presented in figure 4.1, which includes four variables. The figure's six arrows show how the variables are interrelated.

An arrow that goes from one variable to another is directly related to it. Thus, use of resources, resources, and external factors are directly related to outcomes. An arrow that goes from one variable to a third variable through a second variable is indirectly related to the third variable. Thus, resources are indirectly related to outcomes through use of resources, and external factors are indirectly related with outcomes through resources. Therefore, three variables—resources, use of resources, and external factors—can be directly or indirectly linked with outcomes of struggle, negotiation, mediation, arbitration, and adjudication. Below, we consider Gulliver's (1979) four variables in relation to the Ellis process theory diagrammed in figure 4.1.

FIGURE 4.1   Ellis Process Theory of Power

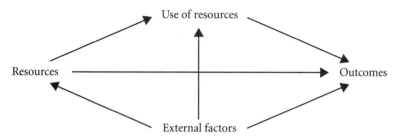

1. *Resources.* The Ellis process theory says that parties involved in a conflict possess or control resources. In some conflicts, the quantity and quality of resources possessed or controlled by Party A are very much greater than the resources possessed or controlled by Party B. Awareness of resource differentials can cause Party B to give in, or give way, before Party A begins to use its resources. For example, a coffee-shop owner located in Collingwood, an Ontario town with many ski resorts, decides not to name her shop Skibucks because she anticipates the possibility of legal action by Starbucks. Alternatively, Party A can achieve the outcomes it desires regardless of how effectively it, or Party B, actually uses its resources. Consider the US invasion and victory over the tiny island of Grenada. Here, the massive differences in resources of the respective parties made the outcome a foregone conclusion.
2. *Use of resources.* Figure 4.1 shows that the power resources available to the parties can be used by them to achieve the outcomes they desire. Frequently, parties who possess and use power resources that are greater than those possessed and used by opposing parties achieve the outcomes they desire. Sometimes, however, they use their greater power resources to achieve outcomes that both parties desired. For example, consider a grandfather who is an expert poker player teaching his 13-year-old granddaughter to play poker. He combines winning most games with losing an occasional game. He is rewarded by the granddaughter's increasing interest in poker and the time they spend together. The granddaughter is rewarded by winning a game occasionally and spending time alone with her grandfather.
3. *External factors.* Figure 4.2 also shows that external factors—that is, factors that are neither possessed nor controlled by the parties— influence outcomes directly and indirectly. They influence outcomes directly by producing them independently of resources and the use of resources. The thunderstorm that caused a barge to destroy the bridge

FIGURE 4.2   A Resource–Process Theory of Negotiating Power

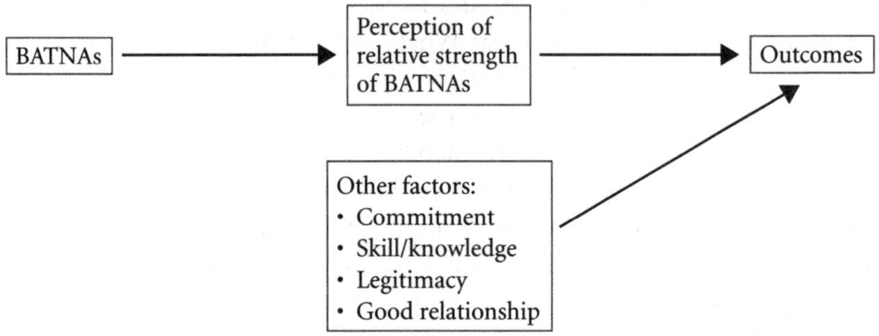

Source: Fisher, Ury, and Patton (1991).

to an island that we considered earlier in this chapter is an example of an external factor directly influencing an outcome.

External factors can also influence outcomes indirectly by creating conditions under which resources used by the parties to a conflict increase the likelihood of achieving the outcomes they desired. For example, three external factors facilitated the renewal of negotiations between Israelis and Palestinians aimed at implementing US President George W. Bush's "Road Map to Peace": Israeli Prime Minister Ariel Sharon's unilateral decision to leave Gaza, the death of Palestinian leader Yassir Arafat, and the re-election of Bush (Erlanger, 2005, p. 5; Kalman, 2005, p. 7).

4. *Outcomes.* Outcomes, the fourth variable in the theory, are the result of the influence of one or more of the other three variables included in figure 4.1. As we indicated earlier, outcomes can be win–win, win–lose, or lose–lose.

APPLICATION OF THE ELLIS PROCESS THEORY OF POWER

The Ellis process theory of power can be applied to any conflict. To facilitate a better understanding of the theory, we have chosen to apply it to the conflict between the Cree of northern Quebec and Hydro-Quebec. This conflict is described in *Power: One River, Two Nations* (1998), a documentary film produced by the National Film Board of Canada. We have already considered this conflict in chapter 1 in the section entitled "Conflict Analysis Illustrated."

Conflict Between the Cree and Hydro-Quebec

Conflict arose between the Cree and Hydro-Quebec as a result of Hydro-Quebec's plans to dam the Great Whale River in northern Quebec. The conflict lasted five years, from 1990 to 1995. Hydro-Quebec wanted to dam the river to generate additional hydroelectricity to sell in Quebec and New York State. The Cree opposed the plan because the flooding caused by the dam would destroy sacred land that supported a traditional lifestyle based on hunting, trapping, and fishing. The dam also would cause significant loss as a result of the relocation of many Cree communities. In 1971, the Cree had experienced the deleterious effects of relocation—such as higher than average rates of crime, spousal abuse, drug abuse, suicide, and teenage pregnancies—when Hydro-Quebec dammed the Le Grande River.

Resources

The power resources available to the Cree were resources they could use to persuade New York and Massachusetts, Hydro-Quebec's largest potential purchasers of hydroelectric power generated by the Great Whale River, to do two things:

1. pressure Hydro-Quebec to complete the environmental impact assessment it was required by law to conduct before asking the Cree to participate in negotiations, and
2. have the New York State legislature cancel the $17 billion contract it had signed with Hydro-Quebec.

The Cree could also use other resources to help them achieve their most important objective, cancellation of Hydro-Quebec's plans to dam the Great Whale River.

Completion of an environmental impact assessment was important to the Cree for two reasons.

1. It would delay the project, which would allow the Cree more time to mobilize support for cancelling Hydro-Quebec's damming plans.
2. The Cree believed that the results of the impact assessment would reveal that the Great Whale damming project would have social and environmental consequences that were at least as harmful as the damming of the Le Grande River, if not more so.

Cancellation of the contract between Hydro-Quebec and New York State was important to the Cree because Hydro-Quebec needed money to begin to dam the Great Whale River.

The Cree believed that they could achieve their two objectives by presenting themselves as David to Hydro-Quebec's Goliath. They were a small indigenous nation of 15,000 people who respected the environment, and whose culture, land, and traditional lifestyle were being threatened. Hydro-Quebec was a large corporation that claimed to represent the interests of over 7 million Quebecers and enjoyed the support of the Quebec government, industry, banks, and the law.

Resources the Cree could use to mobilize support by disseminating this image to legislators and residents in New York State and Massachusetts included the following:

- their description of a 500-year history of victimization by Quebecers and Hydro-Quebec;
- their traditional culture;
- the destructive environmental and social consequences of Hydro-Quebec's earlier damming of the Le Grande River;
- the law that required an environmental impact assessment before Hydro-Quebec could implement its plans to dam the Great Whale River;
- the media; and
- the vote, a political resource.

Hydro-Quebec's power resources included the following:

- a 500-year history of winning conflicts with the Cree and producing what it considered win–win results in projects that the Cree initially resisted;
- great economic, legal, and political resources;
- backing by the coercive power of the state (police, the army, and the courts);
- a provincial population of over 7 million;
- a legally binding contract, signed by the Cree, that permitted the damming of Great Whale River in return for monetary compensation; and
- the media.

In conclusion, the distribution of power resources greatly favoured Hydro-Quebec.

Use of Resources

The Cree used their resources in the following manner:

- Cree leaders in traditional dress attracted international media attention and generated publicity sympathetic to their positions and interests by making traditional "pleadings journeys." By odeyak (a hybrid canoe–kayak devised by their ancestors), they paddled from James Bay to New York Harbour, arriving just in time to participate in Earth Day ceremonies.

- By attracting the attention of environmentalist Robert F. Kennedy Jr. and gaining his political support, they enlisted the support of the New York State and Massachusetts legislatures for conducting an environmental impact assessment before Hydro-Quebec proceeded with the damming of the Great Whale River.
- The Cree used money donated by the Sierra Club and other environmental groups sympathetic to the plight of indigenous peoples to place advertisements in the *New York Times*.
- Cree leaders made presentations in New York State schools and the state legislature, thus mobilizing public support and offering New York State legislators a politically safe reason for cancelling the hydroelectric contract, in addition to cancelling it because of the state's declining demand for electricity.
- The result of the 1995 referendum on separation indicated that over 95 percent of the Cree voted to remain in Canada should Quebec decide to separate. This persuaded Premier Jacques Parizeau that Cree support for Quebec separation was unlikely to be forthcoming in the future if the government continued to alienate the Cree by pushing forward with the Great Whale River project. Consequently, Parizeau indefinitely postponed the damming.

Hydro-Quebec used its resources in the following manner.

- It held formal press conferences in which Hydro-Quebec bureaucrats, including the CEO, answered questions put to them by reporters.
- It completed an environmental impact assessment.

In conclusion, the Cree mobilized and used their power resources far more effectively than Hydro-Quebec used its resources.

Outcomes

- Hydro-Quebec completed an environmental impact assessment and presented it to the Cree before negotiations in an effort to achieve an agreement.
- New York State legislators cancelled the $17 billion contract signed by Hydro-Quebec and New York State in 1989.
- The Great Whale River project was "indefinitely postponed."

In conclusion, linkages between the use of power resources and these major outcomes are far stronger for the Cree than they are for Hydro-Quebec.

External Factors and Outcomes

- The environmental movement was very active during the 1990s, and the conservation of electricity by residents of New York State led to a decreased demand for electricity. Moreover, New York State legislators became convinced that the decreased demand could be met locally without importing hydroelectricity from Quebec. These two factors helped persuade New York State legislators to cancel their contract with Hydro-Quebec. The effective use of resources by the Cree helped legislators make this decision, but the decreased demand for electricity was the determining factor. If the demand for hydroelectric power was increasing beyond New York State's capacity to meet it, the contract would probably not have been cancelled, regardless of the Cree's use of resources.

- Robert Bourassa, premier of Quebec during the first four years of the conflict, died during its fifth and final year. The Parti Québécois, led by Jacques Parizeau, won the election, replacing Bourassa's economic agenda with Parizeau's separatist one. Parizeau ranked a political outcome—separation—more highly than an economic one—the economic development of Quebec. The results of the Cree referendum, which rejected separation, and the Quebec referendum, which came close to supporting it, were responsible for the indefinite postponement of the Great Whale River project. However, they would not have come into play without the untimely death of Bourassa.

In conclusion, external factors played a significant part in bringing about the indefinite cancellation of the contract between Hydro-Quebec and New York State, and the indefinite postponement of the Great Whale River project.

Case Study Postscript

In 2002, seven years after the conflict ended, Ted Moses, grand chief of the Grand Council of the Cree (the position held by Matthew Coon Come during the conflict), signed a $3.4 billion contract allowing Hydro-Quebec to install hydroelectric generating stations on two major rivers in northern Quebec. In the ensuring referendum, over 90 percent of Cree voters concurred with Moses's decision. Quebec Premier Bernard Landry and Grand Chief Moses agreed that the contract represented a win–win result for the Cree and Quebec.

EFFECTS OF THE BALANCE OF POWER
BETWEEN THE PARTIES

Findings reported by researchers such as Beriker and Druckman (1996), Deutsch (1973), and Rubin and Zartman (1995) indicate that the effect of the balance of power between the parties is dependent on the parties' Interpersonal orientation (Rubin & Brown, 1975). Interpersonal orientation includes two dimensions: competitiveness and focus. Parties involved in a conflict resolution procedure can be located on two continuums: one continuum places highly competitive at one end and non-competitive at the other end; the second continuum places focus on self at one end and focus on self and others at the other end.

When power relations are balanced and both parties are competitive and self-focused, conflict escalates; hostility and the time necessary reach settlements increases because the parties are indifferent about their relationship (Rubin & Zartman, 1995, p. 363). When power relations are balanced and the parties are not competitive and focused on both themselves and the other, collaboration increases, and the time necessary to reach a settlement decreases because the parties get along well with each other. When one of the parties is highly competitive and self-focused, and the other is not competitive and focused on both himself and the other, the hostility between them and the time necessary to reach a settlement increases because the parties irritate each other.

Contemporary discussions of power balances and imbalances tend to be informed by two additional contributions to academic literature. First, the process of negotiation makes an important contribution to balancing power relations derived from the unequal distribution of resources because negotiated agreements require not unilateral, but joint, decision making (Lax & Sebenius, 1995). Second, findings reported by Janeway (1981) and Scott (1985) indicate that weaker parties—that is, parties with fewer or less potent resources—regularly obtain some of the outcomes they want or need by adjusting their tactics to the real or perceived power balance. Tactics sometimes adopted by weaker parties include blustering, delaying, threatening to walk out of negotiations, appealing to allies, publicly shaming the stronger party, and meticulously following cumbersome rules (Janeway, 1981; Scott, 1985). If the stronger and weaker parties are interdependent, the likelihood of a desirable result for a weaker party increases. Weaker parties may also benefit from the fact that the focus of stronger parties may be partially diverted by other conflicts in which they are simultaneously engaged. For example, a large trade union may be focused on many negotiations at once. A small employer, however, may be able to devote undivided attention to a single labour relations conflict. In sum, three factors mute the impact of imbalanced power relations on weaker parties:

1. the effective tactics sometimes adopted by weaker parties,
2. the interdependence between weaker and stronger parties, and
3. the focus and effort that weaker parties may be able to devote to settling a conflict with stronger parties.

The negotiations process itself is another factor that may help to mute the impact of imbalanced power relations between the parties (Rubin & Zartman, 1995). Mutual decision making is at the heart of the negotiation process. Parties usually enter negotiations when the net benefits (benefits minus costs) of mutual decision making outweigh the net benefits of uni-lateral decision making. The desirability of mutual decision making balances power relations by regulating both the resources that the stronger party brings to the table and the way in which the stronger party uses them. At the same time, mutual decision making empowers weaker parties because they know that stronger parties depend on them to reach an agreement.

In negotiations facilitated by a mediator, the potential for balancing power relations is increased. In addition to mediation's joint decision-making requirement and a mediator's control over the process of mediation—estab-lishing ground rules, deciding who will speak and for how long, choosing and changing topics for discussion, and identifying the order in which issues are negotiated (Neumann, 1992)—mediators can use a variety of power-balancing skills (Bennett & Hermann, 1996). Some of these are described below.

PRACTICAL IMPLICATIONS OF POWER BALANCING

The research findings reported in this chapter provide an empirical rationale for balancing imbalanced power relations. Research indicates that balanced power relations yield beneficial results for the process and outcomes of nego-tiation and, by extension, mediation. Research also identifies motivational orientation involving self and others as a condition under which balanced power relations are most likely to produce beneficial consequences.

The negotiation process, with its mutual decision-making requirement, encourages the parties to become concerned with each other (Gulliver, 1979). However, there is great diversity in the motivational orientations that the parties bring to the negotiating table and maintain or modify during the pro-cess. Mediators can encourage parties to change their motivational orientation from an exclusive focus on themselves to an inclusive focus on themselves and the other party. Here are two techniques that may assist:

1. Encourage the parties to link desired outcomes more strongly with a self-and-other orientation than with an exclusively self orientation. In other words, get the parties to say to themselves, "I have a better chance of getting what I want by taking the other party's circumstances and desires into account than by focusing exclusively on what I want." A mediator could point out to the parties' the adverse consequences of an exclusively self orientation: increased likelihood of impasses, damage to relationships, more expense, greater stress, delay, uncertainty, and loss of control over the process as a result of having to go to arbitration or to court to settle the case.

2. Encourage the parties to conform with the cross-cultural norm of reciprocity (Gouldner, 1960). Applied to parties everywhere, this norm states, "You should not harm those who help you, and you should help those who help you." The norm of reciprocity is most potent when combined with the rule of graduated risk. This rule states that parties with a self orientation can initiate a cycle of mutually beneficial exchanges by offering a helpful bit of information or an agreement that entails a small risk, such as agreeing to hold the negotiations in a location that is slightly more convenient for the other parties to attend. After actions entailing small risks have been reciprocated, the parties can then move to helpful actions that entail greater risks, such as making the first, or an important, concession.

From the process theory of power, we derive a number of implications for the practice of negotiation. Parties can increase their negotiating power by

- improving the quantity and quality of their alternatives;
- changing the other party's perceptions about the relative strength of their power resources; and
- using their power resources more effectively by making credible commitments, creating win–win options, and obtaining third-party support.

The process theory of power also has major implications for the practice of mediation in the field of assessing power imbalances and intervening to achieve balance.

Assessing Power Imbalances

The process theory of power requires mediators to implement a two-stage assessment process. First, they must assess power resource differentials. Second, they must assess how the parties use their resources. Mediators can assess power resource imbalances at intake by using a resource differential questionnaire (RDQ) (Ellis, 2004). They can assess the parties' use of their power resources by means of a power observation grid (POG) (Gray, 1999) that is scored during the first mediation session at which both parties are present. Because RDQs and POGs are derived from the process theory of power, they are theoretically grounded instruments.

A power imbalances assessment questionnaire (PIAQ), derived from Gewurtz's (2001) redesigned mediation model, includes questions that measure procedural resources, such as education, expertise, information, cognitive ability, and negotiation experience. It also contains questions that measure substantive resources, such as material resources one party can use to reward or punish the other party, feasible alternatives to a negotiated agreement, and legitimacy. The PIAQ also requires a mediator to assess the "relationship context." Answers to relationship context questions reveal:

- the presence or absence of a relationship;
- the power dynamics that define the relationship; and
- whether the relationship has ended or is continuing, voluntarily or involuntarily.

Relationship context questions are important because answers to them predict the likelihood of the abuse of power by the parties, and therefore the power-balancing interventions required. The parties effectively regulate the abuse of power themselves when

- the prior relationship between them is equal;
- they voluntarily choose to continue the relationship; and
- the procedural and substantive resources they possess or control are roughly equal.

Adler and Silverstein (2000) provide two case studies of how these three factors regulate the abuse of power. The first case is entitled "Peter and Paul." Peter and Paul are businessmen who have maintained a good relationship for some years. For this reason, Peter was upset when he returned a large box of widgets to Paul, who also was upset because over half of the widgets were defective. The situation was exacerbated when Paul claimed that the widgets were damaged by Peter's workers, who did not know how to install them properly. During negotiations aimed at settling the conflict, Peter and Paul are unlikely to abuse their power because they are equally intelligent, knowledgeable, and determined businessmen who respect each other as equals (equal prior relationship and equal procedural power) and who manage two similarly sized businesses in ways that have been equally profitable for each of them (equal control over substantive resources). They want to continue doing business with each other after the widget issue is settled (voluntary continuation of the relationship).

Adler and Silverstein's (2000) next case is "The Bicyclist and the Accountant." In this case, the accountant runs his Mercedes into a garbage collector riding a bicycle. There were no witnesses. According to Adler and Silverstein, both parties are unlikely to regulate the abuse of power during negotiations aimed at settling the resulting conflict, because there was no prior relationship between them (absence of an equal relationship), the procedural and substantive resources controlled by the accountant are greater than those controlled by the bicyclist (unequal procedural and substantive resources), and neither party wants to establish and continue a relationship with the other (absence of a voluntary continuing relationship).

Had these cases been mediated, the rate of mediator interventions would have been very high in the case of the bicyclist and the accountant because of the presence of two sources of power imbalances—inequality before and during mediation—and the absence of a continuing relationship to regulate the tactics used by the parties during the mediation sessions. In contrast, the rate of power-balancing interventions would be low in the case of Peter and Paul, because of the equality between the parties before and during mediation and the continuing relationship that regulates the parties' negotiating tactics. Table 4.1 juxtaposes the relative impact of relationship contexts in these two cases.

TABLE 4.1   Relationship Context, Self-Regulation, and Mediator Interventions

Case	Prior relationship		Pre-existing power dynamics			Continuing relationship			Procedural & substantive resources		Rate of mediator power-balancing interventions
	Yes	No	None	Imbal.	Bal.	No	Yes (V)	Yes (I)	Eq.	Uneq.	
1	•				•		•		•		Low
2		•	•			•				•	Very high

Notes:

Case 1 = Peter/Paul	Imbal. = Imbalanced	V = Voluntary	Eq. = Equal
Case 2 = Bicyclist/Accountant	Bal. = Balanced	I = Involuntary	Uneq. = Unequal

The process theory of power requires mediators to balance imbalanced power relations by decreasing differences in resources possessed or controlled by the parties, and by motivating weaker parties to use the resources available to them, and/or to use them more effectively.

Resource Differences

Mediators can change inequalities in the resources possessed or controlled by the parties by referring the parties to relevant community, business, or government resources. Referring both parties provides fairness. However, it is usually the weaker party who benefits more than the stronger party from the referrals because the weaker party's need for advice, information, or support is usually greater. This, however, is not always the case, particularly when the stronger party has an inflated sense of the merits of her case and/or an erroneous impression of a law or governing principle.

Mediators help balance imbalanced power relations by acting as "resource expanders" for the parties (Stulberg and Bridenback, 1981). For example, an ex-partner participating in mediation to divide domestic assets may not know that she is eligible for spousal support, but she can obtain this information when she visits the local women's legal information centre to which she was referred by the mediator. Mediators can effortlessly expand the resources of the parties by providing them with the community resources handbooks that are published by many municipalities.

As many conflict resolution theorists, such as Fisher, Ury, and Patton (1991, p. 22) have stated, conflict is in the minds of people. In a general way, this insight opens the way for mediators to change the parties' perceptions of the power of the resources they possess or control. Thus, during negotiations between a farmer and a developer, the developer presents a "take it or leave it" offer, apparently secure in the belief that a city planning decision favouring his position cannot be overturned. The developer's perception of the power of his resource changes when the mediator asks him in caucus whether he is aware that Ontario's *Planning Act* permits the minister of municipal affairs and housing to overrule municipal planning decisions, and that previous ministers have responded positively to farmers' requests to overrule orders that favour developers.

Moore (1996, pp. 330-331) states that mediators can also motivate the parties to continue mediating and help them reach an agreement by asking questions that change their evaluations of their resources. For example, Party A may threaten Party B with adjudication because she thinks that she will win the case in court. Party A's belief in the potency of adjudication as a power resource may be undermined by a mediator who, in caucus, asks her, "How certain are you that you will win: 90 percent? 50 percent? What risk are you willing to take, and what happens if you lose? Even if you win, what impact will winning have on your relationship with Party B and others who will be affected by the outcome?" (p. 331). Moore's advocacy of "careful questioning" as a means of raising doubts in the minds of parties about the power of their resources and/or the acceptability of the positions they take is accompanied with the following caveat: "If misused, this technique obviously approaches manipulation and raises questions about the ethics of mediator influence" (p. 331).

Use of Resources

Cognitive ability is an important power resource in negotiations because negotiations involve cognitive tasks, such as assessing and analyzing information, and creating bargaining formulas and win–win options. Mediators can help balance imbalanced power relations by encouraging contributions from the party with greater cognitive abilities for two reasons.

1. Their contributions often help both parties achieve objectives that are important to them.
2. Their contributions sometimes result in win–lose outcomes favouring the party with lower cognitive abilities. This counterintuitive intervention is supported by the research findings of Barry and Friedman (1998). Apparently, very smart people get caught up in the problem-solving aspect of the negotiation process and sometimes solve problems in ways that benefit the other party, even at their own expense.

Bennett and Hermann's Power-Balancing Interventions
Mediators Bennett and Hermann (1996) identify 23 power-balancing interventions. Included among them are 8 that focus on the use of resources:

1. assign homework to increase the weaker party's information level;
2. provide education and training before mediation to increase the weaker party's skill level;
3. introduce a time-out to give the weaker party time to assess his predicament and develop options;
4. confront the stronger party in caucus, discussing whether the exercise of her greater power to force an agreement is fair and/or in her overall interest;
5. structure mediation sessions to ensure that the weaker party has an equal opportunity to think and speak;
6. mediate in separate sessions to buffer the weaker party from the stronger party when necessary;
7. allow the weaker party to bring an advocate to the mediation sessions; and
8. tutor the weaker party in an effort to have the party adopt an effective negotiation strategy and tactics during a caucus called for the purpose.

Haynes's Power-Balancing Interventions

Haynes (1988, pp. 289-290) focuses on the mediator as a power resource, and identifies three basic mediator strategies for dealing with power imbalances:

1. identify with the weaker party, intervene by framing power abuses of the stronger party as "inadvertent," and ask the stronger party's permission to intervene in the future should inadvertent abuses of power occur again;
2. prevent the discussion of matters that are not directly relevant to an issue and are brought up by the stronger party for the sole purpose of making personal attacks against the weaker one; and
3. control communications by engaging in shuttle mediation or by using questions and directives to ensure that the weaker party is able to express herself fully, freely, and safely in face-to-face negotiations with the stronger party.

Moore's Power-Balancing Interventions

Moore (1996, p. 337) describes five "empowering moves" that mediators can make. Three of them focus on the use of resources:

1. help the weaker party collect, organize, and analyze data and mobilize her resources;
2. educate and assist the weaker party in planning and carrying out an effective negotiation strategy; and
3. encourage the weaker party to make realistic concessions.

Gewurtz's Power-Balancing Interventions

Gewurtz (2001) contributes to the power-balancing literature by making a distinction between two types of conflict-specific resources: the procedural and substantive resources referred to earlier. He makes an even greater contribution by linking mediator power-balancing interventions with the predominant type of resource that creates the power imbalance.

For example, when an unequally distributed procedural resource—such as a party's ability to think quickly—is the predominant cause of a power imbalance, a mediator can intervene in one or more of the ways described by Bennett and Hermann (1996), and Moore (1996). She can, for example, give the slower thinking party more time by slowing down the pace of mediation or by engaging in shuttle mediation.

When an unequally distributed substantive resource—such as territory—is the predominant cause of a power imbalance, a mediator can intervene by calling a caucus and pointing out to the stronger party some positive consequences of refraining from using his resources to coerce the weaker party.

For example, a mediator could cite Ury's rule, "The harder you make it for them to say 'no,' the harder you make it for them to say 'yes' " (1991, p. 150). Mediators can also influence a stronger party's use of resources by pointing out that imposed outcomes are usually unstable, and characterized by compliance problems and/or the need for detailed monitoring and high enforcement costs.

Perceptions of BATNA

Mediators can also intervene by providing information that changes the stronger and weaker party's perceptions of the relative strength of their BATNAs. Thus, in the context of a conflict between a large supplier and a small manufacturer, a mediator's questions may elicit answers that indicate to both parties that finding another supplier is an easier proposition than finding another manufacturer. For example, answers could reveal that an alternative supplier has been in business longer than the current one, will have more stable costs in the long run, and has an excellent record of reliability in supplying materials on time. In contrast, there may be no alternative manufacturer in the area to whom the supplier can sell his materials.

Adler and Silverstein's Power-Balancing Interventions

Adler and Silverstein (2000) describe 24 ways in which weaker parties can be empowered, 4 of which are described below. Mediators can advise weaker parties about the importance of

1. preparing, which includes determining
   a) what each party wants and needs for the other;
   b) what punitive resources each party can use against the other if there is no agreement;
   c) what alternatives exist for both parties;
   d) whether the party's own alternatives can be improved and, if so, how;
   e) how both parties rank their priorities; and
   f) whether relevant laws can strengthen the party's position;
2. collecting, organizing, and using information effectively;
3. managing the impressions given by verbal and non-verbal communications effectively, and creating a first impression of being a confident, competent, and principled negotiator; and
4. discovering interests shared by both parties and creating elegant solutions, which simultaneously satisfy the interests of both parties.

Aspiration Levels

Another relatively simple and effective way in which mediators can empower weaker parties is to help them set and maintain high, but not unrealistic, aspiration levels (Barry & Friedman, 1998; Pienaar & Spoelstra, 1991; Ury, 1991; Adler & Silverstein, 2000). Aspiration level refers to a highly valued objective that a party realistically expects to achieve through negotiation. Stated positively, "high aspirations, other things being equal, tend to produce favourable results" (Adler & Silverstein, 2000, p. 64). Stated negatively, "low aspirations tend to be self-fulfilling. What you don't ask for, the other side is unlikely to give you" (Ury, 1991, p. 25).

Ethical Considerations in Power Balancing

Moore inserts a caveat into his discussion of "empowering moves" when he notes that a mediator who acts as a "secret advocate" for the weaker party puts her "impartiality and effectiveness as a process intervenor at risk" (1996, p. 337). Moore's solution for eliminating secret advocacy is to have mediators obtain the stronger party's prior approval of their power-balancing interventions. For Moore, power-balancing interventions are ethical when all parties approve them.

One problem with this advice is that it is based on the assumption that mediator power-balancing interventions have only beneficial consequences for the weaker party. However, these interventions may have adverse consequences if they undermine the weaker party's sense of control over the outcome of negotiations. To the extent that weaker parties feel that a mediator was mainly responsible for the way they negotiated and the outcome of mediation, they may also feel that any ensuing agreement is not truly theirs. Agreements perceived to have been produced by mediators may not be as durable as agreements that the parties believe they produced themselves. Moreover, a weaker party whose sense of competence as a negotiator is undermined may be less able to negotiate future conflicts.

With these considerations in mind, we build on Moore's advice by proposing the following: power-balancing interventions are ethical when the stronger party does not perceive the mediator as being aligned with the weaker party, and the weaker party does not perceive the mediator as an agent of his or her disempowerment.

In sum, power-balancing interventions are ethical when

- the mediator is fairly certain that the power imbalances he observes are likely to lead to unfair and unstable agreements,
- the mediator intervenes in ways that neither party perceives as alignment with the weaker party, and

- the weaker party does not perceive the mediator as an agent of his or her disempowerment.

The Power of a Mediator

The outcomes of mediations are not exclusively those sought by the parties to the conflict. This is explicitly acknowledged in a number of definitions of a mediator's role. For example, Schelling (1960, p. 44) defines a mediator as "a third party with a pay-off structure of his own who is given an influential role through his control over communication." In Gulliver's (1979, p. 213) triadic conception of mediation, the mediator "becomes a negotiator and as such, he inevitably brings with him, deliberately or not, certain ideas [and] knowledge." Girdner (1988, p. 52) defines a mediator as "an additional party with preferences, strategies and interests, whose presence turns the process into triadic negotiation."

During negotiations mediators use resources in ways that satisfy their professional and personal interests as well as those of the parties. The results of Kolb and Kressel's (1994) study of mediator profiles indicate this is what environmental, divorce, business, community, and international mediators do. Additional support for Kolb and Kressel's conclusion is provided by Gulliver (1979) and Silbey and Merry (1986).

Research findings, then, indicate that mediators control the process of mediation (Neumann, 1992), as well as the use of resources—such as authority, experience, expertise, and control over information—to bring about convergences on outcomes that are sought by mediators themselves, the parties, and/or the bureaucracy that employs them. Therefore, the role of the mediator involves the exercise of power.

To state that the use of power is inherent in the role of the mediator (Aubert, 1963; Simmel, 1950) is not to state that all or most mediators use their power in the same way and to the same degree. The style of individual mediators varies greatly. The role assumed by individual mediators may be placed on a continuum with facilitation on one end and evaluation on the other. The silent mediator who facilitates negotiations by her mere presence— for example, a respected First Nations elder—at the facilitative end of the continuum. The intrusive mediator who evaluates the strengths and weaknesses of the parties, gives them advice on how their problems should be settled, and emphasizes the consequences of not reaching a mediated settlement can be placed at the evaluative end of the continuum (Riskin, 1996). Findings reported in *When Talk Works: Profiles of Mediators* (Kolb & Associates, 1994) indicate that mediators regarded as among "the best in the business" (Fisher, 1994) adopt different intervention styles.

Evaluation of Resource Theories

Strengths

A resource theory of power has two strong points. It

- identifies resources as a factor that can have a significant impact on the process and outcome of conflict-resolving procedures, and
- is supported by research findings.

Weaknesses

Resource theory also has the following significant weaknesses:

- Factors such as cultural support and motivational orientation can increase or decrease the impact of resources on process and outcomes.
- Resource theorists cannot explain why parties with fewer or less powerful resources ever "win" conflicts.
- Resource theorists cannot predict the outcomes of conflicts when the parties control or possess equally powerful resources.

Evaluation of Process Theories' Strengths

A process theory of power has significant strengths. It

- includes resources and use of resources,
- is supported by research findings,
- helps explain why the impact of resources on outcomes varies because it focuses on how the parties use resources,
- suggests that mediators can assess power imbalances by distributing questionnaires or conducting interviews at intake and by observing the parties' negotiations, and
- offers a theoretical grounding for power-balancing interventions by mediators.

Weaknesses

A process theory of power, which includes only four factors that are interconnected in one direction (arrows going one way), may be too simple to be applied to actual conflicts, which involve feedback among factors (arrows going both ways).

CHAPTER SUMMARY

We began this chapter with a description and evaluation of resource and process definitions of power. The unidimensional resource definition equates power with differences in the possession or control of resources. The multidimensional process definition emphasizes the use of resources, but includes a personal resource: the willingness to use them. We next described resource and process theories and concluded that the major difference between them is that resource theory links only two factors—resources and outcomes—whereas process theory links four factors—resources, use of resources, external factors, and outcomes. We focused on the Ellis–Wight process theory of power and applied it to the conflict between the Cree of northern Quebec and Hydro-Quebec. The application of theories about power raises questions relating to power balances and imbalances. We explored the means by which mediators can regulate the use of resources by stronger parties, and found that one of the most effective means is to point out the instability of imposed outcomes. We noted that research findings provide an empirical rationale for attempting to balance imbalanced power relations. The process theory of power provides a rationale for assessing power imbalances through the use of questionnaires at intake and during observation of the parties in the process of negotiating with each other. We devoted the last part of the chapter to a discussion of the ethics of power balancing and mediator power, and finally we evaluated the theories described earlier in the chapter.

RECOMMENDED READING

Adler, P. and Adler, P. (1998). *Peer power.* New Brunswick, NJ: Rutgers University Press. This book describes peer power and other informal social pressures in the context of social order among preadolescent children in the school community.

Scott, J. (1985). *Weapons of the weak.* New Haven, CT: Yale University Press. This book describes the results of an anthropological study of class conflict in a small rice-farming village in Malaysia. Value/ interest conflicts, and the tactics used by strong and weak adversaries, are described in detail. The book also includes a very good discussion and analysis of resistance (pp. 289-303).

Uviller, H. R. (1999). *The tilted playing field.* New Haven, CT: Yale University Press. This book describes resources and their use by defence and prosecuting lawyers in courtrooms in the context of the balance of power.

FILMS, VIDEOS, AND DVDS

Conflicts in school—Vignettes. Available from triune@triune.ca or http://www.triune.ca.

Power: One river, two nations. Available from the National Film Board of Canada http://www.nfb.ca or 1-800-267-7710 (90 minutes).

The lock out. Directed by N. Rogers and P. Salem. Available from the Program on Negotiation at Harvard Law School (17 minutes).

CHAPTER FIVE

Culture

Chapter Objectives

Define culture.

Describe value orientations theory.

Describe the Costa Rican model of conflict resolution.

Describe the medicine wheel model of mediation.

Compare different cultural models of mediation.

Describe communications theory.

Describe a cultural–situational theory of conflict resolution.

Increase your own cultural sensitivities.

CULTURAL RELATIVITY

In chapters 2 and 3, we described conflict resolution procedures used by members of predominantly Western societies, such as Canada and the United States. In this chapter, we describe conflict resolution procedures used by some members of societies that are not Western. Canada is a multicultural society, incorporating both Western and non-Western elements. The primary objective of this chapter is to increase the cultural sensitivity of students who are, or may become, conflict resolution practitioners. "The Elder and the Farmer" is a short vignette about cultural relativity in the context of negotiation.

The Elder and the Farmer

An Ojibwe elder is participating in negotiations with an English-Canadian farmer in an effort to resolve a conflict about the location of a fence. The elder's terms of negotiation include healing, harmony, and her band's obligation to protect sacred land. The farmer emphasizes the fact that he and his forbears have transformed barren soil into productive and profitable farmland. He speaks of negotiation as a means of achieving results that are important to him, such as keeping the fence in its present location and maintaining its present length and height. He speaks of ownership and of dominance.

Both parties are fluent in Ojibwe and English. The elder chooses to speak Ojibwe, a gentle, non-judgmental language of relationships that is grounded in the understanding that life is a process of transformation, and that people—including the farmer and herself—are "people who are becoming," rather than "people who are." The farmer chooses to speak English, a beautiful language of great subtlety and flexibility, but also a language with many judgmental words—stupid, brilliant, charming, appalling—and the capacity to describe states of being as fixed and unchangeable. English, for example, offers its speakers no single word for "person who is becoming" (Ross, 1996, pp. 101-130).

This brief vignette reveals differences in values (obligations to a group, independence, healing, harmony, winning), cognitions (Earth as sacred, land as commodity), identities, and language. All of these are cultural differences.

Source: Ross (1996).

Definitions of Culture

Western sociologists, such as Brym et al. (2003, p. 68), define culture broadly as "problem solving." Problems are solved through the production of material objects and the sharing of symbols that mean the same thing to all members of a culture. "Material culture" refers to the problems solved by technology. The material problem-solving items produced by technology include cars, computers, and refrigerators. "Non-material culture" refers to symbols used by members of the culture to communicate with and understand each other. Faure and Sjostedt (1993, p. 182) define non-material culture as "a set of shared, enduring meanings, values, [and] beliefs that characterize national, ethnic and other groups and orient their behavior [and] help build and preserve their identity." Chapter 5 focuses on non-material culture, and henceforth, when we refer to culture, we mean non-material culture.

Culture refers to symbols, such as language, cognitions, values, norms, feelings, attitudes, beliefs, and identities that

- are learned and internalized during the process of socialization by parents, relatives, peers, teachers, religious workers, neighbours, artists, and the media;

- are transmitted across generations and places;
- can and do change;
- are shared by members of national, racial or ethnic, gender, religious, class, and other social groupings;
- are often unacknowledged or taken for granted;
- permeate the intentions, motives, actions, and reactions of cultural members (Goffman, 1959; Hall, 1976; Hall & Hall, 1990);
- define people; and
- are present in all societies.

Cultural Definitions of Conflict Resolution

Culture, the "software of the mind" (Hofstede, 1980), is a prerequisite for predictable, coordinated, and regulated interaction among people. It is therefore a prerequisite for the existence of society. At the same time, societies vary with respect to the content of their cultures. Because of differences in cultural content—that is, differences in values, norms, language, meanings, identities, and perceptions—conflict resolution procedures embedded in different cultures also vary.

According to Faure and Sjostedt (1993, p. 1), "the meaning of negotiation [and other conflict resolution procedures] cannot be fully understood unless [they are] interpreted in the cultural context in which [they occur]." This is because the meaning of negotiation differs in different cultures, and these differences have consequences for the process and outcome of negotiations. Meanings and definitions of conflict and conflict resolution, which are instilled in individuals during the process of their socialization, determine how they define struggle, negotiation, mediation, arbitration, and adjudication. Internalized definitions are important because they influence the thoughts, feelings, and conduct of individuals participating in conflict resolution procedures. Cross and Madson (1997) and Derlega et al. (2002) argue that cultural theorists and researchers should focus on "subjective construals of situations" and not the situations themselves. This theory, originally formulated in 1931 by sociologist Thomas (1966), states that if individuals define situations as real, the consequences of the situations become real.

CULTURAL THEORIES

In addition to meanings and definitions, cultural contexts include a number of other elements, one of which is "value orientations." Cross-cultural scholars such as Hofstede (1980) and Triandis (1989), state that an understanding of the value orientations shared by most members of a culture not only contributes to an understanding of the contexts in which conflict-resolving procedures occur, but also contributes to an understanding of the strategies and tactics used by those who participate in them. Other scholars—for example, Cohen (1993), LeBaron Duryea and Grundison (1993), and Hall (1976)—emphasize communication. Taken together, value orientations and communications theories help explain the cultural context in which procedures aimed at ending conflicts occur, and why the strategies and tactics used by members of different cultures vary.

Value Orientations Theory: Collectivism and Individualism

Osyerman, Kemmelmeier, and Coon (2002, p. 114) define value orientations as "internalized cognitive structures" that guide choices by evoking basic moral values (for example, right versus wrong) as well as priorities (for example, the general good is more important than the single individual's pleasure). Consider, for example, how the value orientations of democracy, monogamy, and hierarchy may guide conduct in ways that differ from the value orientations of dictatorship, polygamy, and egalitarianism.

Organizational sociologist Hofstede (1980) identified four basic value orientations, and used them to classify 40 countries according to their relative prominence. Hofstede's value orientations are power/symmetry, risk preference/avoidance, masculinity/femininity, and group/individual. Triandis (1989, p. 42) states that the group versus individual value orientation "is the most important dimension of cultural [value] difference in social behaviour across diverse cultures of the world." Based on their review of a great deal of theorizing and research guided by the individualism–collectivism model, Osyerman, Coon, and Kemmelmeier (2002, p. 44) concluded that "[t]he model focuses on a few central dimensions of cultural difference that provide a powerful explanatory tool for understanding the behaviour of individuals in different parts of the world." Individualism–collectivism values are central to the value orientations theories formulated by cross-cultural scholars such as Triandis (1989) and Ting-Toomey (1988).

Individualism

Individualism refers to "a belief that the individual is an end in himself, and as such ought to realize his self and cultivate his own judgment, notwithstanding the weight of pervasive social pressures in the direction of conformity" (Gould & Kolb, 1964). Of the 40 cultures in Hofstede's 1980 sample, those with the most individualistic cultures were the United States, Australia, Canada, Great Britain, and New Zealand (in descending order).

Cultures based on individualism are characterized by values that emphasize

- the uniqueness of the individual;
- self-reliance or independence; and
- instrumental duty—that is, duty toward groups depending on the degree to which they are perceived as contributing to or detracting from the achievement or maintenance of individual goals and objectives.

Osyerman, Coon, and Kemmelmeier (2002, p. 44) define uniqueness and independence as the "core elements" of individualism.

Collectivism

Collectivism refers to the belief that the "in-group" is an end in itself, and that in-group members behave in ways that meet in-group expectations, not because of what they stand to gain as individuals, but because it is the right thing to do. Triandis (1989, p. 53) defines "in-group" as "a group whose norms, goals and values shape the behavior of its members." Examples of in-groups include families, communities, ethnic groups, and all members of a society who share the values and interests that the society holds to be important. In-group members perceive individuals who share different or opposing values, norms, and interests as being members of out-groups (Triandis, 1989, p. 53).

Cultures based on collectivism are characterized by values that emphasize

- moral duty to the in-group, even if it means personal loss or inconvenience (Schweder & Bourne, 1982); and
- in-group harmony.

Osyerman, Coon, and Kemmelmeier (2002, p. 44) define duty to the in-group and maintenance of harmony as the "core elements" of collectivism.

Hofstede's 1980 ranking of the five most collectivist cultures from a 40-culture sample were Guatemala, Indonesia, Pakistan, Singapore, and Panama (in descending order).

Hofstede and Triandis found none of the cultures they studied to be exclusively individualistic or collectivistic. Instead, they found that both types of value orientations coexist within the same society. For example, in cultures classified as individualistic—such as the Canada and United States—the dominant value orientation was found to co-exist with the collectivistic value orientations of the First Nations (Lajeunesse, 1990; Brant, 1990; Ross, 1996) and immigrants from predominantly collectivistic cultures (LeBaron Duryea & Grundison, 1993).

One of the "most surprising" findings to emerge from the body of research reviewed by Osyerman, Coon, and Kemmelmeier (2002, p. 44) is that "relationality and family orientation is not closely linked with collectivism." Specifically, the findings indicate that Canadians and Americans enjoy their relationships with family members, but do not feel obligated to family members.

Conflict Resolution in Collectivistic and Individualistic Cultures

Cultural value orientations theorists, such as Ting-Toomey (1988) and Triandis (1989), predict that people who are brought up in collectivist cultures are more likely to participate in conflict resolution procedures that are aimed at maintaining relationships with members of different groups than are people who are brought up in individualist societies. Those brought up in individualist societies are more likely to participate in procedures aimed at achieving substantive outcomes. Ting-Toomey's (1988) "value orientations face" theory is described in figure 5.1. This figure illustrates that individualistic value orientations are linked to competitive (distributive) strategies and tactics, and the use of these tactics is linked to the achievement of substantive outcomes. Figure 5.1 also illustrates that collectivistic value orientations are linked to cooperative (integrative) strategies and tactics, and the use of these tactics are linked to maintaining relationships.

The differences between conflict resolution in collectivistic and individualistic cultures can be illustrated by comparing interest-based mediation, a technique used by predominantly individualistic cultures, with mediation models used in two collectivistic cultures: the residents of Puntarenas, Costa Rica (Hofstede, 1980) and the First Nations of Canada (Huber, 1993; Lajeunesse, 1990).

Mediation: A Costa Rican Model

Socio-linguist Lederach (1991, p. 167) lived for a period of time in the Costa Rican town of Puntarenas in order to study how the residents attempted to settle conflicts and how third parties played a role in the conflict resolution process. One of Lederach's first major findings was that residents used the term "conflict" to refer to entanglements that harm relationships (p. 167). The concepts of "conflict as entanglement" and "conflict resolution as disentanglement" are grounded in a holistic view of social life in which individuals are members of networks (families, friends, neighbours, workmates) and are therefore interconnected. The metaphor of a fishing net is used to describe the processes of conflict and conflict resolution.

> In a conflict [network members] are caught in a [tangled] net, with its knots and connections. When tangled, the net must slowly and patiently

Figure 5.1 Ting-Toomey's Value Orientations Theory (1988)

Source: Ting-Toomey (1988).

be disentangled. When it is disentangled, it remains a net. The net is frequently torn, leaving holes. It must be sewn back together, knots once again connecting separated loose ends (p. 168).

Getting from "In" to "Out"

People's motivation to extricate themselves from conflicts arises from the pain that conflict causes. The residents of Puntarenas use the analogy of a nail being driven into their bodies to describe the feeling associated with being involved in a conflict. Thus, individuals frequently start a conversation by saying, "What a nail I've got." The deeper the nail is driven in—that is, the longer, more intense, or more complex the conflict—the more difficult it is to get it out.

"Getting out" can be accomplished in two ways: avoidance and *arreglo*. Avoidance means ignoring the problem or avoiding contact or communication with others who are involved in the conflict. Avoidance helps the individual to extricate himself from the conflict, but it leaves holes in the net because the conflict is not settled. *Arreglo* settles the conflict by sewing the net back together.

There are two steps preliminary to *arreglo*: *ubicase* (getting one's bearings) and *platicar* (dialogue).

Ubicase is a process in which the parties involved in a conflict try to make sense of the conflict. To this end, they may engage in *la ronda*, in which each party sits in a circle, states her perspective on the problem, and offers suggestions as to how it may be solved.

Platicar not only involves talking; it also involves exchanging information in a way that reaffirms the parties' relationship. Most importantly, it helps the parties enter into each other's worlds and prepares them to participate in *dialoga*. *Dialoga* involves a deeper level of exchange designed to reconnect people who have become disconnected by the conflict.

Arreglo means three different things to the residents of Puntarenas:

1. disentangling something that was entangled;
2. understanding, love, and mutual caring for each other; and
3. an arrangement that emerges from a relationship in which each party has partaken of the world of the other.

Rather than creating "techniques of conflict resolution," the culture of Puntarenas creates "a way of being and relating." Third parties can become involved in three ways: by being one who gives *consejo*, by being a *confianza*, or by acting as a *patas*. A third party gives *consejo* when she gives advice, joins another in thinking about the problem and how to solve it, and generally participates as a caring member of a network. A *confianza* is a person whom the parties judge to be trustworthy and in whom they have confidence. People involved in a conflict are more likely to "open up their worlds"—that is, fully disclose their inner thoughts and feelings—to a *confianza* than to other third parties. The greatest challenge faced by *confianzas* who attempt to settle conflicts is to motivate the parties to reveal information about their inner worlds.

A *patas* is an individual in the network who has special knowledge or abilities or who occupies a specific position. He acts as a go-between with a view to getting another party to intervene in a way that would solve the problem. For example, a local priest may approach a mutually respected elder to intervene in a marital conflict by reframing the couple's conflict as a hypothetical one, and asking both parties how they think the hypothetical conflict could best be settled.

In conclusion, the Costa Rican mediation model defines conflict as harmful entanglements, and conflict resolution as a process of disentanglement. One of the most frequently used methods of facilitating disentanglement is *arreglo*, which involves three interconnected processes.

1. The entangled parties attempt to understand the conflict and suggest ways in which it can be settled.
2. The parties engage in a deeper form of communication that facilitates mutual understanding.
3. Third parties can become involved to give advice to the parties, facilitate full disclosure, or act as a go-between to locate a mutually respected third party to help the parties settle the conflict.

Mechanisms that contribute to disentanglement are mutual understanding that repairs the parties' relationship and holistic problem solving that deals with interconnected issues.

Mediation: A First Nations Model

First Nations' "medicine wheel" model, described by Huber (1993), is holistic, collectivistic, grounded in spirituality, and focuses on healing the participants and their communities. The medicine wheel helps First Nations people understand "many diverse aspects of life that can be talked about in terms of four." Four is a significant number: there are four seasons, four directions (East, South, West, and North) and "four parts of the whole person"—spiritual, emotional, physical, and intellectual. All four parts of each participant in the medicine wheel ceremony must be honoured.

The circle is used to assist the process of mediation because it symbolizes

- wholeness and unity,
- equality (everyone around the circle has an equal voice),
- continuity (no beginning and no end), and
- sacredness (those present must obey its rule or remove themselves from the circle).

Problems that brought the parties to mediation are symbolically placed at the centre of the circle "for all to work on." Parties present at the mediation take turns to speak. Interruptions are regulated by means of a "talking stick" or other object, such as a rock or feather. Only the person holding the talking stick or other object may speak, and if she chooses to say nothing, a period of silence speaks for her.

The four directions—East, South, West, and North—have their distinct contributions to the whole. "Setting the climate" for mediation takes place in the East. An opening prayer and "smudging"—that is, directing the smoke of sweetgrass, sage, or other spiritual plant over the body to cleanse it—establishes a peaceful atmosphere that facilitates full and honest communication, clears the mind, diffuses strong emotions, and decreases anxiety by making disclosure safer. The mediator explains the mediation process by engaging in self-disclosure, describing conflicts he has been involved in, and explaining how they were resolved. These revelations humanize the conflict by showing that conflict is a normal part of being alive. They also help to build rapport and trust.

"Telling the story" takes place in the South, the heart of emotional expression. Emotional expression that is sensitive to the feelings of others helps "unblock capabilities for love and warmth." The mediator encourages the participants to express their emotions and carefully listens to the stories that they tell in order to clarify the matters that underlie the conflict and summarize essential aspects of the stories.

"Discovering what is important" takes place in the West because self-reflection and introspection are gifts of the West. The mediator assists the participants in understanding themselves in relation to others and in respecting the vision of elders. She also models and manages power relations between the participants. Power relationships always work for the benefit of all when they are exercised in ways that are in harmony with universal teachings.

"Creating solutions" takes place in the North. The mediator helps to solve the problem by facilitating a sense of detachment. He does this by placing the problem and its solutions in the context of the past, present, and future, and inviting participants to adopt multiple perspectives in order to set aside the strong feelings they may have.

The centre of the circle is a place where the mediator helps the parties adopt a holistic perspective on the problem and the proposed solutions. Participants are invited to select solutions that are "congruent with the values of their respective communities." The centre is also the place where holistic solutions are implemented.

Lajeunesse (1990, p. 16) compared the collectivistic First Nations model of mediation with and the Western interest-based model. We added the Costa Rican model, and tabulated the results in table 5.1.

Migration Between Collectivistic and Individualistic Cultures

The First Nations' collectivistic culture originated in the harsh conditions of life faced by First Nations peoples well over 500 years before the arrival of immigrants from Europe. Survival depended on the group's cooperation and collaboration, and on placing a higher value on collective than on individual interests (Brant, 1990). Today, people of the First Nations who live in reserve communities in northern Canada are more likely to participate in collectivistic cultures than those who live and work in large cities whose cultures are predominantly individualistic (Huber, 1993).

Similarly, the values, norms, and behaviour of (especially younger) immigrants from societies with predominantly collectivistic cultures are likely to be influenced to a greater degree by Canada's predominantly individualistic culture the longer they live, go to school, play sports, and work in Canada. On the other hand, the values, norms, and behaviour of individuals from societies with collectivistic cultures who immigrated to Canada as adults with members of their families are likely to be influenced to a greater degree by the collectivistic cultures of the societies from which they came.

TABLE 5.1   Models of Mediation in Different Cultures

	Western	Costa Rican	First Nations
View of conflict	Individual-based	Individual entangled in a network of relationships	Community ownership of conflict: collective interest
Forum	Office setting; appointments scheduled	Community settings, such as homes and workplaces	Community setting
Mediator's qualifications	Impartiality emphasized	Trusted and knowledgeable connections to the community stressed	Trust emphasized over neutrality
Process	Parties meet face to face or mediator shuttles between them	Parties meet face to face through third parties	Triadic management: parties communicate through the mediator
	Past and present reviewed to determine effects on each party	Past, present, and future explored to disentangle a tangled net (conflict)	Present and future explored to restore balance and harmony to the community
Communication	Direct verbal communication; often confrontational; fact-specific	Dialogue and non-verbal communication	Facts relayed through storytelling or other means; facts not always relayed at outset of mediation
Object of resolution	Obtain results acceptable to parties	Disentangle network of relationships	Obtain settlement to restore balance and harmony to the community

Source: Lajeunesse (1990).

LeBaron Duryea and Grundison (1993) included adult immigrants from four societies with predominantly collectivistic cultures in their study of the link between conflict, culture, and conflict resolution. These researchers interviewed Chinese, Vietnamese, South Asian, and Latin American immigrants. They found that adult immigrants from these societies felt that an educational model of mediation was more culturally appropriates than the widely used interest-based mediation model, which was created by people who were heavily influenced by individualistic cultural values.

An *educational model* of mediation is one in which mediation is viewed as "an educational experience, an educative process that respects individuals as members of communities [and] acknowledges that individuals must return to live within their communities" (LeBaron Duryea & Grundison, 1993, p. 199). In this model, the parties view the mediator, not as a neutral third party, but as a trusted and knowledgeable educator whom they authorize to control the process and make decisions about outcomes. The role of mediator as educator and parties as students gains legitimacy as a result of the customary respect for teachers in many societies with collectivistic cultures.

Cultures and Outcomes

In both collectivistic and individualistic cultures, participation in negotiations or mediation yields results or outcomes. Outcomes can be classified as desired and actual. *Desired outcomes* refer to goals or objectives that the parties believe they are entitled to achieve. Desired outcomes exist in the minds and hearts of parties at the start of their participation in conflict-resolving procedures. Culture defines entitlement, and places a higher value on some desired outcomes than others. The strategies and tactics used by the parties are influenced by the goals they want to achieve. For example, findings reported by Ohbuchi, Fukushima, and Tedeschi (1999) indicated that the collectivistic-minded Japanese wanted to achieve relationship goals more than they wanted to achieve goals related to economic resources or the expression of hostility; moreover, they used non-confrontational tactics more frequently than they used assertive tactics. Individualist Americans wanted to achieve justice more than any other goal, and they used assertive tactics more than they used conciliatory and non-confrontational tactics (p. 58). The study demonstrates that culture influences outcome preferences, which in turn influence the tactics used by the parties.

Actual outcomes refer to the goals or objectives achieved by the parties who participate in conflict-resolving procedures as a result of their strategies and tactics. Because cultural differences are reflected in different strategies and tactics, and because outcomes are the result of their use, culture indirectly influences outcomes. For example, outcomes achieved by individualistic American negotiators were perceived as unfair by collectivistic Japanese parties. The Japanese associated the self-serving biases of the Americans with the use of tactics that they perceived as unfair because the tactics were primarily aimed at achieving outcomes that were important to the Americans, rather than outcomes that were important to both parties (Gelfand et al., 2001).

Fair Outcomes

Culture influences outcomes directly by defining them as fair or unfair. Fairness is used to evaluate outcomes in most cultures, but it is culturally defined (Faure & Rubin, 1993, p. 12). Members of one culture may define a fair outcome as one that distributes gains according to the needs of the parties and losses according to the ability of the parties to bear them. For example, in negotiations over the distribution of river water between a rich country with an abundance of water and a poor country facing mass starvation as a result of a water shortage, some people may think it is fair for the poor country to receive a greater supply of water because its need for water is greater.

Members of another culture may define a fair outcome as one that distributes gains according to the relative contributions of the parties who produce them. For example, according to this view, it is fair for a country that conserves water and invests in ensuring that the river continues to flow without flooding to receive a greater share of the water than a country that neither conserves water nor invests in ensuring its supply.

Members of another culture may define a fair outcome as one that distributes gains equally, regardless of contributions or needs. According to this view, it is fair for the country that neither conserves water nor invests in ensuring a reliable supply to receive the same share as a country that needs water, conserves water, and invests in ensuring a regular water supply.

In collectivistic cultures, parties involved in negotiations or mediations with in-group members are likely to define a fair outcome as one that distributes gains according to need and/or ability to absorb losses. On the other hand, parties involved in negotiations with out-group members are likely to define a fair outcome as one that yields them a greater share of material resources, such as land, property, or water. The definitions are supported by cultural norms.

In individualistic cultures, a party participating in positional bargaining is likely to define an outcome as fair if he believes that the compromises he makes are equally great as those made by the other party, regardless of the other party's position as an in-group or out-group member. Principled negotiation (Fisher, Ury, & Patton, 1991) was the product of an individualistic North American culture, and its creators define a fair outcome as one that reflects the merits of the case and is legitimated by objective standards.

In collectivistic cultures, the healing of damaged relationships is likely to be defined as a fair outcome of negotiations and mediations between members of the same in-groups. In some instances, such a definition may also govern a fair outcome of negotiations and mediations with out-groups. On the other hand, achieving a larger share of material resources—such as land or water—may be a definitive quality of outcomes perceived as fair by parties involved in negotiations or mediations with out-group members. In this regard, consider "The Euphrates in 1991: Fair Outcomes for Turkey, Syria, and Iraq."

The Euphrates in 1991: Fair Outcomes for Turkey, Syria, and Iraq

Research on negotiations aimed at settling the Euphrates River conflict led Slim (1993, p. 151) to the following conclusion: "Decision makers in Turkey, Syria and Iraq [three countries with collectivistic cultures] hold different conceptions of what would be a fair outcome, partly determined by what each party believes to be at stake in the dispute."

Turkish decision makers perceived that Turkish sovereignty was at stake because it is a tenet of international law that Turkey, like all other countries, owns and controls resources, including the Euphrates River, that are located within its territory. Turkey therefore defined a fair outcome as one that recognized Turkish rights of ownership over the Euphrates River.

Decision makers in Iraq perceived the quality of life of its people and Syria perceived the very survival of its people to be at stake. Historically, the three countries shared Euphrates water more equitably, and the distribution of water was related to the countries' needs. Syria and Iraq cited two international conventions—the Helsinki Rules, 1966 and United Nations 172—stating that population size and need for water in accordance with "historical allocation" and "prior usage" should be the criteria used in allocating water that flows across national boundaries. Decision makers in Iraq and Syria used these criteria in defining a fair outcome as one that satisfied the needs of their respective populations for water to drink, grow crops, and generate electricity (Slim, 1993, pp. 151-152).

The Euphrates River case failed to result in a negotiated agreement because different definitions of a fair outcome were used by Iraq and Syria on the one hand, and Turkey on the other.

Source: Slim (1993).

Conclusion

In sum, collectivistic and individualistic orientations are reflected in

- the creation of different mediation models,
- the use of different strategies and tactics, and
- the existence of different ideas about the outcomes of negotiation and mediation.

The combined effect of value orientations and situational factors are reflected in differences in the disclosure and exchange of information during negotiations, and the use of cooperative and competitive tactics by negotiators.

Communications Theories: Meanings and Styles

Meanings

Communications theories that emphasize the meaning of verbal and unspoken communications identify "misunderstandings" as the cause of cognitive conflicts (LeBaron Duryea & Grundison, 1993) and of difficulties in attempting to settle them (Krauss & Morsella, 2000). In Cohen's (1993, p. 24) communications theory, culture is defined as "a set of underlying grammatical rules—guiding perceptions and structuring meanings—in fact creating reality." If human beings are thought of as sophisticated computers, it is the software that translates potential into actuality. Software confers meanings—for example, a wink may mean a "conspiratorial message" (Geertz, 2003, pp. 183-184). It also guides perceptions—for example, the perception of one person as a member of an in-group and another as a member of an out-group. Meanings and perceptions differ greatly across cultures, and the differences create a problem when members of different cultures clash because they do not understand each other. In other words, they do not share meanings and perceptions.

According to former US President Bill Clinton (2004, pp. 912-914), "culture clash" was partly responsible for the breakdown in the peace negotiations between Palestinian Authority Chairman Yassir Arafat and Israeli Prime Minister Ehud Barak in 2000. Clinton reported that Barak's "way of doing things [such as] wanting others to wait until he decided the time was right, then, when he made his best offer, he expected it to be accepted as self-evidently a good deal, was diametrically opposed to honored customs among Arabs." The Palestinian parties with whom he was negotiating "wanted trust-building courtesies and conversations and lots of bargaining."

In *Skeletons on the Zahara*, King (2004, p. 36) describes misunderstandings in communication during positional bargaining between Arab merchants and European buyers in the following manner:

> When two Arabs begin negotiating they expect to reach a deal. Asking the price of an item or making a counter-offer … commits one to a process in which two people acting in good faith should be able to reach an agreement. This explains why Westerners who casually ask the price of an object for sale in an Arab medina often find the merchant overly aggressive: and, on the other hand, when Westerners suddenly break off negotiations, the merchant is insulted.

A communications and meanings theory is also implicit in Ross's (1996, p. 111) description of misunderstandings and misinterpretations caused by language differences between aboriginals and non-aboriginals. Imagine negotiations between First Nations negotiators who learned to speak a language [Ojibwe or Mi'kmaq] replete with double meanings, the relative absence of nouns, and the presence of neutral adjectives that "describe in value-free terms," what the speaker comprehends with her senses. In this connection, Ross quotes a Mi'kmaq woman who says,

> When you're speaking Mi'kmaq, you can go all day long without speaking a noun. … My eyes see nouns. … But that's not what the function of language is. It's not to become another pair of eyes. It's supposed to be speaking to the ear and to the heart.

The English language can also speak to the ear and the heart. The difficulty lies with English-speaking negotiators who use language as a vehicle of judgment rather than wisdom, pronouncement rather than exploration, and deflection rather than openness.

Styles

High-Context and Low-Context Styles

In *Beyond Culture* (1976, p. 39), Hall identifies two major styles of communication: high context and low context. He states:

> Any transaction can be characterized as high or low context. High context transactions feature preprogrammed information that is in the receiver and the setting, with only minimal information in the transmitted message. Low context transactions are the reverse. Most of the information must be in the transmitted message in order to make up for what is missing in the context.

In high-context cultures, values, norms, and meanings are shared by most members. Therefore, the contexts in which interpersonal or inter-group communications occur are well understood by those who are communicating with each other because "meanings and interpretations of a message are vested mainly in the implicitly shared, social and cultural knowledge of the context." An example of a high-context communication is the in-group joke—a joke that is comprehensible only to members of the in-group.

In high-context cultures, a relatively high proportion of messages sent and understood are of the in-group joke type. Moreover, non-verbal means of communicating are emphasized over verbal messages. When members of high-context cultures use speech as a tool of communication, "things that are not said [are] sometimes more important than things that are said" (p. 77).

In low-context cultures, most members share only some values and meanings. Different and opposing values and meanings are shared by members of different ethnic, gender, religious, and social class in-groups. Therefore, people who communicate with each other may not entirely understand the context in which interpersonal or inter-group communications take place. As a result, they use written or spoken messages as a means of conveying meaning. A written contract is an example of a low-context communication. Written contracts are more likely to be found in low-context than in high-context cultures.

As is true of cultures classified as collectivistic and individualistic, no culture is exclusively a high-context culture or a low-context culture. Still, using criteria identified by Hall (1976, p. 76), countries such as Canada, the United States, Germany, and Great Britain have been classified as predominantly low-context cultures, and countries such as Japan, Korea, and Vietnam have been classified as high-context cultures.

According to Gudykunst and Ting-Toomey (1988), collectivistic and individualistic value orientations and high- and low-context communication styles are present in all cultures. Gudykunst and Ting-Toomey theorize that individualistic value orientations are associated with high-context communication styles. This combination is linked with the use of confrontational tactics, such as making "take it or leave it" demands, using threats, interrogating the other party with closed-ended questions (which require yes/no answers), and focusing on substantive outcomes. Gudykunst and Ting-Toomey also posit that collectivistic value orientations and low-context communication styles go together. This combination is associated with the use of collaborative tactics that take the needs and interests of both parties into account, and encourage the expression of feelings and subtle forms of communication.

Brett (2000) and Ting-Toomey (1988) report findings that support this theory. Their research indicates that low-context communicators tend to use confrontational, solution-oriented, distributive, competitive tactics, whereas high-context communicators use polite, collaborative, integrative tactics. During negotiations, low-context communicators tend to make direct statements about their positions on issues. They also attempt to obtain information by asking direct questions about preferences in the expectation that direct communications will help the other party correctly interpret their messages because their meanings are in their messages themselves. High-context communicators tend to make indirect statements about their positions on issues and obtain information about preferences by making offers and counteroffers. They obtain and exchange information through this indirect process in the expectation that the other party will correctly infer their meanings, which are not explicitly stated in the messages themselves (Brett, 2000; Ting-Toomey, 1988).

STRATEGIES AND TACTICS

Data based on questionnaires and laboratory studies using hypothetical situations indicate that people with different communications styles use different strategies and tactics. Low-context communicators tend to use dominating, confrontational, solution-oriented, distributive, competitive tactics, whereas high-context communicators use polite, obliging, collaborative, integrative tactics (Brett, 2000; Ting-Toomey, 1988).

The use of different communications styles increases the likelihood of "communications strain," and misunderstandings caused by communications strain decreases the likelihood of reaching a negotiated or mediated agreement (Cohen, 1993; Gudykunst & Ting-Toomey, 1988).

CONFLICT RESOLUTION PROCEDURES

Building on the contributions of Hall (1976), Jandt and Pedersen (1996) formulated a number of hypotheses about cross-cultural conflict management and mediation in the Asia–Pacific region. Here are two of them:

1. Parties in low-context cultures are more likely to negotiate their conflicts in private, whereas parties in high-context cultures are more likely to settle their conflicts publicly with the assistance of third parties.
2. Parties in low-context cultures are more likely to use adversarial procedures, such as adjudication, than parties in high-context cultures, who regard resorting to such procedures as a failure (1996, pp. 14-15).

Jandt and Pedersen tested these hypotheses in 100 mediations that were conducted in a number of Asian–Pacific countries. Some of their findings are set out below.

In high-context cultures, mediation was likely to be successful when mediators

- paid attention to relationships between the parties, and
- focused on long-term outcomes.

In low-context cultures, mediation was likely to be successful when mediators

- focused on immediate solutions,
- minimized or ignored the impact of process and outcomes on relationships, and
- tended to view the mediation as separate from the social context in which it was being practised.

Jandt and Pedersen also arrived at the following conclusions:

- Members of low-context cultures are more likely to prefer a face-to-face process than members of high-context cultures. Members of high-context cultures are more likely to choose intermediaries than members of low-context cultures.
- Members of low-context cultures are more likely to prefer adversarial procedures, while members of high-context cultures are more likely to prefer non-adversarial alternatives.
- In a low-context culture, such as Canada, immigrants from high-context cultures are more likely to choose the procedure favoured by more numerous and powerful low-context communicators when they are involved in conflicts with them.
- Parties who emigrated from high-context to low-context cultures are unlikely to achieve the outcomes they want by participating in the mainstream mediation processes created in low-context cultures.

SITUATIONAL FACTORS

Findings reported by Aries (1996), Faure and Rubin (1993), and Lind et al. (1994) indicate that the following situational factors are relevant to the strategies and tactics used by members of both high-context, collectivist cultures and low-context, individualistic cultures:

- geographic location (whether located upstream or downstream on a river),
- type of conflict (within or between groups), and
- intensity of conflict (higher or lower).

In-Groups and Out-Groups

Every society, including Canada, has in-groups—whose members share values, norms, and ways of behaving—and out-groups—who, from the perspective of in-group members—are strangers who share different or opposing values, norms, and ways of behaving. Research findings reported by Gudykunst, Nishida, and Schmidt (1989) and Triandis et al. (1988) suggest that in collectivist cultures—such as Hong Kong and Japan—parties are more likely to share relevant information when negotiating with members of their in-group than when negotiating with members of out-groups. (Such sharing is central to negotiations facilitated by interest-based mediators and also central to Gulliver's (1979) cyclical–developmental theory of negotiation.) In individualistic cultures—such as the United States and Australia—

the amount and type of disclosure did not change when negotiators participated in negotiations with in-group or out-group members.

Findings cited by Triandis (1989, p. 87) and reported by Espinoza and Garza (1985) suggest that a similar pattern exists for the use of cooperative and competitive tactics. Collectivists tend to use cooperative tactics when negotiating with in-group members and competitive tactics when negotiating with out-group members. Individualists are equally likely to use cooperative and/or competitive tactics in negotiations with in-group and out-group members.

Taken together, the findings reported here support the conclusion that situational factors exert a greater influence on the strategies and tactics used by negotiators in collectivistic cultures than on those used by negotiators in individualistic cultures.

Separating the person from the problem is the first principle of principled negotiation (Fisher, Ury, & Patton, 1991). Negotiators in individualistic cultures find it difficult to make this separation (Fisher, Ury, & Patton, 1991, pp. 17-39). Findings reported by Rojas (1981) indicate that negotiators in collectivistic cultures experience even greater difficulty in doing so. One possible reason for this difference is that members of in-groups in collectivistic cultures are more likely to be known to each other, a situational factor; they are therefore likely to be in possession of personal information that justifies their linkage of the person and the problem.

Studies of conflicts about water indicate that people with the *same* communication style adopt different strategies and tactics depending on whether the conflict is between in-group members or between in-group and out-group members (Faure & Sjostedt, 1993). Deng (1993, p. 77) studied a conflict between people of northern and southern Sudan (both collectivistic, high-context cultures) over the waters of the Nile River. He found that attempts to settle everyday conflicts between members of in-groups through negotiation or mediation were characterized by the use of gentle, courteous, reasonable, and respectful communications that are hallmarks of integrative negotiation. On the other hand, attempts to settle conflicts between members of in-groups and out-groups were characterized by the use of highly adversarial negotiation tactics.

LeBaron Duryea and Grundison (1993) studied immigrants who came to Vancouver from collectivistic South Asian, Chinese, Vietnamese, and Latin American societies. The procedure selected by members of these collectivistic societies varied with whether the conflict involved in-group or out-group members. For example, the immigrants selected the self-help procedures of avoidance and negotiation when their conflict involved in-group members. They selected procedures such as negotiations through lawyer, arbitration, and adjudication when conflict existed between in-group and (majority) out-group members. LeBaron Duryea and Grundison also found that members of collectivistic, high-context cultures in Vancouver—such as the Chinese and Vietnamese communities—used collaborative, integrative procedures aimed at maintaining relationships when the conflict involved in-group members; however, they used problem-solving tactics aimed at achieving substantive outcomes when they were involved in conflicts with members of out-groups.

Researchers Tyler et al. (1998) studied conflicts between American supervisors and employees. Both supervisors and employees were members of the same individualistic, low-context culture. Some of the employees were members of the same ethnic groups as their supervisors, and others were members of different ethnic groups. The researchers also studied conflicts between Japanese teachers—who were members of a collectivistic, high-context culture—and American teachers—who were members of an individualistic, low-context culture. Tyler et al. reported two major findings:

1. Parties attempting to settle in-group conflicts were more concerned with relationship issues than substantive outcomes, regardless of whether the conflict existed between members of collectivistic, high-context cultures or individualistic, low-context cultures.

2. Parties attempting to settle out-group conflicts were more concerned with substantive outcomes than relationship issues, regardless of whether the conflict was between members of collectivistic, high-context cultures or individualistic, low-context cultures.

These findings led Tyler et al. (1998, p. 146) to conclude that the "nature of the situation, not the participant's [culture], was responsible for the effects observed."

ETHNOCENTRISM AND STEREOTYPING

The presence of racial/ethnic, religious, gender, and class in-groups and out-groups within a society, or among nations, is a situational factor associated with two cultural creations that can cause conflicts between in-groups and out-groups: ethnocentrism and stereotyping. In addition to causing conflict, ethnocentrism and stereotyping also inhibit settlement of existing conflicts.

Ethnocentrism

The term "ethnocentrism" was coined by Sumner (1906). In *Folkways* (pp. 12-13), Sumner defined ethnocentrism as "a view of one's own group as the center, and other groups placed at the margins in relation to it." Groups at the centre regard themselves not only as being different from groups at the margins, but also as being better than them. They use the standards or values of their own culture in making this and other judgments about other cultures (Macionis & Gerber, 2005, p. 71). Members of a group are practising ethnocentrism to the degree that they

- perceive their group as being inherently different from and superior to other groups,
- use their own cultural standards to evaluate other cultures, and
- act and react toward members of other cultures on the basis of these perceptions and evaluations.

Deutsch (1973) and Fisher (2000) state that ethnocentrism not only causes conflict between in-group and out-group members, but also makes it more difficult for in-group and out-group members to settle existing conflicts. Ethnocentrism causes conflict by promoting misunderstanding and encouraging prejudgment of the characters and actions of members of out-groups. It also causes conflict by promoting discrimination—that is, treating people differently simply because they are members of an out-group. Misunderstanding, prejudgment, and discrimination also undermine attempts to settle conflicts through negotiation or mediation because they undermine the creation of collaborative relationships and constructive mutual problem solving.

An example of how ethnocentrism contributes to conflict and inhibits negotiation is provided by Ross (2004, pp. 15-45), chief Middle East peace negotiator for former US presidents George Bush Sr. and Bill Clinton. The Palestinian ethnocentric narrative presents Palestinians as the victims of Israeli oppression, demonizes Israelis, and condemns the conduct of their leaders. The Israeli ethnocentric narrative presents Israelis as survivors taking whatever steps are necessary to ensure the survival of their imperilled state, demonizes Palestinians, and condemns the conduct of their leaders. Ethnocentric mythologies brought to the negotiations by both Israelis and Palestinians were partly responsible for the parties' failure to reach a peace agreement at the Camp David summit initiated by US President Clinton (2004, p. 773).

Another example of the influence of ethnocentrism on strategies and tactics is provided in "Ethnocentrism: The Jonglei Canal Project," based on Deng's (1993) study.

Ethnocentrism: The Jonglei Canal Project

The Jonglei Canal project was designed to retrieve water from a swampy region in southern Sudan and redistribute it to northern Sudan and Egypt. Deng found that conflicting values and ethnocentric biases were reflected in the use of win–lose strategies and related tactics by the two principal negotiators: Nimeri from northern Sudan and Abel Alier from southern Sudan. Nimeri was the representative of a Muslim culture whose members regarded themselves as superior to the "heathen" cultures of the Dinka and Nuer in the south. Historically, the northern Sudanese viewed heathens as "legitimate targets of raids and enslavement" (Deng, p. 74) and as fair game for manipulation by making and breaking promises.

Alieri, a Dinka, was the representative of a culture whose members regarded themselves as morally superior to others and regarded northerners as untrustworthy and morally corrupt. Culturally rooted attempts by the northern Sudanese to impose Islamic superiority were met with culturally rooted resistance by the Dinka and Nuer in the south.

Negotiations reflected cultural outlooks. Nimeri used tactics aimed at imposing superiority, and Alieri, who did not trust Nimeri or the people he represented, resisted them. As a result, the parties participated in distributive negotiation characterized by inflexibility, hard bargaining, and the use of adversarial tactics. For both negotiators, "visions of a bitter past not only govern[ed] the choices made ... but also over-determine[d] the emotions with which negotiation problems were perceived and treated" (Faure & Rubin, p. 211).

Source: Deng (1993); Faure and Rubin (1993).

Stereotyping

Aries (1996, p. 163) defines a stereotype as "a set of beliefs about the characteristics presumed to be typical of [all members of a social category]." Social categories are relatively large groups of people who share a characteristic, such as gender, race/ethnicity, religion, nation, or social class. Rattansi (1992, p. 25) defines stereotyping as "the tendency to assign identical characteristics to all members of social categories or groups regardless of differences between individual members." For example, all Hindus are the same because they are members of the same religion. Stereotyping, then, involves generalizing about individual members of a social category on the basis of their membership in that category.

Some generalizations are relatively accurate in the sense that they are supported by evidence systematically collected by social scientists or government agencies. For example, the generalization that violent crime rates in Canada are higher among aboriginals than among non-aboriginals is supported by government statistics (Ellis & Diamond, 2005). Other generalizations are inaccurate or only partially accurate. For example, generalizations about "the typical man," "the typical woman," "the typical Muslim," or "the typical Jew" are inevitably inaccurate because the categories "man," "woman," "Muslim," and "Jew" are far too broad to support intelligent generalizations, and the adjective "typical" is usually suspect.

Stereotypes influence the strategies and tactics used by parties involved in negotiations and mediations by acting as self-fulfilling prophecies (Aries, 1996, p. 188). For example, consider the operation of stereotyping in an employment environment that expects members of Social Category X to be "neither ambitious nor intelligent." Expectations shape perceptions of members of Social Category X as unambitious and unintelligent. Perceptions shape evaluations of them as unambitious and unintelligent. And evaluations shape reactions. Therefore, employers give members of Social Category X boring, low-prestige jobs that require little intelligence. The concentration of members of Social Category X in these kinds of jobs confirms the expectation that they are unambitious and unintelligent, and adds the notion that they are irresponsible. The original prophecy is at once confirmed and enlarged.

Faure and Sjostedt (1993, pp. 224-225) reviewed the findings reported by scholars who witnessed four conflicts over waterways (the Nile, Rhine, Euphrates, and Jordan rivers). They observed that these case studies "document the fact that we enter into negotiation with stereotypic perceptions and expectations of different cultures ... and these stereotypic expectations may over-determine the very things one sees." Their account of the consequences of stereotyping are worth noting.

A paraphrased and slightly altered version of their account is presented in "The Ravages of Stereotyping." In this account, a mediator reacts differently to identical behaviour by parties from two different cultures because she brought stereotypic expectations with her to mediation, and she was not aware of the degree to which these expectations influenced her reactions.

The Ravages of Stereotyping

A mediator expects parties from Culture A to be fair-minded and parties from Culture B to be untrustworthy and manipulative in the negotiations she is facilitating.

During the course of negotiations, a party from Culture A makes a concession and asks a party from Culture B to do the same. The mediator perceives the request as fair-minded and evaluates it posi-tively, asking the party from Culture B if he would like to reciprocate.

At a later stage in the negotiations, the party from Culture B makes a concession and asks the party from Culture A to recipro-cate. The mediator expects manipulative and deceptive behaviour from the party from Culture B, evaluates the request adversely, and does not ask the party from Culture A to reciprocate.

Source: Faure and Sjostedt (1993, pp. 224-225).

CULTURAL–SITUATIONAL THEORY

Taken together, the findings on values orientations and communication styles presented here suggest that the conflict resolution strategies and tactics used by parties from collectivistic, high-context cultures and individualistic, low-context cultures can best be explained by a theory that takes both cul-tural and situational factors into account. A see-saw cultural–situational theory can accomplish this.

A see-saw theory emphasizes the interaction between cultural and situational factors. It makes the following assertion: the impact of culture is stronger when situational factors are weak; the impact of culture is weaker when situational factors are strong. According to Faure and Sjostedt (1993, p. 216), "Culture's effects on international negotiations are least prominent when structural [situational] factors are strong; and culture exerts its most powerful effects when structural [situational] factors are in remission."

In negotiations about the distribution of river water, the influence of situational factors is strong and the influence of cultural factors is weak when one of the parties represents a collectivistic, high-context culture that is located upstream from an individualistic, low-context culture, which is rep-resented by the other party. This is because the collectivistic, high-context culture can unilaterally decrease or increase the flow of water to the down-stream country. However, the influence of situational factors is weaker and the influence of cultural factors is stronger when these two different cul-tures are located opposite each other on the river because neither culture can unilaterally change the flow of water to the other culture.

In addition to differences in the location of cultures on a river, the intensity of the conflict over the distribution of river water is another important situational factor (Huer & Penrod, 1986). For example, in both of the cases described in the previous paragraph, struggle tactics are more likely to be used when the intensity of the conflict is high, and less likely to be used when the intensity of the conflict is low.

The see-saw theory posits that the choice of procedure—struggle, negotiation, mediation, arbitration, or adjudication—as well as the strategies and tactics used by the parties will be mainly influenced by the intensity of the conflict, regardless of whether the conflict is between in-group members who share the same culture, or between in-group and out-group members who do not share the same culture (Deng, 1993; Huer & Penrod, 1986).

ADVICE FOR PRACTITIONERS

Keep a Dual Focus on Cultural and Situational Factors

The see-saw theory should encourage negotiators and mediators to obtain information that helps them understand the thoughts, feelings, attitudes, beliefs, myths, and values of the parties, as well as the situational factors that influence them. Evaluating both sources of information will help negotiators and mediators avoid the "fundamental attribution error," which Aries (1996, pp. 19-20) defines as "a pervasive tendency to attribute the cause of behavior to personal dispositions rather than to the situational context." With culture in mind, we define the fundamental attribution error as the pervasive tendency to attribute the causes of strategies and tactics used by parties participating in conflict resolution procedures to either culture *or* situational factors rather than to both culture *and* situational factors.

Facilitate Information Sharing and Alternation

The advice we derived from theories of negotiation described in chapter 2 is also relevant here. For example, Gulliver's (1979) cross-cultural theory of negotiation advises practitioners to facilitate the dynamic processes inherent in negotiation—information sharing and alternation—that propel negotiations toward agreements in all cultures.

Reconcile Interests

We derive the following advice to negotiators and mediators from principled negotiation (Fisher, Ury, & Patton, 1991): Facilitate the reconciliation of interests (values or basic needs) because they are shared by individuals in all cultures. Be mindful of the criteria used by individuals in many different cultures in selecting procedures and evaluating them: procedural fairness, conflict reduction, expectation of a favourable outcome, and control over the process (Lind, Huo, & Tyler, 1994; Leung, Au, Fernandez-Dols, & Iwawaki, 1992).

Be Sensitive to the Nuances of Culture

In multicultural societies, such as Canada, inter-cultural conflicts are not uncommon. The advice given by Cohen (1993, p. 23) to mediators who participate in their resolution is to adopt a culturally sensitive approach. Cohen advises mediators to learn the languages of the parties involved in the conflicts that they most frequently mediate and/or learn about their cultures. In the context of a conflict between parties from collectivistic, high-context and individualistic, low-context cultures, culturally knowledgeable and sensitive mediators can "save the face of the more honor-conscious party, smooth the friction between their adversarial and conciliatory [approaches], ease the [communications] strain between them [and] above all act as cultural interpreters, explaining the parties to each other" (p. 35).

Abandon Ethnocentrism, But Uphold the Rule of Law

Knowledge of cultural differences not only helps undermine ethnocentrism—that is, the tendency to use the standards of one's own culture in evaluating the conduct of individuals from other cultures—but also facilitates the celebration of cultural diversity. At the same time, mediators in Canada should not condone by their silence conduct by members of other cultures that violates Canadian criminal laws or the *Charter of Rights and Freedoms*. Examples of such conduct include assaults against wives by their husbands—defined as an entitlement (Preisser, 1999).

Assist the Parties in Abandoning Stereotypes by Abandoning Them Yourself

Stereotyping is rooted in prejudgment and ignorance. Parties who are strangers to each other can undermine stereotyping by getting to know each other through participation in pre-negotiation dialogues or the exchange of pre-negotiation memos that contain personal information that is not prejudicial to their cases.

Mediators can abandon their own tendencies to stereotype by collecting personal information from the parties at intake. They can inhibit these tendencies in the parties by obtaining their permission to share personal information and by frequently reminding them that they are participating in a *mutual* decision-making process. Findings reported by Lang (1993) and Kremenyuk (1993) suggest that professional negotiators from different cultures who come to each other as individuals and who are dependent on each for solving problems are unlikely to engage in stereotyping.

Use the Elicitive Model of Conflict Resolution Where Appropriate

Activist researchers, such as Lajeunesse (1990, p. 16), and practitioners, such as Huber (1993), point out that "western/anglo/majority group" models of mediation tend to be imposed on First Nations. These models are perceived as being inappropriate because they emphasize substantive outcomes over relationships, problem solving over healing, and individuality over membership in a community.

Findings reported by other researchers—for example, Avruch, Black, and Scimecca (1991), Just (1991), and Lajeunesse (1990)—indicate that ways of settling conflicts vary across cultures in different societies and across different cultures within the same society. In a multicultural society, one of the most effective ways of implementing culturally appropriate models of conflict resolution is to use the "elicitive model" created by Lederach (1990, p. 5). This model

> [i]s designed to enable groups to access their own cultural ways of disputing and resolving conflict and to apply these understandings to the development of their own training programs without any prescribed models being introduced by the trainers. This approach seeks to provide a means to insure that culture can shape the dispute resolution process, rather than simply adapting foreign structures and tools of mediation to other cultural groups.

Lederach's elicitive model is appropriate for conflicts between members of the same culture and inappropriate for conflicts between members of different cultures.

EVALUATION OF CULTURAL THEORIES OF CONFLICT RESOLUTION

Strengths

Cultural explanations of differences in the parties' preferences for conflict resolution procedures and their strategies and tactics have a number of strengths. The most obvious is that without culture there would be no society, and therefore no conflict resolution procedures to select or strategies and tactics to use in settling conflicts. Other, less obvious strengths include the following:

- preferences for conflict resolution procedures and the use of strategies and tactics vary across different cultures; and
- an understanding of culture contributes to an understanding of the differences in preferences and the use of strategies and tactics, even when situational factors are taken into account.

Weaknesses

Cultural theories also have some weaknesses. They

- ignore situational factors;
- tend to focus on why conflict resolution procedures fail (culture was ignored), rather than on why they succeed (culture was taken into account) (Versi, 2004; Zartman, 1993, p. 17); and
- rarely measure cultural meanings and definitions in studies comparing the consequences of individualistic and collectivistic value orientations.

CHAPTER SUMMARY

We began by defining non-material culture as values, norms, identities, beliefs, language, meanings, and ways of communicating that are learned and internalized by individuals during the process of their socialization. We next focused on theories of culture that described value orientations and communication styles. Value orientations theory links differences between cultures that emphasize collectivism or individualism with differences in preferences for conflict resolution procedures and strategies and tactics. Communications theory links differences between high- and low-context cultures with preferences, strategies, and tactics. We noted that these two theories can be usefully modified by including both cultural and situational factors. We then identified two types of conflict: conflict confined to an in-group and conflict between an in-group and an out-group. Next we examined the dangers of ethnocentrism and stereotyping in the context of conflict resolution among different cultures. We devoted the final part of the chapter to describing some of the implications for practice that we derived from our examination of theory and research on the links between culture and conflict resolution. Finally, we presented an analysis of the strengths and weaknesses of cultural theories of conflict resolution.

Recommended Reading

Forbes, H.D. (1997). *Ethnic conflict: Commerce, culture and the contact hypothesis.* New Haven: Yale University Press. This book integrates contradictory findings about the impact of culture and contact on ethnic conflict, thereby increasing the cultural sensitivity of those who participate in procedures aimed at ending intercultural conflicts.

Moran, M. (2003). *Rethinking the reasonable person.* Toronto: University of Toronto Press. This book describes how judges' rulings about how a "reasonable person" acts reproduces cultural stereotypes.

Rosen, L. (1984). *Bargaining for reality.* Chicago: University of Chicago Press. This book describes how Sunni Moroccans in Sefrou routinely negotiate social conflicts.

Ross, R. (1996). *Returning to the teachings.* New York: Penguin. This book, written by a First Nations prosecutor, describes how indigenous conflict resolution processes are embedded in the history and culture of First Nations people.

Films, Videos, and DVDs

Black robe. Feature film directed by Bruce Beresford, 1991 (190 minutes).

Breaking barriers. Available from LaMarsh Research Centre on Violence and Conflict Resolution, York University, desellis@yorku.ca (60 minutes).

Developing multicultural awareness. Available from Insight Media, New York, cs@insight_media.com, #20X1089 (105 minutes).

Do the right thing. Feature film directed by Spike Lee, 1989 (190 minutes).

Smoke signals. Feature film directed by Chris Eyre, 1998 (180 minutes).

CHAPTER SIX

Gender

{
Chapter Objectives

Define gender and present a rationale for the definition.

Describe the socialization theory of gender and apply it to findings about conflict resolution procedures.

Describe the interactionist–situational theory of gender and apply it to findings about conflict resolution procedures.

Describe the structural theory of gender and apply it to findings about conflict resolution procedures.

Derive implications for the practice of mediation from the findings.
}

DEFINITIONS OF GENDER

West and Zimmermann define gender (1987, p. 127) in terms of a person's management of his conduct in the presence of others "in the light of normative conceptions of attitudes and activities appropriate to [his] sex categorization." This frequently cited definition is noteworthy because it conceives of gender as an everyday activity: gender as performance rather than as state of being. For West and Zimmermann, gender is not something that is firmly entrenched in people by the age of 3 or 13, but something that must be achieved throughout a person's life by engaging in gender-appropriate actions and interactions.

At birth, most individuals are classified as female or male on the basis of their genitalia. The sex categories of female and male become the foundations upon which society constructs feminine and masculine genders. Society constructs the feminine gender, for example, by attaching an identity and expectations to the sex category "female" that are different from those it attaches to the sex category "male." Gender identities, expectations, values, and communication styles exist within culture. Through the process of socialization into their culture, women and men learn and internalize identities, values, and expectations that society defines as appropriate for their respective genders. By publicly acting in socially sanctioned ways throughout their lives, women and men achieve or maintain membership in the gender categories feminine and masculine, respectively. Women and men can choose to leave their categories, and are doing so in increasing numbers as gender takes on an ever-increasing fluidity within diverse societies.

The West and Zimmermann definition of gender can be made more useful for examining links between gender and conflict resolution procedures by implementing changes suggested by two criticisms:

1. The authors ignore the link between gender inequality and "doing gender." Collins (1997), Giddens (1991, p. 209), and Mackinnon (1987, p. 54) conceive of gender as "doing domination." "Doing domination" refers to conforming with gender expectations that justify the domination of the feminine by the masculine.

2. The authors ignore the fact that women and men do not do one gender in all situations; they do a variety of genders in accordance with gender's inherent fluidity. Findings cited by Connell (1987) and Messerschmidt (1993) indicate that women and men do gender differently in different situations. Instead of "doing gender," they "do genders." Femininities and masculinities performed in the home often differ from masculinities and femininities performed while working as a business executive, soldier, or nurse (Cross & Madson, 1997, p. 27). In addition, women do gender differently from other women, just as men do gender differently from other men, even while remaining within the scope of socially sanctioned norms.

For the purposes of this chapter, we broaden West and Zimmermann's definition by defining gender as *the activities associated with managing conduct in the light of social norms appropriate for one's sex category and using gender as a power resource.* The activities associated with managing conduct in the light of social norms draw attention to differences in conduct. The activities associated with power focus attention on power imbalances.

THEORIES OF GENDER

There are a number of theoretical perspectives on gender. We focus on three of them:

1. socialization theory,
2. interactionist–situational theory, and
3. structural theory.

We have selected these theories because they are frequently cited, and they have generated a substantial amount of research on gender aimed at testing the hypotheses derived from them. A description of them will assist readers in understanding where the questions asked by researchers originate (Lips, 2002, p. 80).

Socialization Theory

At three years of age, children are aware of feminine and masculine gender roles. Female and male three-year-olds imitate the behaviour of the parent or parents with whom they share their sex more frequently than they imitate the behaviour of an opposite-sex parent (Bussey & Bandura, 1984). Gender roles refer to a set of cultural expectations that define how individuals occupying the position of female or male should behave (Stark, 1992, p. 675). Developmentally, the learning of gender roles precedes the emergence of gender identities.

In the social learning theory formulated by Bandura (1997), three mechanisms facilitate learning of social roles and the internalization of gender identities: modelling, imitation, and reinforcement. The family is the earliest and one of the most important contexts for the learning of gender roles. Through the process of family socialization, mothers and/or fathers serve as role models that children identify with, observe, and imitate. According to Bandura, parents also reward gender-appropriate performances and punish gender-inappropriate performances. Through socialization and a system of rewards and punishment, children learn appropriate gender identities and role conduct. Social learning and internalization of appropriate gender roles is highly effective because young children are completely dependent on parents, who are perceived as available, powerful, and nurturing. Bandura (1997) reports that masculine parents are more effective gender role socialization agents for male children, and feminine parents are more effective gender role socialization agents for female children.

Bandura's social learning theory seems to assume that parents are active teachers and children are passive learners of gender roles and identities. Maccoby (1992) questions this assumption. Specifically, she conceives of children as learning from and teaching parents, and parents as teaching and learning from their children. In other words, not "gender role learning" but "reciprocal gender role learning" is going on. Reciprocal gender role learning takes place through social interaction between parents and children. For example, small differences in female and male infant levels of activity are reinforced by parents who devote greater attention to the more active male infant, whose level of activity increases, which in turn attracts even more parental attention. As a result, parents come to expect male children to be more active than female children, and to define activity as appropriate for masculine roles and passivity as being appropriate for feminine roles. According to Maccoby (1992), children tend to conform with parental expectations in part because parents reward gender-appropriate conduct and punish gender-inappropriate conduct. In a heterosexual household, reciprocal gender role learning by parents and children is greatly facilitated when a daughter's conduct meets her father's expectations and a son's conduct meets his mother's expectations.

Maccoby's reciprocal gender role-learning theory modifies Bandura's role learning theory by emphasizing interaction between parents and children as the mechanism facilitating gender role learning and the internalization of gender identities. At the same time, both gender role learning theories are similar to each other in two ways.

1. They focus on the acquisition of gender identities and gender-appropriate conduct.
2. They attempt to explain stability in gender identities throughout the life of individuals.

It seems that childhood socialization is so potent that once female and male children have learned to act according to feminine and masculine genders respectively, most of them will act like women and men throughout their lives.

Gender role-learning theory has been used to explain gender differences in language and communication styles. Tannen (1990) postulates that women and men learn to speak different languages, and that miscommunication instigates conflicts and makes it more difficult to settle them fairly. For example, as a result of cultural indoctrination in feminine gender behaviour, during negotiations many women tend to take the feelings of others into account when they communicate. As a result of indoctrination in masculine gender behaviour, many men tend to communicate by attempting "to maintain the one-up position or at least avoid appearing one-down" (Tannen, 1994, p. 121). As a result, negotiated agreements tend to favour men who "do masculine" over women who "do feminine" by neither seeking a "one-up" position nor avoiding a "one-down" position.

Kolb and Coolidge (1995) offer the theory that women's place during negotiations is "under the table" because their learned feminine communication style places them at a disadvantage in negotiations with masculine men. The theory places masculine men squarely "at the table" because their learned communication style gives them a communicative advantage in negotiations. Kolb and Coolidge (1995, p. 220) assert that negotiation calls for "clear, direct, authoritative communication about goals, interests, [and] problems" and that a masculine communication style—"self-enhancing, confident, linear, legalistic, direct and depersonalized"—is uniquely suited to the purpose. They note that women's "self-effacing, indirect, relational, [and] personalized" voice, which "includes many qualifiers" (p. 269) puts them at a negotiating disadvantage, as does their general reluctance to seize the opportunity to speak. Subsequent research by Gray (1999) contradicts the hypotheses of Kolb and Coolidge (see below under the heading "Effect of Violence and Abuse").

Interactionist–Situational Theory

While social learning theory focuses on the acquisition of gender roles, gender interactionist–situational theory—such as that created by Deaux and Major (1987)—focuses on gender as performances that conform to or deviate from societal expectations. For example, in a family context, the theory would examine the degree to which activities such as caring for children, earning an income, taking out the garbage, or cooking are expected to be performed by one or other of the domestic partners, and how conforming to or deviating from these societal expectations influences the interaction between the partners.

Instead of assuming a stability in gender identity and gender role acquisition, interactionist–situational theory focuses on explaining changes in gender identities and role performances during a person's lifetime. The context for these changes is interactions, during which gender-appropriate performances are rewarded and gender-inappropriate performances are punished. "Interactional continuity" exists when individuals are rewarded for behaving in ways that meet societal expectations throughout their lives, and they continue to conform to these expectations because of the rewards they receive. This conformity supports rather than challenges societal patterns of gender role performances.

Interactional discontinuity exists when individuals are either rewarded for behaving in ways that do not meet gender expectations or punished for behaving in ways that meet them. The first type of discontinuity is evident when a woman seeks and obtains a job as an engineer because she is assertive, competitive, demonstrates high technical competence, and places career over family. The second type of discontinuity is evident when a woman demonstrates high technical competence but is not hired because she gives the impression that her family is more important to her than her career and her demeanour is perceived to be too emotional and passive.

Interactional continuity and discontinuity helps account for both stability and change in gender identities and gender role performances.

Structural Theory

Social structure refers to the characteristics of societies, organizations, and groups—not to the characteristics of individuals. For example, the social structure of a business organization refers to the set of differentiated, hierarchically arranged, and interrelated roles that are described in the business's organizational chart. In an organizational chart, the president occupies the top position. Under this, vice-presidents occupy different positions in finance, marketing, law, technology, and human resources, for example. Departmental managers who report to vice-presidents are located under vice-presidents. Support staff, salespeople, computer programmers, and production workers who are supervised by managers are located below the managers.

The structure of a hierarchical society includes occupational roles that are differentiated—such as truck drivers, nurses, and construction workers—and ranked in terms of the income, authority, and status that society attaches to them. The social structure of a society can also include categories that link individuals on the basis of gender, race or ethnicity, and social class; these categories can also be differentiated from each other, and ranked according to the income, authority, and status that society attaches to them. Gender structural theory links membership in gender categories with gender differences in behaviour generally and negotiating behaviour in particular.

Structural theories of gender differences and gender hierarchy have been formulated by Eagly and Wood (1999) and Smart and Smart (1978), respectively. In Smart's structural theory, occupations are the source of power resources. Occupations that provide higher income, authority, and status are disproportionately filled by men, while those that provide lower income, authority, and status are disproportionately filled by women (Babcock & Laschever, 2003, pp. 23-27). The accessibility for men of greater power resources creates and perpetuates gender inequality that is reflected in legal and social/gender norms. As a result women are doubly disadvantaged: first, when they participate in legal systems created by and for men; second, when their role performances during negotiations with men outside legal systems are influenced by societal expectations that favour men.

Eagly and Wood (1999, p. 408) formulate a structural theory of gender differences in behaviour in which biological factors (such as strength and the capacity to bear children), cultural factors (such as beliefs and norms), and the demands of the economy (such as those reflected in the change from a manufacturing to a service economy) are identified as causes of "the differing placement of men and women in the [occupational] structure [of society]." Specifically, more men than women occupy high income, authority, and status occupations, and more women than men occupy low income, authority, and status occupations. Occupations are "the engine of sex differentiated behaviour because they summarize the social constraints and opportunities under which men and women carry out their lives" (Eagly & Wood, 1999, p. 409). Women and men adjust to the constraints and opportunities attached to their occupations. In the process, they develop different emotional, relational, and communication styles and other differences that can be observed during their participation in conflict resolution procedures.

APPLICATION OF GENDER THEORIES TO CONFLICT RESOLUTION

In the following sections, we apply socialization theory, interactionist–situational theory, and structural theory to women's and men's choices of conflict resolution procedures, strategies, and tactics. Note that with the exception of negotiations about safe sex, the studies on struggle, negotiation, mediation, and adjudication were conducted in Western individualistic cultures.

Struggle

Kurz (1995) studied the tactics used by heterosexual couples in settling their marital conflicts by interviewing 129 randomly selected, recently divorced women residing in Philadelphia. Findings revealed that husbands used violent tactics more frequently than wives (39 percent versus 21 percent), and they inflicted serious injuries three times more frequently than wives (23 percent versus 7 percent). Kurz (1995, p. 71) reports that "almost all" of the 27 divorced women who used violent tactics used them in response to violence initiated by their husbands. She attributed gender differences in initiating the use of violent tactics to differences in socialization (p. 74). Finally, Kurz found gender differences in the reasons given for using violent tactics. Men use them as a means of settling conflicts and controlling their wives; women use them in self-defence.

Findings reported by Kurz were based on data collected from wives only. Another study that included both wives and husbands found that both sexes reported the use of violent tactics in self-defence in equal proportions (Ellis and Stuckless, 1996). Studies that involve husbands only find that husbands frequently blame wives ("she knows which buttons to push") for their own use of violent tactics (Arendell, 1995). Studies that involve wives only reveal that the wives' attempts to "act independently" are the most frequently cited reason for husband-initiated violence (Kurz, 1995, p. 67).

Beneria and Roldan (1987, p. 20) studied working class families in Mexico City. They interviewed "140 women home based workers who belonged to

137 households with a total population of 870." Their interviews revealed that gender expectations regulated negotiations between husbands and wives. That is, the parties negotiated and renegotiated the marriage contract using tactics defined as legitimate or appropriate for their genders. It was only when gender expectations were not complied with that wives and husbands resorted to the use of coercive tactics in negotiating changes to their original marriage contract (p. 138).

In some cases, domestic partners attempt to settle conflicts by using violence that results in death. Wilson and Daly (1992, p. 93) state that "most spousal homicides are the relatively rare and extreme manifestations of the same basic conflicts that inspire sub-lethal marital violence." If this is true, then a far higher proportion of men in Canada (37 percent) than women (12 percent) settle conflicts with intimate partners by killing them (Ellis & DeKeseredy, 1996, p. 84; Wilson & Daly, 1994, p. 5). Among the First Nations, however, the proportions are reversed. Findings reported by Ellis and DeKeseredy (1996, p. 84) indicate that "for every 100 killings of aboriginal female partners by aboriginal male partners there are 152 killings of aboriginal male partners by aboriginal female partners."

The difficult and impoverished circumstances—including high rates of unemployment, drug and alcohol use, and poverty-level incomes—under which many people live on and off reserves (Anderson, 2003) are associated with high rates of violence and abuse by men against women partners. Statistics from the General Social Survey (Statistics Canada, 2002) reveal that spousal violence rates for aboriginal peoples are six times higher than the rates for non-aboriginals. The use of violent and abusive tactics by men elicits violent and abusive tactics by women partners, either in self-defence or retaliation.

Findings reported in these studies support both gender socialization and interactionist–situational theories in explaining gender differences in the use of struggle tactics.

Negotiation

Sexual intercourse between heterosexual couples is an increasingly frequent way in which HIV/AIDS is transmitted (Pape, 2000, p. 230). Findings reported by *The Economist* (2004, pp. 82-83) indicate that the risk is greater for women than it is for men in some countries. For example, in sub-Saharan Africa, "57 percent of those infected are female [and] among young South Africans, Zambians and Zimbabweans, 75 percent are female." Negotiations between heterosexual partners over the use of condoms yield outcomes that increase or decrease the risk of HIV/AIDS transmission to both male and female partners.

Pulerwitz et al. (2002, p. 1) studied negotiations about condom use involving "388 mainly Latina women at an urban community health center in Massachusetts." They found a very strong relationship between "sexual relationship power" and condom use. Women with greater sexual relationship power—that is, women who exercised greater control in their relationships with male partners and who made more decisions about matters relating to condom use, sexual activities, other shared activities, and the friends with whom they socialized with "were five times as likely as women with low sexual relationship power to report consistent condom use" (p. 5). Other researchers—for example, Amaro (1995), Amaro and Raj (2000), and Wingood and DiClemente (1998)—also report findings that link low female partner negotiation power with less frequent condom use.

Pape (2000) studied the link between relationship power, negotiation power, and condom use in Haiti. Haiti has one of the highest reported rates of HIV/AIDS cases in the Caribbean. In the city of Carrefour, "a center of prostitution," the rate is 200.8 per million Haitians. In Haiti's capital, Port-au-Prince, the rate is 110.7 (Pape, 2000, p. 229). In Haiti, sexual intercourse with infected men is the main cause of the high rate of infection in women. The problem of gender inequality and its effects on negotiation is described in "Negotiating Safe Sex in Haiti."

Negotiating Safe Sex in Haiti

When researchers interviewed members of 12 focus groups of Haitian women and men, they found that Haitian women were knowledgeable about HIV/AIDS, high HIV/AIDS rates in Haiti, and the role played by unsafe sex in its transmission. However, the women were frequently unable to negotiate a safe-sex outcome by persuading their partners to use condoms. Cultural and structural factors that contributed to the women's relatively low negotiating power were responsible this result.

Cultural values that emphasize harmony and the maintenance of long-term relationships with intimate partners undermined women's negotiating power by providing women with reasons for acquiescing to their partner's refusal to use condoms. They feared that resistance to these demands for unsafe sex would result in disharmony and possibly lead to their partner's ending the relationship. Cultural norms that condone male sexual activity with other women encouraged female partners to ignore it. The presence of alternative sexual partners also influenced female partners not to press their demands for condom use too strongly in case their male partners left them for women who were willing to participate in unsafe sex. In addition, cultural norms required women to be sexually faithful to their long-term male partners. Men valued female partners who were sexually faithful to them. If their partners insisted on the use of condoms too strongly or persistently, they might end the relationship because of their suspicions that their partners were having sex with other men. Female partners therefore felt that they were protecting their relationships by not making strong and persistent demands for safe sex.

Structural factors also contributed outcomes that Haitian male partners considered desirable in negotiations over condom use. Male partners provide most, if not all, of the household income. In most homes, female partners are responsible for taking care of the home and the children, and are dependent on their male partners for money. Male partners' control of income and their willingness to use this control as a negotiating tool by threatening to decrease financial support often persuaded female partners to agree to participate in unsafe sex.

These findings support an interactionist–situational theory of gender, such as the one formulated by Deaux and Mead [*sic*] (1987). The gender differences in negotiation behaviour and outcome are greater in relationships where women are economically dependent on male partners and smaller in relationships where women are economically independent.

Ulin, Cayemittes, and Metellus's findings also support socialization and structural theories. Like the cultures of most patriarchal societies, Haitian culture defines the roles of men and women involved in sexual and marital relationships in ways that favour men. Haitian men and women learn gender roles and internalize values that their society considers appropriate to their gender through the process of socialization. Haitian culture also reflects and legitimates the structural positions of men as income earners and women as household labourers who earn no income.

Source: Ulin, Cayemittes, and Metellus (1993).

The findings cited here suggest that condom use is likely to be lowest when male partners make condom use decisions unilaterally, and highest when female partners make these decisions unilaterally. Findings reported by Harvey et al. (2002) link shared or women's decision making with more frequent condom use.

Harvey et al. studied 112 women in Los Angeles and Oklahoma. Over half of them were self-identified African-Americans (55 percent) and over one-third (35 percent) were self-identified Hispanics. One of the researchers' major findings was that women who reported making the decision to use condoms alone or jointly with their male partners were far more likely to report using condoms (and using them more frequently) than women who reported that their male partners made the decision to use condoms.

Fair Salaries

The findings of Babcock and Laschever (2003, pp. 1-15) indicate that women's starting salaries are lower than those of men with equivalent qualifications and experience. For example, the authors found that the average starting salaries of men with master's degrees were $4,000 or 7.6 percent higher than the average starting salaries of women with master's degrees from the same university. Assuming equivalent annual percentage increases in salaries over the course of a 38-year career, the incomes of male graduates will exceed the incomes of female graduates by over $250,000.

Babcock and Laschever (2003, pp. 3-4) identify women's tendency to accept the salaries they are offered, rather than negotiate the salaries they want, as the immediate cause of salary differences. For example, findings from an Internet survey conducted by Babcock, Gelfand, Small, and Stayn (2002) indicate that "men may be initiating four times as many negotiations as women." Babcock and Laschever also report that 57 percent of men graduating with master's degrees from Carnegie Mellon University asked for more money than they were offered. The comparable figure for female graduates was 7 percent. And for every salary negotiation initiated by female graduates, eight were initiated by male graduates.

Babcock and Laschever (2003, pp. 119-122) identify four causes for women's failure to negotiate their salaries: the desire to avoid conflict, the desire not to damage relationships, a low sense of entitlement, and fear of punishment for assertive behaviour.

Babcock and Laschever concluded that women do not negotiate as effectively as men because of liabilities created by gender expectations (p. 86). During their socialization, many women learn that they are expected to place a high value on relationships and being liked by others. They may adopt society's expectation that they should behave passively. These findings harmonize with the socialization learning theory of gender.

An interactionist–situational theory of gender is demonstrable by considering a woman who arrives at a job interview with a firm offer of another job at a good salary in hand. This woman has a better BATNA (best alternative to a negotiated agreement) than someone who approaches a job interview with no such offer. Women with good BATNAs are likely to be more assertive and ask for what they want than those without (the same is no doubt true of men). Here, a situational factor is the source of differences in the negotiation behaviour of people who are members of the same gender category.

Communication

Communication, as we stated in chapter 2, is fundamental to negotiation. One way in which parties participating in negotiation is by disclosing information about themselves. Aries (1996, p. 157) reviewed a number of studies designed to test the degree to which self-defined feminine and masculine gender role orientations predicted differences in self-disclosure. The results of her review led Aries to conclude that "masculinity and femininity used as predictors account for [a maximum of] 11% of the variance in self-disclosure" (p. 158). The remaining 89 percent is explained by other factors, including the following situational ones:

- *Closeness of the relationship.* Women and men disclose more when they are negotiating with family members than when they are negotiating with strangers.
- *Gender of the listener.* Women disclose more to other women than they do to men. Men disclose less to women than women disclose to them, and men disclose even less to other men.
- *Formality.* When participating in informal conversations, men disclose more to women than men. However, when men participate in more formal communications, such as negotiation, they disclose the same amount to men and women.
- *Social class.* Middle-class women and men disclose more than working-class women and men.
- *Role requirements.* Female and male interviewers, for example, use the same forms and styles of speech.
- *Content of communication.* In conversations between people of the same sex, women are more likely than men to disclose personal information (Aries, 1996, pp. 150-159).

On the basis of her review of over 60 studies of gender differences in behaviour relevant to negotiation, Aries (1996, p. 92) reached two major conclusions.

1. Gender differences in the way men and women communicate are situationally variable. For example, women interviewers communicate in one way when they are doing their jobs and in other ways when they are interacting with their partners or children. Parents of either sex may have unique ways of communicating with their children but similar ways of communicating when they are doing their jobs as interviewers.

2. "[S]imilarities in communication between men and women are far greater than the differences ... [and] ... knowledge of a person's gender

does not enable us to accurately predict how a person will behave in many situations, including negotiations."

Findings reported by Aries (1996) support an interactionist–situational theory of gender.

Negotiation Power

Gender inequality in patriarchal societies is the starting point for many analyses of the relative impact of gender and power on the negotiation tactics used by women and men. Watson (1994, p. 79) reviewed 34 studies "conducted since 1975 that addressed … gender differences in negotiation, conflict or power." One of her major findings was that when researchers provided women with more effective resources than men, by designating them as managers, giving them strategic information, or providing them with better alternatives, women tended to negotiate according to the stereotypic masculine model. The threatening and "tit for tat" tactics used by women in superordinate positions were similar to the tactics used by men in superordinate positions. Specifically, women were dominant, assertive, competitive, and successful. Female and male negotiators with high situational power—that is, parties who possessed greater resources and/or who were provided with information on how they could use their resources most effectively—were equally successful in achieving desired outcomes. These findings led Watson (1994, p. 81) to conclude that "situational power is a better predictor of negotiator behaviour and outcomes than gender." Watson's findings support a interactionist–situational power theory of gender differences in negotiating behaviour.

Aries (1996) reported findings that reveal significant gender differences in the use of tactics during negotiations, such as the following:

- *Speech.* Women were gentle, friendly, open, emotional, and polite; men were loud, aggressive, authoritarian, blunt, angry, and used slang and swear words more frequently than women.
- *Persuasive tactics.* Women used promises, moral appeals, and altruism; men used threats and verbal aggression.
- *Interruptions.* Women were less likely to interrupt than men.

These findings support the socialization theory that gender stereotypes have direct effects on interactions between women and men, including the interaction that takes place during negotiations. Other research findings, however, indicate that the strength of these effects varies in accordance with particular situations (Echabe & Castro, 1999). Thus, gender stereotypes are stronger in the following situations:

- *Gender is more salient to the matter at hand.* Gender stereotypes may be stronger when negotiations involve job discrimination on the basis of gender than when they involve environmental issues.
- *The parties are strangers.* Gender stereotypes may be stronger when strangers are negotiating than when intimates or friends are negotiating, and they may be stronger earlier in the negotiations process, before the parties get to know each other, than later, once the parties know each other better.
- *Stereotypes are activated.* Gender stereotypes can become more pronounced when they are activated, for example, by an authoritarian third party, such as a judge, who acts and reacts to the parties in stereotypical ways.

Mediation

In chapter 3, we defined mediation as a conflict resolution procedure in which a third party facilitates negotiations between parties in conflict, who make decisions on outcomes. Years ago, Bottomley (1984), a structural theorist, published a report that indicated that married heterosexual women brought gender liabilities with them to mediation. She, like other theorists who have addressed this subject (such as Fischer, Vidmar, & Ellis, 1993; Hart, 1990; Grillo, 1991), focused on divorce mediation. According to Bottomley, the major source of these liabilities was women's "continuing position of disadvantage in society" and their "lack of bargaining power *vis-à-vis* individual men," which made them "particularly vulnerable in [mediation] procedures." However, more recent studies that focus on issues of self-determination of outcomes, empowerment, and levels of satisfaction appear to indicate that Bottomley's conclusions are no longer reflective of contemporary social reality.

For example, Kelly (2004, pp. 3-35) reviewed major family mediation projects in Colorado, California, Charlottesville, Virginia, and Hamilton, Ontario. Findings on self-determination in family mediations at the California divorce and mediation project reveal that "[female and male] mediation clients had high levels of self-determination with respect to selecting and ordering issues for discussion and negotiation, length of sessions, the pace of mediation, the use of outside counsel and additional experts, and all temporary and final decisions" (p. 16).

With respect to empowerment, Kelly reports, "Mediation clients, particularly women, viewed mediation as more empowering than did the adversarial men and women (that is, men and women who hired lawyers to negotiate or litigate their divorces) in helping them assume greater responsibility in managing their financial affairs, and in better understanding their spouse's point of view" (p. 17).

With respect to satisfaction, 69 percent of female and male partners reported being "somewhat to very satisfied" with the divorce mediations they participated in. The comparable figure for adversarial men and women was 47 percent.

Satisfaction was not measured in divorce mediations conducted in Colorado's 10th Judicial District, but it was measured in the Charlottesville custody mediation project (Emery, 1994). Data collected one year after divorce mediations were completed indicate that "[w]omen in both groups remained more satisfied than [men] on a number of measures of outcome" (p. 120). Emery (1994, p. 187), the lead author on this one-year follow-up study, concluded that "the majority of the study's findings point to the disadvantage of men in litigation, not to the disadvantage of women in mediation." In addition, Kelly (2004, p. 12) cites findings from the follow-up study (Emery, Matthews, & Wyer, 1991) that revealed that both mothers and fathers who participated in mediation felt that they obtained some of the outcomes they wanted, but mothers felt "they won quite a bit" of what they wanted and fathers felt they won only "a little" (Kelly, 2004, p. 13).

The Ontario family mediation pilot project (Ellis, 1994; Ellis & Stuckless, 1996) resulted in two conclusions:

1. Mothers who value sole custody above all other outcomes are more likely to achieve this outcome through lawyer negotiations, court hearings, or trials; they are therefore more likely than fathers to express satisfaction with adversarial procedures than fathers.
2. Fathers who value joint custody or sole custody with liberal access arrangements are more likely to achieve these outcomes through mediation; they are therefore more likely than mothers to express satisfaction with mediation.

Findings reported by other researchers indicate that factors related to process as well as those related to outcome contribute to differences in satisfaction levels reported by mediation and adversarial clients. For example, Pearson and Thonnes (1989, p. 437) report findings indicating that 77 percent of female and male parties participating in mediation reported being satisfied with the process. The comparable figure for clients participating in adversarial proceedings was 40 percent. These findings suggest that process factors may be as important or more important than outcomes in influencing satisfaction with mediation and adjudication.

Another situational factor that influences levels of satisfaction with divorce mediation is the involvement of lawyers or judges in the mediation process. The less the involvement, the greater the satisfaction of both female and male participants (Ogus et al., 1989). In the Hamilton study (Ellis &

Stuckless, 1996, pp. 97-98), lawyers acted as co-mediators in some cases; they gave advice about contentious issues and reviewed agreements reached by the parties in all cases. Findings indicate that a relatively high proportion of clients, over 40 percent, were dissatisfied with their lawyers. This may have contributed to their dissatisfaction with the mediation process (Kressel & Pruitt, 1989, p. 413).

One situational factor that contributes to women's greater satisfaction with adversarial procedures is that mediation emphasizes compromise and joint or collective outcomes. Adversarial procedures place greater emphasis on winning and outcomes desired by each parent. Male or female parties who "win" without having to give up anything in return are more likely than parties who make compromises to express satisfaction with the procedure that helped them win.

It is clear from these findings that situational factors are far more significant that gender issues in mediations that involve the breakdown of family relations. The sex of participants cannot be used to predict differences in either process or outcome.

Effect of Violence and Abuse

Some researchers state that the ex-partners who are most likely to bring serious liabilities with them to divorce mediation are those who have been victims of violence and abuse (Fischer, Vidmar, & Ellis, 1993; Grillo, 1991; Hart, 1990). Ellis and Stuckless (1996, p. 30) found that the majority of divorcing wives (56 percent of 127 wives) in their Hamilton study cited violence and/ or abuse by their male partners as a major reason for ending the relationship. Most of these women had probably been victimized more than once by their partners. Fischer, Vidmar, and Ellis (1993, pp. 2161-2162) claim that ex-partners who have been the victims of repeated violence and abuse are unable to participate as equal parties in mediation because "[t]he mediation session may be a safe as well as a powerful setting for the abuser to intimidate and control his victim through hidden symbols of impending violence."

However, this claim is tempered by the following findings of Ellis and Stuckless (1996):

1. Wives who were victims of violence and/or abuse during their marriages were as likely to achieve the outcomes they wanted as other wives (1996, pp. 69-70).
2. Female victims of male partner violence and/or abuse were as likely as others to state that they can "stand up for [themselves] and state [their] position" in the event of a disagreement as well as or better than their ex-partner.

3. Female ex-partners, whether abused or not, obtained the child support they wanted in the face of strong resistance by male ex-partners (Ellis & Stuckless, 1996, p. 83).

Gray's (1999, p. 56) study of couples who participated in family court-based divorce mediation revealed that women who engaged in face-to-face negotiations with male partners obtained a greater proportion of the outcomes they wanted than did their male ex-partners (20 of 43 women versus 11 of 48 men). No evidence indicated that the ratio was different for the four women who cited their ex-partner's violence as the major reason for separating. This finding must be interpreted with some caution because the sample is a small one. However, it provides some support for the thesis that women and men can participate with equal strength in mediation regardless of their domestic history.

Gray's (1999) findings also cast doubt on Kolb and Coolidge's (1995) hypothesis that women's "weak advocacy" was partly responsible for the relatively poor negotiated outcomes of female negotiators participating in negotiations with males. Gray found that the women she studied strongly contended for the outcomes they wanted and in fact achieved a higher proportion of the outcomes they wanted than the men who also participated. Moreover, Gray found that women's advocacy was not diluted or undermined by the experience of living with abusive male partners.

Conclusion

In sum, gender differences are not evident, or only weakly evident, in mediation when

- the mediation involves the custody of children and the quality of life after divorce,
- the mediator attempts to ensure that the process and outcomes are fair (Davis & Davis, 1989), and
- parties for whom mediation may be inappropriate are screened out (Ellis, 1994; Girdner, 1990).

Taken together, the findings reported here tend to support a situational theory of gender differences in mediation.

Adjudication

Small claims courts, which deal with between 70 and 80 percent of non-criminal cases, have been the setting for studies of communications by female and male litigants. Following the publication of Gilligan's (1982) socialization theory of gender, researchers classified women's verbal communications as mainly "relationally oriented" and men's verbal communications as mainly "rule-oriented." Rule-oriented communication "mainly frames problems around legal categories and concerns." Relationally oriented communication "mainly frames problems around appeals to affiliation, relational consequences and personal needs" (Morrill, Harrison, & Johnson, 1998, p. 640). The qualifier "mainly" is used because there is some overlap between the two communication frames. Conley and O'Barr (1988, 1990) found that rule-oriented communications were more effective than relationally oriented communications in achieving outcomes desired by litigants. However, they found no significant or stable differences in the use of these communication styles by female and male litigants.

In an attempt to isolate differences besides gender that could have influenced the results reported by Conley and O'Barr (1988), Morrill, Harrison, and Johnson (1998) conducted an experimental study using four small claims court cases, and 39 female and 33 male student subjects as litigants. In two of the cases the litigants were relationally close: they were friends. In the other two cases, the litigants were relationally distant: they were neighbours. The researchers found no differences in relational and rule-oriented communications by female and male litigants. Instead, they found "relational context" to be the factor that most strongly influenced the use of relational and rule-oriented communications. Females and males who were involved in litigation with friends were equally likely to use relationally oriented communications. Females and males involved in litigation with neighbours were equally likely to use rule-oriented communications. Here a situational factor—relational context—overwhelmed the impact of gender on the use of relational and rule-oriented communications.

Moving from small claims courts to family courts, Jacob (1992, p. 584) looked for gender differences in how 90 separating or divorcing couples framed custody and support issues at the start of legal proceedings: 56 percent of women framed these issues relationally, and 46 percent used a rule-oriented frame. The comparable figures for men were 59 percent and 41 percent, respectively. The differences are not significant. On the basis of these findings, Jacob concluded that "[g]ender by itself did not appear to have any tendency to push respondents towards a legalistic or relational frame."

Situational factors made a much greater contribution than gender in accounting for differences in the use of relational and rule-oriented communications. For example, close to 75 percent of the women who used a rule-oriented frame and just over 50 percent of women who used a relational frame were economically dependent on the men from whom they were separating. Economic self-sufficiency was the situational factor that accounted for differences in the women's choice of frame.

Findings from both small claims and family courts support an interactionist–situational theory gender differences in tactics used by women and men.

EVALUATION

Findings on the part played by gender in struggle, negotiation, mediation, and adjudication do not offer consistent support for one theory of gender. Instead, they support a theory that integrates socialization, interactionist–situational, and structural theories. In so far as structural differences—that is, differences in the positions occupied by women and men in society—reflect differences in socialization and cultural values, we suggest formulating a see-saw theory of gender that integrates social and situational factors. The see-saw theory of gender posits that gender stereotypic behaviour is weak when situational pressure to display other behaviour is strong, and gender stereotypic behaviour is strong when situational pressures to display other behaviour is weak or when situational pressure to display gender stereotypic behaviour is strong.

Socialization Theory

Strengths

This theory has a number of strengths. It

- indicates that gender differences are present when men and women participate in conflict resolution procedures; and
- links socialization and gender role learning with occupational and income differences that favour men over women.

Weaknesses

This theory's most significant weakness is that it fails to take situational factors into account.

Interactionist–Situational Theory

Strengths

This theory has two important strengths. It

- indicates that gender differences vary with the relative strength of situational factors; and
- avoids the "fundamental attribution error" (Aries, 1996, p. 19) of attributing causes to gender, when in fact they lie within the situations in which women and men struggle, negotiate, mediate, and litigate.

Weaknesses

Like most theories, this theory also has some weaknesses, the most import-ant of which is that it fails to take socialization and gender role learning into account in explaining gender differences in participation in conflict resolu-tion procedures.

Structural Theory

Strengths

Structural theory has one major strength. It emphasizes the influence on individuals of the social categories into which they are born (for example, race/ethnicity) or of which they become members (for example, social class). Specifically, structural theorists hypothesize that membership in social cat-egories such as gender, race/ethnicity, social class, and religion influences the conduct of individual members, including their conduct during nego-tiations and mediation. To some extent, membership in these categories does influence conduct, and knowledge of these "background factors" provides negotiators and mediators with information that helps them understand each other better.

Weaknesses

Set against this major strength of structural theory are these weaknesses:

- It ignores cultural and situational factors that influence the thoughts, feelings, and conduct of individuals;
- It does not take into account the great deal of variation in the thoughts, feelings, and conduct of individual members of the same social category—for example, male or female—that includes millions of individuals. Structural theorists ignore individuals and individual differences, yet these are far more significant than membership in a social category to negotiators and mediators.
- It may facilitate the use of stereotyping to close the gap between more or less accurate knowledge about social categories and a lack of knowl-edge about individual members of those categories.

IMPLICATIONS FOR PRACTICE

Several guidelines for the practice of mediation emerge from the findings presented here:

1. *Be aware of underlying situations and stereotypes.* Mediators should be alert to specific situational factors that are, or may be, underlying

mediation sessions. They should also be aware of gender stereotypes that the parties may be enacting to the detriment of a fair outcome.

2. *Emphasize the parties' interdependence.* Mediators should promote interdependence by describing negotiation as a joint decision-making process and continuing to remind the parties of their mutual responsibilities to reach a stable outcome that is satisfactory to them both.

3. *Know the parties and help them know each other.* Mediators can decrease the likelihood that stereotypes will interfere with negotiations by getting to know the other parties as individuals and by facilitating the parties' knowledge of each other (Young et al., 1999). Mediators can facilitate the disclosure of personal information and, with the permission of the parties, the exchange of non-strategic information.

4. *Eradicate stereotypes from your own psyche.* Mediators must examine their own thought processes to ensure that they do not harbour views that might prompt them to react to any negotiator—female or male—in stereotypical ways.

CHAPTER SUMMARY

We began this chapter by discussing definitions of gender, and concluded that gender refers to activities associated with managing conduct in the light of society's (ever-changing) notions about appropriateness and inappropriateness on the basis of sex categorization and using gender as a power resource. We then presented three theories of gender: socialization theory, interactionist–situational theory, and structural theory. Later, we used these theories to interpret findings about women's and men's participation in procedures aimed at ending conflicts through struggle, negotiation, mediation, and adjudication. Findings from all four conflict resolution procedures supported an integrated theory of gender that incorporates social and situational factors. Mediation and adjudication are most strongly supported by an interactionist–situational theory. Findings about struggle and negotiation supported all three theories. We concluded the chapter with an examination of the implications of gender theories on the practice of mediation.

RECOMMENDED READING

Green, R., & Elffers, J. (1999). *The 48 laws of power*. New York: Penguin. This book is a historical and cross-cultural account of strategies used in courts by well-known historical figures, such as Catherine the Great and Machiavelli, as well as by lesser-known people.

Oates, J.C. (1993). *Foxfire: Confessions of a girl gang*. New York: Dutton. This book tells the story of a girls' gang from the point of view of its leader Margaret "Legs" Saudovsky. It is a story of resistance, compassion, and friendship that involves freeing a dog from a pet shop and using graffiti as a weapon.

Woolf, V. (1938). *Three guineas*. London: Hogarth Press. This book describes the persistent and pervasive attempts made by middle-class men to maintain and reproduce patriarchy.

WEBSITES

Feminist Majority Foundation. http://www.feminist.org. This website promotes the safety of women and provides links to resources about violence against women.

Status of Women Canada. http://www.swc-cfc.gc.ca. This website promotes gender equality and the safety of women and children.

CHAPTER SEVEN

Personality

{ **Chapter Objectives**

Define personality.

Describe the five-factor (CANOE) theory of personality.

Indicate how agreeableness and extroversion influence the process and outcome of distributive and integrative negotiations.

Identify situational factors that change the impact of personality on the process and outcome of negotiations.

Describe how the see-saw model integrates personality and situational factors.

Explain how mediators can use the parties' cognitive abilities and aspiration levels to balance their power relationships.

DEFINITION OF PERSONALITY

Costa and McCrae (1992, p. 23) define personality traits as "dimensions of individual differences in tendencies to show consistent patterns of thoughts, feelings and actions." A personality trait, then, is a consistent way of thinking, feeling, and acting in different situations. For example, a person who obtains a high score in the category "aggressiveness" is aggressive at home, at work, while driving home from work, and while cooking or playing poker after work. Dimensions of personality are not only manifested across different situations during a specific period of time; they are also "relatively enduring" throughout a person's life. A person who obtains a high score on "agreeableness" at age 5 will also obtain one at ages 17, 29, 48, and 105, for example (Costa & McCrae, 1992, p. 2).

Moreover, McCrae and Costa (1999) report that the five "basic tendencies" or personality dimensions they discovered have been "found in all cultures studied so far" (p. 144). Since the 1950s, findings from hundreds of studies conducted by personality researchers working independently of each other have confirmed the existence of the "big five" personality traits, which together form the acronym CANOE (Costa & McCrae, 1992):

- conscientiousness,
- agreeableness,
- neuroticism,
- openness, and
- extroversion.

Each trait has a number of facets. A 44-item inventory is used to measure these traits. On the basis of their responses, individuals are classified as low or high on each trait. Goldberg (1990) describes cognitive, emotional, motivational, and behavioural differences among individuals who score high and low on each trait and the facets that, taken together, constitute the trait (see appendix 7A). For a more detailed description of individual differences in the big five personality traits, see John and Srivastava (1999, p. 113). These authors also identify the statements included in the 44-item inventory (Costa & McCrae, 1992).

THE FIVE-FACTOR THEORY OF PERSONALITY

The five-factor theory of personality (FFT) focuses on characteristics that differentiate individuals from each other, such as the CANOE factors, and not on characteristics that all individuals share, such as the universal characteristics that are the focus of theorists who advocate principled negotiation (Fisher, Ury, & Patton, 1991) (see chapter 2 under the heading "Principled Negotiation"). The FFT explains enduring differences among individuals in terms of mental characteristics or traits within individuals. It assumes that each of these traits varies along a different continuum with, for example, extreme introverts and extreme extroverts located at either end of one continuum. It posits that individuals who are more or less introverted or extroverted will exhibit these traits to the same degree in all situations in which they are involved. This reasoning applies equally to the other continuums: agreeableness–disagreeableness and openness–closedness.

The FFT is grounded in an assumption of proactivity, which is the opposite of reactivity. For example, proactivity is evident when individuals search out situations that suit their personalities, and reactivity is evident when individuals simply react to the situations in which they find themselves. The proactivity of the personality is not the same thing as the proactivity of the person. The proactivity of personality refers to "proactive basic tendencies";

the proactivity of the person refers to "conscious goals." For example, the proactivity of the person is expressed when someone achieves, or fails to achieve, his goal of losing 20 pounds by attending a weight-loss program for a variety of reasons. The proactivity of the personality is expressed when someone with high scores on conscientiousness loses 20 pounds because he consistently "focus[es] on fewer goals and exhibit[s] the self-discipline associated with such a focus" (McCrae & Costa, 1999). The proactivity of personality is part of a person's lifestyle, whereas the proactivity of the person is goal-specific and may reflect different levels of motivation or aspiration.

Theories of personality emphasize differences among individuals. McCrae and Costa's (1999) FFT predicts that people who participate in procedures aimed at ending conflicts will behave differently, and that these differences are caused by aspects of their personalities.

PERSONALITY AND NEGOTIATIONS

Researchers have studied personality in the context of actual negotiations, as well as negotiations that they created and manipulated in laboratories.

Personality in Actual Negotiations

In *My Life* (2004), former US president Bill Clinton describes the peace negotiations between Israelis and Palestinians held at Camp David in July 2000. Clinton reported that the "chemistry" between the Israeli and Palestinian teams of negotiators was good. They "exchanged offers and counter-offers as well as stories, jokes and family histories." However, the chemistry between Ehud Barak and Yassir Arafat, leaders of the two negotiation teams was not good. According to Clinton, "Barak … was brilliant and brave and he was willing to go a long way on Jerusalem and on territory. But he had a hard time listening to people who didn't see things the way he did, and his way of doing things was diametrically opposed to honored [Palestinian] customs … of trust-building, courtesies, conversations and lots of bargaining. Barak wanted others to wait until he decided the time was right, then, when he made his best offer, he expected to be accepted as self-evidently a good deal." Arafat, according to Clinton, "was famous for waiting until the last minute before making a decision" in the hope of squeezing more out of Israel before showing his hand (pp. 913-914). Negotiations ended without reaching a peace agreement.

Dennis Ross (2004) concluded that a peace agreement was not reached because "Arafat could not do a deal that ended the conflict … he was not up to it. He could live with a [peace] process, but not a conclusion"(p. 767).

Barak, on the other hand, could live with a conclusion but not with a process that required a lot of bargaining. The "personality clash" between Barak and Arafat contributed to the failure of the Camp David negotiations.

In 1988, Eastern Airlines, a large business corporation, went bankrupt. According to McKersie (1995), the people responsible for the demise of the corporation were Charles Bryant, president of the Machinists Union and Frank Lorenzo, the CEO of Eastern. Both Bryant and Lorenzo were described as "assertive" and "tough-minded." Their clashing personalities resulted in a breakdown in negotiations. During union–management negotiations, neither party would compromise. As a result, there was an impasse in negotiations when Bryant refused to make the additional wage concessions demanded by Lorenzo. The impasse was followed by Bryant's taking his union out on strike and Lorenzo's taking Eastern into bankruptcy.

In both cases described here, the personalities of the leaders contributed to the failure of negotiations. Implicit in the accounts of Clinton, Ross, and McKersie is the fact that the thoughts, feelings, and actions of the participants remained consistent over a number of negotiation sessions.

In addition to personality, situational factors also contributed significantly to the outcome of the negotiations. Arafat and Barak were influenced by pressures placed on them by the United States, world public opinion, and opposing political groups in Israel and Palestine (Ross, 2004, p. 769). They were also influenced by significant external events, such as Ariel Sharon's visit to the Haram/Temple Mount and suicide bombings by militant Palestinian groups timed, as was Sharon's visit, to disrupt negotiations (Ross, 2004, pp. 617-618). In the case of Eastern Airlines, situational factors such as difficult economic times and increased competition from other airlines also contributed to the failure of negotiations.

Personality in Simulated Negotiations

Barry and Friedman (1998) studied the link between personality and negotiation in a laboratory by administering the FFT inventory created by Costa and McCrae (1992) to 485 graduate students enrolled in a management course. They randomly assigned students into negotiating pairs: 49 pairs participated in win–win negotiations, and 184 pairs participated in win–lose negotiations that yielded outcomes measurable in dollars.

In this study, Barry and Friedman attempted to test the impact of two personality traits—agreeableness and extroversion—on the process and outcomes of integrative (win–win) and distributive (win–lose) negotiations. Agreeableness refers to "the number of sources from which [people] take norms for right behavior" (appendix 7A). Students who scored high on agreeableness tended to follow norms or rules that originated from sources outside themselves, such as spouses, friends, parents, and supervisors. Extroversion refers to "the number of relationships with which [people] are comfortable." Students who scored high on extroversion were involved in a larger number of relationships and spent more enjoyable time in them than students who scored low (appendix 7A).

Integrative negotiation requires negotiators to focus both on establishing and maintaining a good working relationship and on problem solving. Distributive negotiation requires negotiators to focus exclusively on getting the best deal they can get for themselves.

When students with high agreeableness scores participated in integrative negotiations, they were more adept at establishing and maintaining good working relationships than students with low agreeableness scores. For example, agreeable students were more likely to attend to the needs of the other party, make fewer extreme demands, and engage in fewer personal attacks than less agreeable students. On the other hand, they were also more likely to make more concessions and less likely to clearly state what they wanted. The positive effects of their contribution to relationships was cancelled by the negative effects of their failure to use effective tactics to achieve the outcomes that were important to them. As a result, a high agreeableness score had no impact on the distribution of outcomes.

In distributive negotiations, where getting along well with others is not crucial to obtaining the best deal, students with high agreeableness scores achieved less favourable outcomes than students with low agreeableness scores, because highly agreeable students were more likely to be "anchored" by first offers than their less agreeable colleagues. Figure 7.1 illustrates the impact of agreeableness and extroversion on the outcomes of distributive negotiations.

Anchoring means making a counteroffer that is closer to the initial offer made by the other party than the merits of the initial offer warrant on rational or objective grounds. Anchoring is important because first offers and counteroffers contribute significantly to negotiated outcomes (Carnevale & Pruitt, 1992). For example, a person with a high agreeableness score who is negotiating a payment for damage to her bicycle might respond to an initial offer of $200 with a counteroffer of $220, even though she knows that the deductible on her insurance policy is $300, and the estimated cost of repairing the bicycle is $419. In the same situation, a person with a low agreeableness score is more likely to make a counteroffer of, for example, $600, and receive $500 because she is less likely to be anchored by the initial offer.

Students with high extroversion scores who were participating in distributive negotiations were more likely than students with low extroversion scores and students with high agreeableness scores to use effective negotiating

FIGURE 7.1   Impact of Agreeableness and Extroversion on the Outcomes of Distributive Negotiations

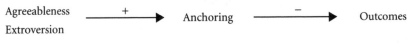

+   Facilitates.
−   Has no effect or decreases.

tactics, such as making credible commitments and stating their demands clearly. However, the contribution made by the use of these tactics during later stages of negotiations was cancelled by anchoring during the earlier stages. Outcomes did not favour highly extroverted students, but they favoured highly agreeable students less.

When students participated in integrative negotiations, where getting along with others was supposed to promote win–win outcomes, highly extroverted and highly agreeable students made only a marginal contribution toward achieving their objectives because friendliness and agreeableness contributed little to creative problem solving. Cognitive ability was a more key asset in this regard.

Cognitive ability refers to a person's ability to understand and solve problems quickly. Students with high cognitive ability made a significant contribution to problem solving, but a non-significant contribution to establishing and maintaining good working relationships with other students who participated in integrative negotiations.

Figure 7.2 shows that high agreeableness and extroversion have no impact on problem solving and, therefore, on the achievement of desired outcomes. High cognitive ability facilitates creative problem solving. Consequently, it facilitates the achievement of desired outcomes, including win–win outcomes.

Findings relating to agreeableness, extroversion, and cognitive ability are summarized below.

Agreeableness

- Students with high agreeableness scores made a significant contribution in establishing and maintaining good working relationships with other students involved in negotiations.
- High agreeableness scores had no impact in integrative negotiation because the attributes of those who achieved them—the proclivity to attend to the needs of the other party, make fewer extreme demands, and engage in fewer personal attacks—were cancelled by their disabilities—the proclivity to make concessions and their relative inability to make clear demands.

FIGURE 7.2   Relative Impact of Agreeableness, Extroversion, and Cognitive Ability on the Outcomes of Integrative Negotiations

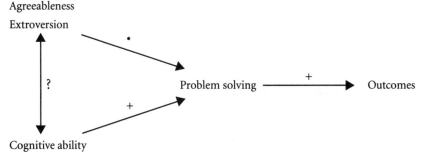

? Factors are unrelated to each other.
• Has no effect.
+ Facilitates.

- A high agreeableness score proved to be a liability in distributive negotiations because people who achieved these scores were more likely to be anchored by the first offers of the other party, less likely to make extreme first offers, and more likely to reveal information that was helpful to the other party than students with low agreeableness scores.

Extroversion

- Students with high extroversion scores made a significant contribution to establishing and maintaining good working relationships by taking the wishes of others into account.
- High extroversion scores had no impact on the outcome of distributive negotiations because the negative effects of anchoring, to which those with high scores were susceptible during the early stages of negotiation, were offset by the positive effects of using effective tactics—such as making credible commitments—during the later stages of negotiations.
- High extroversion scores had no impact on the attainment of win–win outcomes in integrative negotiations because the qualities of gregariousness, friendliness, and communicativeness contribute little to the creative solution of problems.

Cognitive Ability

- Cognitive ability facilitated win–win outcomes in integrative negotiations, and facilitation was greater if both negotiating parties had high cognitive abilities.

- Cognitive ability had no impact on the outcomes of distributive negotiations, partly because this process involved concession, convergence, and compromise, rather than full disclosure and cognitively complex problem solving.

SITUATIONAL FACTORS

Situational factors in struggle, negotiation, mediation, arbitration, and adjudication elicit particular behaviours in the parties and/or influence the emergence and maintenance of specific types of communication and interaction. For example, a person may enter a grocery store with no intention of buying candy, but the display near the checkout counter may prove irresistible. Aries's (1996, pp. 19-20) "fundamental attribution error" is applicable to personality. It arises when people attribute to personality causes that are located in the situations in which individuals act and interact. In the case of Jama Jama (see later in this chapter), we would be making a fundamental attribution error if we attributed the assault to Constable Preston's "aggressive personality" instead of to the two situational factors that were present—peer support and perceived immunity.

Social psychologists who are primarily interested in formulating explanations that emphasize situational factors agree that behaviours associated with personality traits can influence the process and outcomes of negotiations. However, they also point out that

- behaviours associated with any personality trait can be invited, permitted, required, or demanded by a situation in everyday settings, such as grocery stores, and
- situational factors in artificial situations, such as research experiments, can change behaviours associated with personality traits (Funder & Colvin, 1991).

Motivational and Interpersonal Orientations

Deutsch (1973, 1994), Pruitt and Rubin (1986), Rubin and Brown (1975), and Rubin and Zartman (1995) identify two situationally induced orientations: motivational orientation and interpersonal orientation.

Deutsch (1994, p. 16) identifies the following three *motivational orientations*:

1. *Cooperative.* A person with a cooperative motivational orientation (win–win) is interested in the outcomes of the other party as well as in her own outcomes.
2. *Individualistic.* A person with an individualistic motivational orientation (win–win/lose) is interested in achieving outcomes important

to herself, regardless of the impact this has on the outcomes achieved by the other party.

3. *Competitive.* A person with a competitive motivational orientation (win–lose) is interested in achieving more and/or better quality outcomes than the other party.

Rubin and Brown (1975, p. 199) identify a distinctive personal attribute that they call "interpersonal orientation." *Interpersonal orientations* denote "the extent to which [the parties] are sensitive to the interpersonal aspects of their relationship." People with high interpersonal orientations are especially sensitive to variations in the behaviour of other people. People with low interpersonal orientations are relatively insensitive to variations in another's behaviour. Descriptions of specific facets of these orientations by Deutsch (1973, 1994), Pruitt and Rubin (1986), Rubin and Brown (1975), and Rubin and Zartman (1995) suggest to us that facets of high and low motivational orientations are very similar to the facets of agreeableness and extroversion, respectively.

High and low interpersonal orientations, and by extension agreeableness and extroversion scores, have been manipulated or induced by researchers. Rubin and Brown (1975) and Rubin and Zartman (1995) reviewed the results of studies designed to assess the impact of interpersonal orientations on the effectiveness of negotiations. Their findings are set out below.

1. Negotiators with a cooperative (win–win) motivational orientation were more effective than negotiators with an individualistic orientation (win–win/lose), and a lot more effective than negotiators with a competitive orientation (win–lose).

2. Excessive cooperation was costly to one or both parties because

   a) the excessively cooperative people failed to state their needs and preferences clearly and honestly as a result of their concerns about being nice, and

   b) impasses arose when negotiators obtained incorrect information about preferences and preference rankings as a result of the undue reliance on empathy by excessively cooperative people.

3. Negotiators with high interpersonal orientations were effective in negotiations only when they adopted a cooperative motivational orientation.

4. Negotiations were most effective among students who shared a cooperative motivational orientation and a high interpersonal orientation.

These findings indicate that facets of agreeableness and extroversion can be elicited by researchers in conducting experiments on the effectiveness of negotiations. They also indicate that the benefits and liabilities associated with high and low interpersonal orientations are similar to those associated with agreeableness and extroversion.

Motivational orientations and interpersonal orientations influence the effectiveness of negotiations through their impact on other factors.

Motivational orientation influences the effectiveness of negotiation directly and also indirectly through its impact on trust, and the perception that resources will be fairly allocated. Interpersonal orientation influences the effectiveness of negotiation in interaction with motivational orientation and through its impact on sensitivity to social relational cues. These, in turn, increase the likelihood of perceiving and responding to opportunities for problem-solving win–win exchanges. For example, in domestic separation negotiations facilitated by negotiators, a party with a cooperative motivational orientation trusts and engenders trust in the other party. As a result, he makes a risky first offer in which he states his willingness to fully share parenting responsibilities with his ex-partner. The ex-partner responds to the trust reposed in her by offering to share the use of the cottage that her parents gave her after the couple separated. Because the party with cooperative motivational orientation also has a high interpersonal orientation, he is very sensitive to the meaning of the verbal and unspoken communications of his ex-partner. As a result, he perceives more opportunities for achieving win–win outcomes than his partner does during the course of negotiations. Therefore, when the ex-partner signalled that she was favourably disposed to increase child support payments beyond the level set by federal guidelines by clasping her hands together, he agreed to her request that the children spend an equal amount of time in each of their respective residences.

Neither Rubin and Brown (1975) nor Rubin and Zartman (1995) report that cognitive ability influences the effectiveness of negotiations. This is surprising in view of the fact that problem-solving ability makes a significant contribution to integrative negotiations. Findings reported by Barry and Friedman (1998) indicate that cognitive ability is strongly associated with the distribution of win–win outcomes in integrative negotiations.

Level of Aspiration

Level of aspiration refers to the strength of a person's desire to achieve a goal. In the context of negotiation, Barry and Friedman (1998, p. 348) define "level of aspiration" as "the value of the goal toward which the [negotiator] is striving."

Level of aspiration is a situational factor because it can change as a result of other factors operating in particular circumstances (Barry & Friedman, 1998). For example, at the start of negotiations facilitated by a divorce mediator, a mother's level of aspiration for sole custody of her two young children may be greater than her level of aspiration for spousal support or division of property. During the course of negotiations, her level of aspiration for sole custody may decrease and her level of aspiration for joint custody may increase as she realizes that shared parenting may be in the best interests of the children. Her level of aspiration changes further when she learns that her ex-husband is willing to change his shift-work job, sell his home, and buy another in the area in which the children go to school.

In the Barry and Friedman (1998) study, students were randomly assigned to the role of buyer or seller of an industrial product we shall call a widget. Seller were instructed that the reservation price (bottom line) per unit was $10. Buyers were instructed to buy the widgets if they could purchase them for $35 (bottom line) or less per unit. Before the start of negotiations, students were asked if they had "a target price or aspiration level in excess of a minimum requirement for a deal" (p. 350). Students playing the buyer role who stated dollar amounts at or just below the bottom line of $35 (for example, $34) were identified as "low aspiration level" students, while those who stated an amount well below the bottom line (for example, $20) were identified as "high aspiration level" students.

Barry and Friedman (1998) found that aspiration level, a situational factor, interacted with agreeableness scores in producing outcomes. Table 7.1 shows the outcomes that we predict on the basis of their findings. Students with low agreeableness scores and high aspiration scores will earn the highest amounts because low agreeableness will prevent students who are highly motivated to earn money from anchoring. Students with high scores in both agreeableness and aspirations will earn the second highest amounts because anchoring will be reduced or prevented by the high value that the students place on earning money. Students with low scores in both agreeableness and aspirations will receive the next lowest amounts. Even though low agreeableness prevents anchoring, these students do not value money highly enough to obtain large amounts. Students with high scores in agreeableness and low scores in aspirations will obtain the lowest amounts because high agreeableness facilitates anchoring, and the students are not particularly interested in earning money.

Findings based on correlating agreeableness, extroversion, and aspiration level led Barry and Friedman (1998, p. 354) to conclude that "personality effects matter more when bargainer aspirations are low rather than high." The personality trait of agreeableness influences outcomes when aspirations levels are low, but does not influence them as much when aspiration levels are high. In other words, aspirations, a situational factor, change personality trait behaviour when they are high, but not when they are low.

TABLE 7.1   Agreeableness, Aspirations, and Outcome Predictions

Agreeableness	Aspirations	Outcome amount
Low	High	Highest
High	High	High
Low	Low	Low
High	Low	Lowest

Source: Barry and Friedman (1998).

Social Value Orientations

Research on social value orientations provides another indication of how situational factors interact with personality factors. Allison and Messick (1990) identify social value orientation as a personality dimension. Social value orientation refers to an ideal of interpersonal conduct. Negotiators with a high pro-social value orientation tend to

- behave cooperatively,
- judge other pro-social individuals as moral and honest, and
- judge pro-self individuals as immoral and dishonest.

Negotiators with a high pro-self value orientation tend to

- behave competitively,
- judge other pro-self individuals as strong and competent, and
- judge pro-social individuals as weak and stupid.

Pro-self and pro-social value orientations are associated with differences in the behaviour of individuals, as well as differences in how individuals judge others. Pro-self individuals tend to judge others according to their might—that is, their perceived strength or power—while pro-social individuals tend to judge others according to their perceived morality. Individuals who score high on might are judged by other pro-self individuals to be dominant, tough, determined, powerful, strong, smart, and assertive. Individuals who score high on morality are judged by pro-self individuals to be empathic, cooperative, friendly, honourable, trustworthy, fair, and collaborative.

Researchers Smeesters, Warplop, Avermat, and Corneille (2003) led pro-self and pro-social participants in a cooperative–competitive game to believe that the individuals with whom they were interacting were either mighty or moral, or not mighty or not moral. Some of the research findings are presented below.

High pro-selfs who expected their partners to be moral and cooperative exploited them. High pro-selfs who expected their partners to be mighty competed with them. They expressed themselves fully when they judged others to be weak and moral, but held back when they judged others to be as tough as they were, and they believed that retaliation for attempted exploitation was a distinct possibility. The expectations created by the experimenters changed the behaviour of individuals with the same high-self personality dimension.

Pro-social participants behaved cooperatively when they expected others to be moral and to behave cooperatively toward them. They became more competitive when they expected others to behave competitively toward them.

In general, the experiments determined that pro-self and pro-social expectations created by the researchers influenced individuals with different personality dispositions to behave in the same way. For example, pro-self individuals became less competitive when they believed that the other party was also a pro-self person, and pro-social individuals became more competitive when they believed that the other party was a pro-self person. On the other hand, personality also influenced the behaviour of participants. Thus, pro-socials behaved more cooperatively than pro-selfs. High pro-selfs behaved less cooperatively than low pro-selfs, high pro-socials, and low pro-socials. Moreover, the more that high pro-selfs believed that others were moral and cooperative, the more they exploited them.

The pro-social and pro-self personality dimensions and the situational factors identified by Barry and Friedman (1998) and Smeesters et al. (2003) both influence behaviour indirectly. According to Smeesters et al., personality dimensions and situational factors "guide [negotiators'] impressions about [each other] and these impressions may in turn determine [their] behaviour" (p. 984).

PERSONALITY AND STRUGGLE

Social psychologist Toch (1969, p. 169) studied a number of conflicts that arose when police officers entered "explosive situations such as contacts between [themselves] and suspects ... and situations in which citizens are already engaged in fighting each other." Toch used peer interviews, in which police professionals interviewed 32 police officers who had been assaulted by civilians, and convicted offenders interviewed 75 convicted offenders and parolees with violent criminal records, including some who had assaulted police officers more than once. Toch (1969, p. 133) concluded that struggle tactics involving the use of violent acts are expressive of personality.

Toch's analysis revealed two personality types:

1. *Ego-enhancing.* These individuals use violence "to bolster and enhance [their] ego in the eyes of [self] and others" (p. 135).
2. *Egoistic.* These individuals "saw themselves (and their own needs) as being the only fact of social relevance," and they used violence as a means of settling conflicts regardless of its consequences for others.

Other researchers (Ellis & DeKeseredy, 1996) report findings that indicate that situational factors play an important part in accounting for the use of violence by police officers. For example, findings reported by Westley (1953) suggest that police officers are more or less likely to use violence as a means of settling conflicts depending on the degree to which it helps their prospects for promotion, brings rewards from their peers, or helps them remain in a position or role they find rewarding. A more recent example is provided by the case of "Jama Jama."

Jama Jama

Jama Jama is a slightly built 22-year-old male who was born in Somalia. On July 28, 2005, Ontario Supreme Court Justice Peter Wilkie found Constable Roy Preston guilty of assaulting Jama, even though three other officers present at the scene gave evidence in court that did not support Jama's version of events. Unknown to Preston and the other officers, the scene had been videotaped by a tourist, who handed the tape over to the Crown attorney. Preston's personality may have played a part in his use of struggle tactics (excessive use of force), but two situational factors—the presence of brother officers who would support his version of events, and the perception that his conduct was "private," that is, not being videotaped or otherwise credibly recorded—probably played a more significant part.

Source: Powell (2005).

The June Bug Study: Situational Factors

"The June Bug Study" does not deal directly with conflict resolution. However, this "classic study" (Pervin, 1999) reveals interaction among personality traits, situational factors (such as relationships), subjective factors (such as stress), and societal factors (such as marital status) that can guide the strategies, tactics, and outcomes of procedures aimed at settling conflicts.

The June bug study is theoretically and methodologically sophisticated. Gender was not included as a factor because all the workers in the factory were women. Therefore, cultural differences between women and men could not be included as a factor. The inclusion of gender would yield a four-factor theory that could be used to guide research on linkages between personality and conflict resolution, taking cultural, structural, situational, and personal factors (such as cognitive ability and subjective feelings of stress) into account. None of the studies we reviewed were guided by this kind of multifactor model.

The June Bug Study

In June 1962, workers in a dressmaking plant alleged in statements read by researchers Kerchoff and Back (1968) that they were being bitten by insects. As evidence, they pointed to such symptoms as severe nausea, rashes, dizziness, and fainting. Medical experts could find no evidence to indicate that insect bites caused the symptoms reported by the affected workers. "Just anxiety," or perhaps psychosomatic, the medics concluded. The affected workers held fast to their belief that insect bites caused their sickness.

The 59 affected workers represented approximately 9 percent of the 674 workforce. What differentiated them from the majority of workers who did not report experiencing symptoms? Some of the workers who experienced symptoms sought medical attention (official affecteds), others did not, choosing to cope with their symptoms themselves (self-affecteds). What differentiated the treatment choices of official affecteds from those of self-affecteds?

A multifactor model—that is, one that includes situational strain (factor 1), position in a network of relationships (factor 2), and personality (factor 3) provided answers to both questions. Situational strain was associated with such things as being a single parent, working overtime, and working during periods of increased production. Workers were classified as high strain, medium strain, or low strain, depending on the amount of strain they reported. Researchers measured workers' position in a network of relationships by asking them about social ties with "three best friends" and other co-workers. The researchers classified the workers in groups of high, medium, and low, depending on the number of relationships they reported being involved in.

The researchers defined personality as "persistent patterns of behavioural tendency" (p. 86) and measured two personality traits or personal qualities: denial and agreeableness. Deniers persistently denied the existence of their symptoms and other health problems. Agreeables were more susceptible to being influenced by their friends and members of other work groups they belonged to. Findings reported by Kerchoff and Back are presented in table 7.2.

TABLE 7.2   Impact of Personality, Situational, and Relational Factors on Affected Workers

Strain	Relationships[*]	Denier	Agreeable	Affected	Affected type
High	High	High	High	Yes	Official
Medium	High	Low	Low	Yes	Self
Low	Low	**	**	No	

[*]   With affected others.
**   Not reported in findings.

Row 1 in the body of table 7.2 shows that the official affecteds—that is, workers who sought medical attention—

- experienced high strain;
- had relationships with a number of other workers who reported being affected by insect bites;
- coped with strain by denying that it was caused by external factors;
- tended to agree with suggestions made by others; and
- reported being affected by insect bites.

Row 2 in table 7.2 shows that the self-affecteds—that is, workers who dealt with their symptoms themselves in preference to seeking medical attention—

- experienced medium strain because they worked on less stressful shifts in less stressful departments than some of their co-workers;
- had relationships with a number of workers who reported being affected by insect bites;
- coped with strain in other ways than denying its external sources;
- did not always or frequently agree with suggestions made by others; and
- reported being affected by insect bites.

Row 3 in table 7.2 shows that workers who were not affected by insect bites

- experienced low strain because they worked on less stressful shifts in less stressful departments; and
- had fewer relationships with affected co-workers.

The major implication of the findings reported by Kerchoff and Back (p. 144) is that "different kinds of people, under different kinds and amounts of strain, with different patterns of relationships respond differently."

Source: Kerchoff and Back (1968).

Evaluation

Personality Theory and Research

Strengths

Personality theory and research have made a positive contribution by

- demonstrating consistency in the behaviour of individuals participating in negotiations and struggle;
- identifying differences in the behaviour of participants engaged in negotiations and struggle;
- providing evidence of the same (CANOE) personality dimensions in a number of different cultures (Church, 2000, pp. 654-655); and
- providing negotiators with inventories they can use to obtain information about themselves that will help them increase their effectiveness.

Weaknesses

These contributions co-exist with the failure to adequately explain

- variations in the behaviour of individuals participating in integrative and distributive negotiations; and
- why the link between personality dimensions such as extroversion and outcomes of negotiations changes when situational factors are taken into account.

Situational Theory and Research

Strengths

Situational theory and research have made a positive contributing by

- demonstrating differences in the behaviour of individuals participating in negotiations and struggle; and
- identifying situational factors that account for these differences.

Weaknesses

These contributions co-exist with the failure to adequately explain consistent differences in the behaviour of individuals who participate in the same situation when, presumably, situational factors are held constant.

Chapter Summary

We began the chapter by defining personality as consistency in behaviour in different situations throughout a lifetime. We then examined the five-factor

CANOE theory. Next, we described links between personality and failure to reach agreement in two negotiations. This was followed by the presentation of laboratory research findings aimed at testing the impact of two personality traits—agreeableness and extroversion—on the process and outcomes of distributive and integrative negotiation. We devoted the following section to describing the contribution made to the process and outcomes of negotiation by three situational factors: motivational orientation, interpersonal orientation, and social value orientation. Subsequently, we examined the link between personality factors and struggle tactics, finding that both personality and situational factors influenced the use of struggle as a means of settling conflict. In the final part of the chapter, we evaluated personality and situational theory and research.

APPENDIX 7A: THE "BIG FIVE" PERSONALITY TRAITS

Extroversion

Extroversion refers to the number of relationships with which one is comfortable. A larger number of relationships and a larger proportion of one's time spent enjoying them characterize high extroversion. A smaller number of relationships and a smaller proportion of one's time spent in pursuing those relationships characterize low extroversion.

Six Facets of Extroversion	INTROVERT E−	EXTROVERT E+
Warmth	Reserved, formal	Affectionate, friendly, intimate
Gregariousness	Seldom seeks company	Gregarious, prefers company
Assertiveness	Stays in background	Assertive, speaks up, leads
Activity	Leisurely pace	Vigorous pace
Excitement seeking	Low need for thrills	Craves excitement
Positive emotions	Less exuberant	Cheerful, optimistic

Agreeableness

Agreeableness refers to the number of sources from which one takes one's norms for right behaviour. High agreeableness describes a person who defers to a great many norm sources, such as spouse, religious leader, friend, boss, or pop culture idol. Low agreeableness describes one who, in the extreme, only follows one's inner voice. High agreeableness persons will march to the beat of many different drummers, while low agreeableness persons march only to their own drumbeat.

Six Facets of Agreeableness	CHALLENGER A−	ADAPTER A+
Trust	Cynical, skeptical	Sees others as honest and well-intentioned
Straightforwardness	Guarded, stretches truth	Straightforward, frank
Altruism	Reluctant to get involved	Willing to help others
Compliance	Aggressive, competitive	Yields under conflict, defers
Modesty	Feels superior to others	Self-effacing, humble
Tender-mindedness	Hardheaded, rational	Tender-minded, easily moved

Conscientiousness

Conscientiousness refers to the number of goals on which one is focused. High conscientiousness refers to a person who focuses on fewer goals and exhibits the self-discipline associated with such focus. Low conscientiousness refers to one who pursues a larger number of goals and exhibits the distractibility and spontaneity associated with diffuse focus.

Six Facets of Conscientiousness	FLEXIBLE C−	FOCUSED C+
Competence	Often feels unprepared	Feels capable and effective
Order	Unorganized, unmethodical	Well-organized, neat, tidy
Dutifulness	Casual about obligations	Governed by conscience, reliable
Achievement striving	Low need for achievement	Driven to achieve success
Self-discipline	Procrastinates, distracted	Focused on completing tasks
Deliberation	Spontaneous, hasty	Thinks carefully before acting

Openness

Openness refers to the number of interests to which one is attracted and the depth to which those interests are pursued. High openness refers to a person with relatively more interests and, consequently, relatively less depth within each interest, while low openness refers to a person with relatively few interests and relatively more depth in each of those interests.

Six Facets of Openness	PRESERVER O−	EXPLORER O+
Fantasy	Focuses on here and now	Imaginative, daydreams
Aesthetics	Uninterested in art	Appreciates art and beauty
Feelings	Ignores and discounts feelings	Values all emotions
Actions	Prefers the familiar	Prefers variety, tries new things
Ideas	Narrower intellectual focus	Broad intellectual curiosity
Values	Dogmatic, conservative	Open to re-examining values

Negative Emotionality

Negative emotionality refers to the number and strength of stimuli required in eliciting negative emotions in a person. More resilient persons are bothered by fewer stimuli in their environment, and the stimuli must be strong in order to bother them. More reactive persons are bothered by a greater variety of stimuli, and the stimuli do not have to be as strong in order to bother them.

Six Facets of Negative Emotionality	RESILIENT R+	REACTIVE R−
Worry	Relaxed, calm	Worrying, uneasy
Anger	Composed, slow to anger	Quick to feel anger
Discouragement	Slowly discouraged	Easily discouraged
Self-consciousness	Hard to embarrass	More easily embarrassed
Impulsiveness	Resists urges easily	Easily tempted
Vulnerability	Handles stress easily	Difficulty coping

RECOMMENDED READING

Kerchoff, A.C., & Back, K.W. (1968). *The June bug: A study of hysterical contagion.* New York: Appleton-Century-Crofts. This book described a field study of an event in which a number of factory workers reported symptoms of illness that they attributed to insect bites. The authors integrate structure, culture, the work situation, and personality in their explanation of contagion and individual differences in reporting symptoms.

McNamee, E. (1994). *Resurrection man.* New York: Picador. This book, which is set in Belfast, tells the story of a member of a Protestant paramilitary organization that specializes in the struggle with Catholics. Historical, contemporary, situational, and personality factors combine to explain the protagonist's use of extreme violence.

References

Abel, R. (1974). A comparative theory of dispute institutions in society. *Law and Society Review, 8,* 217-247.

Adams, G.W. (2003). Report submitted to the Ontario English Catholic Teachers Association, Toronto.

Adler, R.S., & Silverstein, E.M. (2000). When David meets Goliath: Dealing with power differentials in negotiations. *Harvard Negotiation Law Review, 5,* 1-112.

Allen, C.M., & Straus, M.A. (1980). Resources, power and husband–wife violence. In M.A. Straus & G. Hotaling (Eds.), *The social causes of husband–wife violence* (pp. 188-205). Minneapolis, MN: University of Minnesota Press.

Allison, S.T., & Messick, D.M. (1990). Social decision heuristics in the use of shared resources. *Journal of Behavioural Decision Making, 3,* 195-204.

Amaro, H. (1995). Love, sex and power: Considering women's power in HIV prevention. *American Psychologist, 50,* 437-447.

Amaro, H., & Raj, A. (2000). On the margin: Power and women's HIV risk reduction strategies. *Sex Roles, 42,* 723-749.

Anderson, D. (2003) After Gladue: Are judges sentencing aboriginal offenders differently? Doctoral dissertation, York University, Department of Sociology.

Antes, J.R., & Saul, J.A. (2001). Evaluating mediation practice for a transformative perspective. *Mediation Quarterly, 18,* 313-323.

Arbitration and Mediation Institute of Canada. (1996). *The arbitration practice handbook.* Winnipeg: Arbitration and Mediation Institute of Canada.

Arendell, T. (1995). *Fathers and divorce.* Thousand Oaks, CA: Sage.

Aries, E. (1996). *Men and women in interaction: Reconsidering the differences.* New York: Oxford University Press.

Aubert, V. (1963). Competition and dissensus: Two types of conflict and of conflict resolution. *Journal of Conflict Resolution, 7,* 26-42.

Avruch, R., Black, P.W., & Scimecca, J.A. (1991). *Conflict resolution: Cross-cultural perspectives.* New York: Greenwood Press.

Babcock, L., Gelfand, M., Small, D., & Stayn, H. (2002). Propensity to initiate negotiations: A new look at gender variation in negotiation behaviour. Unpublished paper, Carnegie Mellon Univeristy, Pittsburgh, PA.

Babcock, L.M., & Laschever, S. (2003). *Women don't ask: Negotiation and the gender divide.* Princeton, NJ: Princeton University Press.

Bagnell, J. (2004). What every ACR member should know about ethics. *ACResolution, Spring,* 11-13.

Bahr, S. (1972). Comment on "The study of family power structure: A review 1960-1969." *Journal of Marriage and the Family, May,* 239-243.

Baker, D. (2002a, June 23). Blue Jays quitters. *Toronto Star,* p. C1.

Baker, D. (2002b, June 24). Halliday tossed in sixth. *Toronto Star,* p. C1.

Bandura, A. (1997). *Social learning theory.* Englewood Cliffs, NJ: Prentice Hall.

Barry, B., & Friedman, R.A. (1998). Bargainer characteristics in distributive and integrative negotiation. *Journal of Personality and Social Psychology, 74,* 345-359.

Beedham, B. (1999, July 31). A survey of the new geopolitics: The road to 2050. *The Economist,* pp. 1-15.

Beneria, L., & Roldan, M. (1987). *The crossroads of class and gender: Industrial homework, subcontracting and household dynamics in Mexico City.* Chicago: University of Chicago Press.

Bennett, M.D., & Hermann, M.S.G. (1996). *The art of mediation.* Notre Dame, IN: National Institute for Trial Advocacy, Notre Dame Law School.

Beradi-Coletta, B., Buyer, L., Dominowski, R.L., & Rellinger, E.R. (1995). Metacognition and problem solving: A process-oriented approach. *Journal of Experimental Psychology: Learning, Memory and Cognition, 21,* 205-223.

Berger, J. (2004, August 1). In Mideast politics, flip-flopping is a strength, not a weakness. *New York Times,* p. 7.

Beriker, N., & Druckman, D. (1996). Simulating the Lausanne peace negotiations, 1922-1923: Power asymmetries in bargaining. *Simulation and Gaming, 27,* 162-179.

Black, D. (1983). Crime as social control. *American Sociological Review, 48,* 34-45.

Blalock, H.M. (1967). *Toward a general theory of minority group relations.* New York: Wiley.

Blalock, H.M. (1989). *Power and conflict: Toward a general theory.* Newbury Park, CA: Sage.

Blau, P. (1964). *Exchange and power in social life.* New York: Wiley.

Blood, R.O., & Wolfe, D.M. (1960). *Husbands and wives: The dynamics of married living.* New York: Free Press.

Blumberg, R.L. (Ed.). (1991). *Gender, family and economy: The triple overlap.* Newbury Park, CA: Sage.

Blumberg, R.L., & Coleman, M.T. (1989). A theoretical look at the gender balance of power in the American couple. *Journal of Social Issues, 10,* 225-250.

Blumstein, P., & Schwartz, P. (1983). *American couples.* New York: William Morrow.

Bok, D. (1983). A flawed system of law practice and training. *Journal of Legal Education, 330,* 530-542.

Bond, M.H., Leung, K., & Schwartz, S. (1990). Explaining choices in procedural and distributive justice across cultures. *International Journal of Psychology, 27,* 211-227.

Bossy, J. (Ed.). (1983). *Disputes and settlements: Law and human relations in the west.* Cambridge, UK: Cambridge University Press.

Bottomley, A. (1984). Resolving family disputes: A critical review. In M. Freedman (Ed.), *State, law and the family: Critical perspectives* (pp. 293-303). London: Tavistock.

Brant, C.C. (1990). Native ethics and rules of behaviour. *Canadian Journal of Psychiatry, 35,* 534-539.

Breslin, J.W., & Rubin, J. (Eds.). (1995). *Negotiation theory and practice.* Cambridge, MA: Harvard Program on Negotiation.

Brett, J.M. (2000). Culture and negotiation. *International Journal of Psychology, 35,* 97-104.

Brislin, R. (1993). *Understanding culture's influences on behaviour.* New York: Harcourt Brace Jovanovich.

Broad, W.J. (1999, July 6). Playful Flipper can be ferocious, dolphin experts say. *New York Times,* p. A7.

Broverman, I.K., Vogel, S., Broverman, D.M., Clarkson, F.E., & Rosenkrantz, P.S. (1972). Sex-role stereotypes: A current appraisal. *Journal of Social Issues, 28,* 59-78.

Bruser, D. (2004, July 22). Egos are always involved. *Toronto Star*, p. C1.

Brym, R.J., Lie, J., Nelson, A., Guppy, N., & McCormick, C. (2003). *Sociology: Your compass for a new world.* Toronto: Nelson.

Burton, J. (1994). *Conflict resolution.* New York: St. Martin's Press.

Bush, B.R., & Folger, J. (1994). *The promise of mediation.* San Francisco: Jossey-Bass.

Bussey, K., & Bandura, A. (1984). Influence of gender constancy and social power on sex-linked modeling. *Journal of Personality and Social Psychology, 47,* 1292-1302.

Cairns, E., & Darby, J. (1998). The conflict in Northern Ireland: Causes, consequences and controls. *American Psychologist, 53,* 754-760.

Campbell, K. (2004, July 22). A failure to communicate. *Toronto Star*, p. E4.

Canadian Broadcasting Corporation. (2002). *The siege of Bethlehem.* Toronto.

Canadian Charter of Rights and Freedoms. Part I of the *Constitution Act, 1982,* RSC 1985, app. II, no. 44.

Canan, P., & Pring, D. (1996). *Strategic lawsuits against public participation.* Belmont, CA: Wadsworth.

Carli, L. (1990). Gender, language and influence. *Journal of Personality and Social Psychology, 59,* 941-951.

Carnevale, P.J., & Pruitt, D.G. (1992). Negotiation and mediation. *Annual Review of Psychology, 43,* 531-582.

Catalyst Foundation of New York. (1999, September 19). Boosting women to the top. *Toronto Star*, p. A7.

Cavalluzzo, P.J. (1999). Strikes in the public sector in the second millennium —Employee right or government policy. Unpublished paper.

Cernetig, M. (1999, August 16). Beijing, Taipei wage psychological warfare. *Globe and Mail.*

Chafets, J. (1980). Conflict resolution in marriage: Toward a theory of spousal strategies and marital dissolution rates. *Journal of Family Issues, September,* 397-421.

Church, A.T. (2000). Culture and personality: Toward an integrated cultural trait psychology. *Journal of Personality, 68,* 651-694.

Clinton, B. (2004). *My life.* New York: Knopf.

Cohen, R. (1993). An advocate's view. In G.O. Faure & J.Z. Rubin (Eds.), *Culture and negotiation: The resolution of water disputes* (pp. 22-37). Newbury Park, CA: Sage.

Cohn, D. (2005, April 14). Japan and China: Old grievances emerge. *Globe and Mail*, p. A2.

Coleman, P.T. (2000). Power and conflict. In M. Deutsch & P.T. Coleman (Eds.), *The handbook of conflict resolution: Theory and practice* (pp. 108-130). San Francisco: Jossey-Bass.

Collins, P. (1997). On West and Fenstermaker's "Doing difference." In M.R. Walsh (Ed.), *Women, men and gender: Ongoing debates* (pp. 73-78). New Haven, CT: Yale University Press.

Coloroso, B. (2002). *The bully, the bullied and the bystander*. New York: Harper-Collins.

Conley, J.M., & O'Barr, W.M. (1988). Fundamentals of jurisprudence: An ethnography of judicial decision making in informal courts. *North Carolina Law Review, 66*, 467-507.

Conley, J.M., & O'Barr, W.M. (1990). *Rules versus relationships: The ethnography of legal discourse*. Chicago: University of Chicago Press.

Connell, R.W. (1987). *Gender and power*. Stanford, CA: Stanford University Press.

Contenda, S. (2004, September 8). Chilling video shows plight of hostages. *Toronto Star*, p. A3.

Coser, L. (1956). *The functions of social conflict*. New York: Free Press.

Coser, L. (1965). Realistic and nonrealistic conflict. In L.A. Coser (Ed.), *Georg Simmel* (pp. 171-180). Englewood Cliffs, NJ: Prentice Hall.

Costa, P.T., Jr., & McCrae, R.R. (1992). *Revised NEO and NEO five factor inventory professional manual*. Odessa, FL: Psychological Assessment Resources.

Cox, D. (2004, August 5). Players' union hardens stance against NHL. *Toronto Star*, p. E2.

Crawford, M., & Gartner, R. (1992). *Woman killing: Intimate femicide in Ontario, 1974-1980*. Report prepared for the Women We Honour Action Committee, Toronto, Ontario.

Cromwell, R.E., & Olson, D.H. (Eds.). (1975). *Power in families*. New York: Halstead Press.

Crosariol, B. (2005, February 7). Business turns to real-time litigation. *Globe and Mail*, p. B14.

Cross, S.E., & Madson, L. (1997). Models of self: Self-construals and gender. *Psychological Bulletin, 122*, 5-37.

Dahl, R. (1957). The concept of power. *Behavioural Science, 2*, 201-215.

Dahl, R. (1968). Power. *International Encyclopedia of the Social Sciences, 12,* 405-415.

De Santis, S. (1999). *Life on the line.* New York: Doubleday.

De Villiers, M. (1999). *Water.* Toronto: Stoddart.

Dean v. Dean. (1978), 7 RFL (2d) 338 (Nfld. TD).

Deaux, K., & Major, B. (1987). Putting gender into context: An interactive model of gender-related behaviour. *Journal of Personality and Social Psychology, 94,* 369-389.

DeDreu, C. (1995). Coercive power and concession making in bilateral negotiation. *Journal of Conflict Resolution, 39,* 646-666.

Deng, F.M. (1993). Northern and southern Sudan: The Nile. In G.O. Faure & J.Z. Rubin (Eds.), *Culture and negotiation: The resolution of water disputes* (pp. 62-96). Newbury Park, CA: Sage.

Derlega, V.J., Cukur, C.S., Kuang, J.C., & Forsyth, D.R. (2002). Interdependent construal of self and the endorsement of conflict resolution strategies in interpersonal, intergroup and international conflicts. *Journal of Cross-Cultural Psychology, 33,* 610-625.

Deutsch, M. (1973). *The resolution of conflict: Constructive and destructive processes.* New Haven, CT: Yale University Press.

Deutsch, M. (1994). Constructive conflict resolution: Principles, training and research. *Journal of Social Issues, 50,* 13-32.

Deutsch, M., & Coleman, P.T. (Eds.). (2000). *The handbook of conflict resolution: Theory and practice.* San Francisco: Jossey-Bass.

Diamond, J. (1999). *Guns, germs, and steel: The fates of human societies.* New York: Norton.

Dobash, R.E., & Dobash, R. (1979). *Violence against wives.* New York: Free Press.

Douglas, A. (1957). The peaceful settlement of industrial and intergroup disputes. *Journal of Conflict Resolution, 1,* 69-81.

Douglas, A. (1962). *Industrial peacemaking.* New York: Columbia University Press.

Drohan, M. (2004). *Making a killing: How and why corporations use armed force to do business.* Toronto: Vintage Canada.

Drohan, M. (2003, June 30). War: Greed not grievance. *Globe and Mail,* p. A15.

Durkheim, E. (1947). *The division of labour in society.* Glencoe, IL: Free Press (originally published in 1893).

Dyer, G. (2003, April 11). Who's next for global vigilante? *Toronto Star*, p. A6.

Eagly, A.H., & Wood, W. (1999). The origins of sex differences in human behaviour: Evolved dispositions versus social roles. *American Anthropologist, 54*, 408-423.

Eagly, A.H., Makhijani, M.G., & Klonsky, B.G. (1992). Gender and the evaluation of leaders: A meta-analysis. *Psychological Bulletin, 111*, 3-22.

Echabe, A.E., & Castro, J.L. (1999). The impact of context on gender identities. *European Journal of Social Psychology, 29*, 287-304.

The Economist. (1999). Give war a chance. *147 #3.*

The Economist. (2004). AIDS in South Africa. *152 #5.*

Edelsky, C. (1981). Who's got the floor? *Language in Society, 10*, 383-421.

Efron, J. (1989). Alternatives to litigation: Factors in choosing. *Modern Law Review, 52*, 480-486.

Ellis, D. (1994). Ontario family mediation pilot project. Report submitted to the Attorney General of Ontario, Toronto.

Ellis, D. (1997). Violence prevention in a secure detention facility for young offenders. Report submitted to the Solicitor General and Minister of Corrections, Ontario, Canada.

Ellis, D. (1999a). Evaluation of a family mediator skills pilot certification project. Report presented to Family Mediation Canada, Guelph, ON.

Ellis, D. (1999b). Water, culture and peacemaking between Israelis and Palestinians. In A. Godenzi (Ed.), *International conflict* (pp. 37-48). Fribourg, Switzerland: University of Fribourg Press.

Ellis, D. (2000). Safety, equity and human agency. *Violence Against Women, 6*, 1012-1027.

Ellis, D. (2003). *The Ontario Human Rights Commission mediation service: An evaluation study.* Report presented to the Ontario Human Rights Commission, Toronto.

Ellis, D. (2004). Assessing power imbalances. Unpublished paper, La Marsh Research Centre on Violence and Conflict Resolution, York University.

Ellis, D., & Beaver, D. (1994). The effect of formal-legal and traditional interventions on woman abuse in a first nations community. Paper presented at the annual meeting of the Society for Applied Sociology, Cleveland, OH.

Ellis, D., & DeKeseredy, W. (1996). *The wrong stuff: An introduction to the sociological study of deviance.* Toronto: Allyn and Bacon.

Ellis, D., & Diamond, F. (2005). Crime in Canada. Unpublished, chapter 1 in manuscript submitted for publication by Pearson Canada.

Ellis, D., & Stuckless, N. (1996). *Mediating and negotiating marital conflicts.* Thousand Oaks, CA: Sage.

Ellis, D., & Wight, L. (1998). Theorizing power in divorce negotiations: Implications for practice. *Mediation Quarterly, 15,* 227-244.

Elster, J. (1991). *Nuts and bolts for the social sciences.* New York: Cambridge University Press.

Emerson, R. (1962). Power-dependence relations. *American Sociological Review, 27,* 31-41.

Emery, R.E. (1994). *Renegotiating family relationships: Divorce, child custody and mediation.* New York: Guilford Press.

Emery, R.E., Matthews, S.G., & Wyer, M.M. (1991). Child custody mediation and litigation: Further evidence on the differing views of mothers and fathers. *Journal of Consulting and Clinical Psychology, 62,* 410-418.

Engel, M. (1994). *With good reason: An introduction to informal fallacies.* New York: St. Martin's Press.

England, P., & Kilbourne, B.S. (1990). Markets, marriages and other mates: The problem of power. In R. Friedland & A.F. Robertson (Eds.), *Beyond the marketplace: Rethinking economy and society* (pp. 163-188). New York: Aldine de Gruyter.

Erickson, B., Lind, E.A., Johnson, B.C., & O'Barr, O.M. (1978). Speech style and impression formation in a court setting: The effects of "powerful" and "powerless" speech. *Journal of Experimental Social Psychology, 14,* 266-279.

Erlanger, H., Chambliss, E., & Melli, M. (1987). Participation and flexibility in informal process: Cautions from the divorce context. *Law and Society Review, 21,* 585-604.

Erlanger, S. (2005, February 13). It's the Middle East. Don't expect much. Right? *New York Times,* p. 5.

Espinoza, J.A., & Garza, R.T. (1985). Social group salience and interethnic cooperation. *Journal of Experimental Social Psychology, 21,* 697-715.

Etzioni, A. (1996). *The new golden rule: Community and morality in a democratic society.* New York: Basic.

Faure, G.O., & Rubin, J.Z. (Eds.). (1993). *Culture and negotiation: The resolution of water disputes.* Newbury Park, CA: Sage.

Faure, G.O., & Sjostedt, G. (1993). Culture and negotiation: An introduction. In G.O. Faure & J.Z. Rubin (Eds.), *Culture and negotiation: The resolution of water disputes* (pp. 1-16). Newbury Park, CA: Sage.

Felstiner, W.L., Abel, R.L., & Sarat, A. (1981). The emergence and transformation of disputes: Naming, blaming, claiming. *Law and Society, 15,* 42-65.

Felstiner, W.L., & Williams, L. (1978). Mediation as an alternative to criminal prosecution. *Law and Human Behaviour, 2,* 223-239.

Fischer, K., Vidmar, N., & Ellis, R. (1993). The culture of battering and the role of mediation in domestic violence cases. *SMU Law Review, 46,* 2117-2174.

Fisher, R. (1972). Third-party consultation: A method for the study and resolution of conflict. *Journal of Conflict Resolution, 16,* 67-94.

Fisher, R. (1994). Review comment on cover of Kolb & Associates (1994), *When talk works: Profiles of mediators.* San Francisco: Jossey-Bass.

Fisher, R.T. (2000). Intergroup conflict. In M. Deutsch & P.T. Coleman (Eds.), *The handbook of conflict resolution: Theory and practice* (pp. 166-184). San Francisco: Jossey-Bass.

Fisher, R., Ury, W., & Patton, W. (1991). *Getting to yes* (2nd ed.). Toronto: Penguin.

Fisher, R., Ury, W., & Patton, W. (1992). Objective standards. In S.B. Goldberg, F.E. Sander, & N. Rogers (Eds.), *Dispute resolution: Negotiation, mediation and other processes* (2nd ed.). Boston: Little, Brown.

Fiske, S.T. (1993). Controlling other people: The impact of power on stereotyping. *American Psychologist, 48,* 621-628.

Fiske, S.T., Bersoff, D., Deaux, K., & Heilman, M. (1991). Social science research on trial: Use of sex stereotyping research in Price Waterhouse vs. Hopkins. *American Psychologist, 46,* 1049-1060.

Fiske, S.T., Morling, B., & Stevens, L.E. (1996). Controlling self and others: A theory of anxiety, mental control and social control. *Personality and Social Psychology Bulletin, 22,* 115-123.

Fiss, O. (1984). Against settlement. *Yale Law Journal, 93,* 1073-1092.

Fiss, O. (1992). Against settlement. In S.B. Goldberg, F.E. Sander, & N. Rogers (Eds.), *Dispute resolution: Negotiation, mediation and other processes* (2nd ed.) (pp. 244-249). Boston: Little, Brown.

Folberg, J., & Taylor, A. (1984). *Mediation: A comprehensive guide to resolving conflicts without litigation.* San Francisco: Jossey-Bass.

Freed, D.A. (2003, October 24). Negotiator could become key player. *Toronto Star,* p. A19.

French, J.R., & Raven, B.H. (1959). The bases of social power. In D. Cartwright (Ed.), *Studies in social power* (pp. 48-62). Ann Arbor, MI: University of Michigan Press.

Freund, J.C. (1992). *Smart negotiating: How to make good deals in the real world.* New York: Simon & Schuster.

Friedman, R. (1994). Missing ingredients in mutual gains bargaining theory. *Negotiation Journal, July,* 266-280.

Fuller, L. (1962). Collective bargaining and the arbitrator. *Proceedings, 15th Annual Meeting, National Academy of Arbitrators,* Washington, DC.

Fukuyama, F. (2005, March 13). The Calvinist manifesto. *New York Times Book Review,* p. 35.

Funder, D., & Colvin, C.R. (1991). Explorations in behavioral consistency: Properties of persons, situations and behaviors. *Journal of Personality and Social Psychology, 60,* 773-794.

Gee, M. (2004, July 15). Not talking is no barrier to settlement. *Globe and Mail,* p. A15.

Geertz, C. (2003). Thick description: Toward an interpretive theory of culture. In K. Endicott & R.L. Welsch (Eds.), *Taking sides: Clashing views on controversial issues in anthropology* (pp. 182-191). Toronto: McGraw Hill.

Gelfand, M.J., Nishii, L., Holcombe, K., Dyer, N., Ohbuchi, K., Kukumo, M., & Toyama, M. (2001). Cultural influences on cognitive representations of conflict: Interpretations of conflict episodes in the United States and Japan. *Journal of Applied Psychology, 86,* 1059-1074.

Gerhart, B., & Rynes, S. (1991). Determinants and consequences of salary negotiations by male and female MBA graduates. *Journal of Applied Psychology, 76,* 256-262.

Gewurtz, I.G. (2001). (Re)designing mediation to address power imbalances. *Conflict Resolution Quarterly, 19,* 135-162.

Giddens, A. (1991). *Introduction to sociology.* New York: Norton.

Giddens, A. (1993). Domination and power. In P. Cassell (Ed.), *The Giddens reader* (pp. 213-283). New York: Macmillan.

Gilligan, C. (1982). *In a different voice.* Cambridge, MA: Harvard University Press.

Girdner, L. (1988). How people process disputes. In J. Folberg & A. Milne (Eds.), *Divorce mediation: Theory and practice* (pp. 45-57). New York: Guilford Press.

Girdner, L. (1990). Mediation triage: Screening for abuse in divorce mediation. *Mediation Quarterly, 7*, 365-376.

Glaberson, W. (2000, October 8). Legal shortcuts run into some dead ends. *New York Times*, p. 4.

Goddard, P. (2002, December 19). Paul's ego trip is so yesterday. *Toronto Star*, p. A43.

Goffman, E. (1959). *The presentation of self in everyday life.* New York: Doubleday Anchor.

Goldberg, L.R. (1990). An alternative "description of personality": The big five factor structure. *Journal of Personality and Social Psychology, 59*, 1216-1229.

Goldberg, S.B. (1989). Grievance mediation: A successful alternative to labor arbitration. *Negotiation Journal, 5*, 8-17.

Goldberg, S.B. (1990). The case of the squabbling authors: A med-arb response. *Negotiation Journal, October*, 391-396.

Goldberg, S.B., Sander, F.E., & Rogers, N. (Eds.). (1992). *Dispute resolution: Negotiation, mediation and other processes* (2nd ed.). Boston: Little, Brown.

Gordon, M. (2003, May 13). Film, TV industry hit hard. *Toronto Star*, p. E5.

Gould, J., & Kolb, W.L. (Eds.). (1964). *A dictionary of the social sciences.* Glencoe, IL: Free Press.

Gould, S.J. (1992). *Bully for brontosaurus.* New York: Norton.

Gouldner, A.W. (1960). The norm of reciprocity: A preliminary statement. *American Sociological Review, 25*, 161-178.

Gray, E. (1999). *Power dynamics between separating couples participating in divorce mediation.* Unpublished doctoral dissertation, Department of Sociology, York University.

Grillo, T. (1991). The mediation alternative: Process dangers for women. *Yale Law Journal, 100*, 1545-1610.

Gudykunst, W.B., Nishida, T., & Schmidt, K.L. (1989). The influence of cultural variability on perceptions of communication behavior associated with relationship terms. *Human Communication Research, 13*, 147-166.

Gudykunst, W.B., & Ting-Toomey, S. (1988). *Cultural and interpersonal communication.* Newbury Park, CA: Sage.

Gulliver, P. (1979). *Disputes and negotiations: A cross-cultural perspective.* Burlington, MA: Academic Press.

Hall, E.T. (1959). *The silent language.* Greenwich, CT: Fawcett.

Hall, E.T. (1976). *Beyond culture.* Garden City, NY: Doubleday.

Hall, E.T., & Hall, M.R. (1990). *Understanding cultural differences: Germans, French, and Americans.* Yarmouth, ME: Intercultural Press.

Hanson, V.D. (2003). *Ripples of battles.* New York: Doubleday.

Hargrove, B. (1998). *Labour of love.* Toronto: Macfarlane, Walter, and Ross.

Hart, B. (1990). Gentle jeopardy: The further endangerment of battered women and children in custody mediation. *Mediation Quarterly, 7,* 316-327.

Harvey, S.M., Bird, S.T., Galavotti, C., Duncan, E.A., & Greenberg, D. (2002). Relationship power, sexual decision-making and condom use among women at risk for HIV/STDs. *Women & Health, 36,* 69-84.

Haynes, J.M. (1981). *Divorce mediation: A practical guide for therapists and counsellors.* New York: Springer.

Haynes, J.M. (1988). Power balancing. In J. Folberg & A. Milne (Eds.), *Divorce mediation: Theory and practice* (pp. 278-296). New York: Guilford Press.

Haynes, J.M. (1992). Mediation and therapy: An alternative view. *Mediation Quarterly, 10,* 21-31.

Heer, D.M. (1963). The measurement and bases of family power: An overview. *Marriage and Family Living, May,* 33-39.

Henderson, E.A. (1997). Culture or contiguity? Ethnic conflict, the similarity of states and the onset of war. *Journal of Conflict Resolution, 91,* 649-668.

Hobbes, T. (1651). *Leviathan.* Republished (1966) with an introduction by J. Plamenatz. Cleveland, OH: Meridian Books.

Hofstede, G. (1980). *Culture's consequences: International differences in work related values.* Newbury Park, CA: Sage.

Hofstede, G. (1991). *Culture and organizations: Software of the mind.* London: McGraw-Hill.

Houck, S. (1992). Complex commercial arbitration: Designing a process to fit the case. In S.B. Goldberg, F.E. Sander, & N. Rogers (Eds.), *Dispute resolution: Negotiation, mediation and other processes* (2nd ed.) (pp. 207-221). Boston: Little, Brown.

Hovius, B. (1992). *Family law: Cases, notes and materials* (3rd ed.). Scarborough, ON: Carswell.

Huber, M. (1993). Mediation around the medicine wheel. *Mediation Quarterly, 10,* 357-367.

Huer, L.B., & Penrod, S. (1986). Procedural preference as a function of conflict intensity. *Journal of Personality and Social Psychology, 51,* 700-710.

Huler, S. (1999). *A little bit sideways: One week inside a NASCAR Winston Cup race team.* Osceola, WI: Motorbooks International.

Human Rights Code, RSO 1990, c. H.19.

Huntingdon, S. (1993). The clash of civilizations? *Foreign Affairs, Summer,* 22-49.

Ibbitson, J. (2004, August 11). Highway tiff threatens Canada-EU deal. *Globe and Mail,* p. A1.

Jacob, H. (1992). The elusive shadow of the law. *Law and Society Review, 26,* 565-581.

Jandt, F.E., & Pedersen, P.B. (1996). The cultural context of mediation and constructive conflict management. In F.E. Jandt & P.B. Pedersen (Eds.), *Constructive conflict management: Asia-Pacific cases* (pp. 249-280). Thousand Oaks, CA: Sage.

Janeway, E. (1981). *The powers of the weak.* New York: Morrow Quill Paperbacks.

Jensen, L. (1984). Negotiating strategic arms control. *Journal of Conflict Resolution, 28,* 535-559.

John, O.P., & Srivastava, S. (1999). The big five trait taxonomy: History, measurement and theoretical perspectives. In L.A. Pervin & O.P. John (Eds.), *Handbook of personality: Theory and research* (pp. 102-138). New York: Guilford Press.

Johnson-Steeves v. Lee. (1997). Alberta Court of Appeal.

Just, P. (1991). Conflict resolution and moral community among the Dou Donggo. In K. Avruch, P.W. Black, & J.A. Scimecca (Eds.), *Conflict resolution: Cross-cultural perspectives* (pp. 107-143). New York: Greenwood Press.

Kalinowski, T. (2003, May 14). 69,000 teachers face board lockout. *Toronto Star,* p. A3.

Kalman, M. (2005, February 7). Mideast adversaries raise hopes of ceasefire. *Globe and Mail,* p. A1.

Kane, J. (1995). *Savages.* Toronto: Douglas & McIntyre.

Kaplan, R. (1994). The coming anarchy. *Atlantic Monthly, 272 #2,* pp. 44-76.

Kelley, H.H., & Schenitzke, D.P. (1972). Bargaining. In C.G. McClintock (Ed.), *Experimental social psychology*. New York: Holt, Rhinehart & Winston.

Kelly, J.B. (2004). Family mediation research: Is there empirical support for the field? *Conflict Resolution Quarterly, 22*, 3-36.

Kelly, K., & Homer-Dixon, T. (1995). *Environmental scarcity and violent conflict: The case of Gaza*. Washington, DC: Amercian Association for the Advancement of Science.

Kenrick, D.T., & Funder, D.C. (1988). Profiting from controversy: Lessons from the person-situation debate. *American Psychologist, 43*, 23-34.

Kerchoff, A.C., & Back, K.W. (1968). *The June bug: A study of hysterical contagion*. New York: Appleton-Century-Crofts.

Kesterton, M. (1998, February 8). Social studies. *Globe and Mail*, p. A16.

Kesterton, M. (2003, February 5). Social studies. *Globe and Mail*, p. A14.

Kesterton. M. (2003, March 27). Social studies. *Globe and Mail*, p. A16.

Kesterton, M. (2004, August 16). Social studies. *Globe and Mail*, p. A12.

King, D. (2004). *Skeletons on the Zahara: Suffering and survival*. Halifax: Fernwood Press.

Kirkwood, C. (1993). *Leaving abusive partners*. Thousand Oaks, CA: Sage.

Kirn, W. (2004, September 12). Forget it? *New York Times Magazine*, p. 19.

Kochman, T. (1981). *Black and white styles in conflict*. Chicago: University of Chicago Press.

Kolb, D.M., & Associates (Eds.). (1994). *When talk works: Profiles of mediators*. San Francisco: Jossey-Bass.

Kolb, D.M., & Coolidge, G.G. (1995). Her place at the table: A consideration of gender issues in negotiation. In J.W. Breslin & J. Rubin (Eds.), *Negotiation theory and practice* (pp. 261-278). Cambridge, MA: Harvard Program on Negotiation.

Kolb, D.M., & Kressel, K. (1994). The realities of making talk work. In D.M. Kolb & Associates (Eds.), *When talk works: Profiles of mediators*. San Francisco: Jossey-Bass.

Kollock, P., Blumstein, P., & Schwartz, P. (1985). Sex and power in interaction: Conversational privileges and duties. *American Sociological Review, 50*, 34-46.

Komter, A. (1989). Hidden power in marriage. *Gender and Society, 3*, 187-216.

Koole, S., Smeets, K., van Kippenberg, A., & Dijksterhus, A. (1999). The cessation of rumination through self-affirmation. *Journal of Personality and Social Psychology, 77*, 111-125.

Koring, P. (2003, January 14). US relents in Korean crisis. *Globe and Mail*, p. A7.

Kozan, M.K., & Ergin, C. (1998). Preference for third party help in conflict management in the United States and Turkey: An experimental study. *Journal of Cross-Cultural Psychology, 29*, 525-539.

Kramarae, C. (1981). *Men and women speaking.* Rowley, MA: Newbury House.

Kramer, C. (1977). Perceptions of female and male speech. *Language and Speech, 20*, 151-161.

Krauss, R.M., & Morsella, E. (2000). Communication and conflict. In M. Deutsch & P.T. Coleman (Eds.), *The handbook of conflict resolution* (pp. 131-143). San Francisco: Jossey-Bass.

Kremenyuk, V.A. (1993). A pluralistic viewpoint. In G.O. Faure & J.Z. Rubin (Eds.), *Culture and negotiation: The resolution of water disputes* (pp. 47-56). Newbury Park, CA: Sage.

Kressel, K. (1989). Mediation. In K. Kressel & D.G. Pruitt (Eds.), *Mediation research: The process and effectiveness of third party intervention* (pp. 520-534). San Francisco: Jossey-Bass.

Kriesberg, L. (1992). *International conflict resolution.* New Haven, CT: Yale University Press.

Kurz, D. (1995). *For richer, for poorer: Mothers confront divorce.* New York: Routledge.

Lacey, M. (2004, August 22). In Sudan, hunter and hunted alike invoke the prophet. *New York Times*, p. 3.

Laghi, B., & Fagan, D. (2003, October 15). Alliance, Tories gain momentum in unity bid. *Globe and Mail*, p. A1.

Lajeunesse, T. (1990). Cross-cultural issues in the justice system: The case of aboriginal peoples in Canada. *Conciliation Quarterly Newsletter, 9*, 6-13.

Lakoff, R.J. (1990). *Talking power: The politics of language in our lives.* New York: Basic Books.

Lang, W. (1993). A professional's view. In G.O. Faure & J.Z. Rubin (Eds.), *Culture and negotiation: The resolution of water disputes* (pp. 38-46). Newbury Park, CA: Sage.

Lang, M., & Taylor, A. (2000). *The making of a mediator.* San Francisco: Jossey-Bass.

Lax, D.A., & Sebenius, J.K. (1995). The power of alternatives or the limits to negotiation. In J.W. Breslin & J.Z. Rubin (Eds.), *Negotiation theory and practice* (pp. 97-113). Cambridge, MA: Harvard Program on Negotiation.

Le Baron, M. (2002). *Bridging troubled waters.* San Francisco: Jossey-Bass.

Le Baron, M., & Carstarphen, N. (1997). Negotiating intractable conflict: The common ground dialogue process and abortion. *Negotiation Journal, October,* 341-361.

LeBaron Duryea, M., & Grundison, J.B. (1993). *Conflict and culture: Research in five communities in Vancouver, British Columbia.* Victoria, BC: University of Victoria Institute for Dispute Resolution.

Lebrun, P. (2004, September 10). Contract talks on road to nowhere. *Toronto Star,* p. B2.

Lederach, J.P. (1990). Training on cultures: A survey of the field. *Conciliation Quarterly, 9,* 6-13.

Lederach, J.P. (1991). Of nets, nails and problems: The folk language of conflict resolution in a central American setting. In K. Avruch, P.W. Black, & J.A. Scimecca (Eds.), *Conflict resolution: Cross-cultural perspectives.* New York: Greenwood Press.

Lee, G., & Petersen, L. (1983). Conjugal power and spousal resources in patriarchal cultures. *Journal of Comparative Family Studies, 2,* 28-38.

Leung, K., Au, Y., Fernandez-Dols, J.M., & Iwawaki, S. (1992). Preference for methods of conflict processing in two collectivist cultures. *International Journal of Psychology, 27,* 195-209.

Leung, K., & Iwawaki, S. (1988). Cultural collectivism and distributive behaviour. *Journal of Cross-Cultural Psychology, 19,* 35-49.

Levy, H. (2004, June 1). Three unions at impasse. *Toronto Star,* p. B5.

Lewicki, R.J., Saunders, D.M., Barry, B., & Minton, J.W. (2004). *Essentials of negotiation* (3rd ed.). New York: Irwin.

Lewicki, R.J., Saunders, D.M., & Minton, J.W. (1997). *Essentials of negotiations.* Chicago: Irwin.

Lewicki, R.J., Weiss, S.E., & Lenin, D. (1992). Models of conflict, negotiation and third party intervention: A review and a synthesis. *Journal of Organizational Behaviour, 13,* 209-250.

Lieberfeld, D. (1999). Conflict "ripeness" revisited: The South African and Israeli-Palestinian cases. *Negotiation Journal, January,* 63-82.

Lim, R.G., & Carnevale, P.J. (1990). Contingencies in the mediation of disputes. *Journal of Personality and Social Psychology, 58,* 259-272.

Lind, E.A., Huo, Y.J., & Tyler, T.R. (1994). And justice for all: Ethnicity, gender and preferences for dispute resolution procedures. Working paper, American Bar Foundation, Chicago.

Lips, H.M. (2002). *Sex and gender: An introduction*. Toronto: Mayfield.

Lowie, M., & Rothman, J. (1993). Arabs and Israelis: The Jordan River. In G.O. Faure & J.Z. Rubin (Eds.), *Culture and negotiation: The resolution of water disputes* (pp. 156-175). Newbury Park, CA: Sage.

Lukes, S. (1974). *Power: A radical view*. London: Macmillan.

Lukes, S. (1986). *Power*. Oxford: Basil Blackwell.

Lund, B., Morris, C., & Duryea, M.L. (1994). *Conflict and culture*. Report of the Multiculturalism and Dispute Resolution Project, University of Victoria Institute for Dispute Resolution, Victoria, BC.

Luttwak, E. (1999). Give war a chance. *Foreign Affairs, July/August*, 36-44.

Luxton, M. (1980). *More than a labour of love*. Toronto: Women's Press.

Lytle, A., Brett, J.M., & Shapiro, D. (1999). The strategic use of interests, rights and power to resolve disputes. *Negotiation Journal, January*, 32-51.

Maccoby, E.E. (1992). The role of parents in the socialization of children: An historical overview. *Developmental Psychology, 28*, 1006-1017.

Macfarlane, J. (2003). *Dispute resolution: Readings and case studies*. Toronto: Emond Montgomery.

Macionis, J.J., & Gerber, L.M. (2005). *Sociology*. Toronto: Prentice Hall.

Mackinnon, C. (1987). *Feminism unmodified: Discourses on life and the law*. Cambridge, MA: Harvard University Press.

MacMillan, M. (2003). *Paris 1919: Six months that changed the world*. New York: Random House.

Magnum Photos. (2003). *A group exhibition celebrating 5 decades*. Toronto: Stephen Bulger Gallery.

Marx, K., & Engels, F. (1848). *Communist manifesto*. Republished (1948). New York: Pantheon.

McCarthy, W. (1995). The role of power and principle in getting to yes. In J.W. Breslin, & J.Z. Rubin (Eds.), *Negotiation theory and practice* (pp. 115-122). Cambridge, MA: Harvard Program on Negotiation.

McCrae, R.R., & Costa, P.T. (1999). A five factor theory of personality. In L.A. Pervin & O.P. John (Eds.), *Handbook of personality: Theory and research* (pp. 139-153). New York: Guilford Press.

McKersie, R.B. (1995). The Eastern Airlines saga: Grounded by a contest of wills. In J.W. Breslin & J.Z. Rubin (Eds.), *Negotiation theory and practice* (pp. 211-215). Cambridge, MA: Harvard Program on Negotiation.

McLean, B., & Elkind, P. (2003). *The smartest guys in the room: The amazing rise and scandalous fall of Enron.* New York: Penguin.

McNamee, E. (1994). *Resurrection man.* New York: Penguin.

Mead, G.H. (1934). *Mind, self and society.* Chicago: University of Chicago Press.

Menkel-Meadow, C. (1995). The many ways of mediation. *Negotiation Journal, July,* 217-242.

Merton, R.K. (1957). *Social theory and social structure.* New York: Free Press.

Messerschmidt, J.W. (1993). *Masculinities and crime: Critique and reconceptualization of theory.* Lanham, MD: Rowman & Littlefield.

Miller, A. (1984). The adversary system: Dinosaur or phoenix. *University of Minnesota Law Review, 69,* 1-37.

Miller, J.B. (1985). Patterns of control in same-sex conversations: Differences between men and women. *Women's Studies in Communication, 8,* 62-69.

Miller, R.E., & Sarat, A. (1980-81). Grievances, claims and disputes: Assessing the adversary culture. *Law and Society Review, 15,* 525-546.

Millson, L. (1997, February 14). Arbitrator calls the shots. *Globe and Mail,* p. S5.

Mnookin, R.H. (1979). Bargaining in the shadow of the law: The case of divorce. Working paper 3, Berkeley School of Law, University of California.

Mnookin, R.H. (1993). Why negotiations fail: An exploration of barriers to the resolution of conflict. *Ohio State Journal of Dispute Resolution, 8,* 235-249.

Mnookin, R.H., Peppet, S.R., & Tulumello, A.S. (2000). *Beyond winning: Negotiating to create value in deals and disputes.* Cambridge, MA: Belknap Press.

Moore, C.W. (1996). *The mediation process: Practical strategies for resolving conflict* (2nd ed.). San Francisco: Jossey-Bass.

Morrill, C., Harrison, T., & Johnson, M. (1998). Voice and context in everyday legal discourse: The influence of sex differences and social ties. *Law and Society Review, 32,* 639-665.

Morris, C. (1997). The trusted mediator: Ethics and interaction in mediation. In J. Macfarlane (Ed.), *Rethinking disputes: The mediation alternative* (pp. 301-348). Toronto: Emond Montgomery.

Moskowitz, D.S., Jung-Suh, E., & Desaulniers, J. (1994). Situational influences on gender differences in agency and communication. *Journal of Personality and Social Psychology, 66,* 753-761.

Muldoon, B. (1993). *The heart of conflict.* New York: Putnam.

National Film Board of Canada. (1998). *Power: One river, two nations.* Ottawa.

National Film Board of Canada. (2003). *The siege of Bethlehem.* Ottawa.

Naylor, D. (2004, August 7). NHL's arbitration process could be on the line. *Globe and Mail,* p. S3.

Neumann, D. (1992). How mediators can effectively address the male–female power imbalance in divorce mediation. *Mediation Quarterly, 9,* 227-240.

Nicholson, L. (1990). *Feminism/postmodernism.* London: Routledge.

Nolan-Haley, J. (1992). *Alternative dispute resolution.* St. Paul, MN: Westwood.

Nowak, M., & Sigmund, K. (1998). No man is a failure so long as he has friends. *Nature, 393,* 573-577.

Nye, J.S. (2002). *The paradox of American power: Why the world's only superpower can't go it alone.* Oxford: Oxford University Press.

Ogus, A., Jones-Lee, M., Walker, J., & Associates. (1989). *Report to the Lord Chancellor on the costs and effectiveness of conciliation in England and Wales.* London: Lord Chancellor's Department.

Ohbuchi, K., Fukushima, O., & Tedeschi, J.T. (1999). Cultural values in conflict management: Goal orientation, social attainment and tactical decision. *Journal of Cross-Cultural Psychology, 30,* 51-71.

Ontario Human Rights Commission. (1999). *Guide to the Human Rights Code.* Toronto: Ontario Human Rights Commission.

Osyerman, D., Coon, H.M., & Kemmelmeier, M. (2002). Rethinking individualism and collectivism: Evaluation of theoretical assumptions and meta-analysis. *Psychological Bulletin, 128,* 3-72.

Osyerman, D., Kemmelmeier, M., & Coon, H.M. (2002). Cultural psychology, a new look: Reply to Bond (2002), Fiske (2002), Kitayama (2002) and Miller (2002). *Psychology Bulletin, 128,* 110-117.

Pape, J.W. (2000). AIDS in Haiti, 1980-1996. In G. Howe & A. Cobley (Eds.), *The Caribbean AIDS epidemic* (pp. 226-242). Cave Hill, Barbados: University of West Indies Press.

Pavri, T. (1997). Help or hindrance: Third parties in the Indo-Pakistani conflict. *Negotiation Journal, October,* 369-388.

Pearson, J.A., & Thoennes, N. (1989). Divorce mediation: Reflections on a decade of research. In K. Kressel and D. Pruitt (Eds.), *Mediation research: The process and effectiveness of third party intervention.* San Francisco: Jossey-Bass.

Perkins, D. (2003, May 13). Weir's way fits Butch to a tee. *Toronto Star,* p. C8.

Pervin, L.A. (1999). Epilogue: Constancy and change in personality theory and research. In L.A. Pervin & O.P. John (Eds.), *Handbook of personality: Theory and research* (pp. 689-704). New York: Guilford Press.

Picard, C., Bishop, P., Ramkay, R., & Sargent, N. (2004). *The art and science of mediation.* Toronto: Emond Montgomery.

Pienaar, W., & Spoelstra, M. (1991). *Negotiation: Theories, strategies and skills.* San Francisco: Jossey-Bass.

Powell, B. (2005, July 29). Officer guilty of assault. *Toronto Star,* p. A1.

Powell, B., & Small, P. (2004, May 28). Tragedy over a $10 cover. *Toronto Star,* p. B1.

Powers, M.S., & Lipschutz, R. (2004). Resolving ethical dilemmas. *ACResolution, 3,* 24-25.

Preisser, A.B. (1999). Domestic violence in south Asian communities in America: Advocacy and intervention. *Violence Against Women, 5,* 684-699.

Pritchard, D., & Lysaght, A. (2002). *The Beatles: An oral history.* Pittsburgh: Diane Publishing.

Provis, C. (1996). Interests vs. positions: A critique of the distinction. *Negotiation Journal, October,* 305-323.

Pruitt, D.G. (1995). Strategic choice in negotiation. In J. Breslin & J. Rubin (Eds.), *Negotiation theory and practice* (pp. 27-46). Cambridge, MA: Harvard Program on Negotiation.

Pruitt, D.G., & Rubin, J.Z. (1986). *Social conflict: Escalation, stalemate and settlement.* New York: Random House.

Pulerwitz, J., Amaro, H., De Jong, W., Gortmaker, S.L., & Rudd, R. (2002). Relationship power, condom use and HIV risk among women in the USA. *AIDS Care, 14,* 789-800.

Radford, J., & Russell, D.E. (Eds.). (1992). *Femicide: The politics of woman killing.* New York: Twayne.

Rattansi, A. (1992). Changing the subject? Racism, culture and education. In J. Donald & A. Rattansi (Eds.), *Race, culture and difference* (pp. 11-48). Newbury Park, CA: Sage.

Raven, B.H., & Rubin, J.Z. (1983). *Social psychology* (2nd ed.). New York: Wiley.

Reuters News Agency. (2004, July 28). Road from hell leads to prosperity. *Toronto Star*, p. E3.

Riskin, L.L. (1996). Mediator orientations, strategies and techniques: A grid for the perplexed. *Harvard Negotiation Law Review, 1,* 7-51.

Roberts, S. (1983). The study of dispute: Anthropological perspectives. In J. Bossy (Ed.), *Disputes and settlements: Law and human relations in the west* (pp. 1-24). Cambridge, UK: Cambridge University Press.

Rodman, H. (1972). Marital power and the theory of resources in cultural context. *Journal of Comparative Family Studies, 3,* 50-69.

Rojas, L. (1981). *An anthropologist examines the navy's recruiting process.* Technical report #4. Champaign, IL: University of Illinois, Department of Psychology.

Ross, D. (2004). *The missing peace: The inside story of the fight for Middle East peace.* New York: Farrar, Straus & Giroux.

Ross, R. (1996). *Returning to the teachings: Exploring aboriginal justice.* Toronto and New York: Penguin.

Rothman, J. (1997). *Resolving identity-based conflict in nations, organizations and communities.* San Francisco: Jossey-Bass.

Rubin, J.Z. (1980). Experimental research on third party intervention in conflict: Toward some generalizations. *Journal of Applied Social Psychology, 1,* 205-239.

Rubin, J.Z. (1992). Some wise and mistaken assumptions about conflict and negotiation. In J.W. Breslin & J.Z. Rubin (Eds.), *Negotiation theory and practice* (pp. 3-12). Cambridge, MA: Harvard Program on Negotiation.

Rubin, J.Z., & Brown, B. (1975). *The social psychology of bargaining and negotiations.* New York: Academic Press.

Rubin, J.Z., & Zartman, I.W. (1995). Asymmetrical negotiations: Some survey results that may surprise. *Negotiation Journal, October,* 349-364.

Rubin, L.B. (1976). *Worlds of pain: Life in the working class family.* New York: Basic Books.

Rudman, L.A. (1998). Self-promotion as a risk factor for women: The costs and benefits of counterstereotypical impression management. *Journal of Personality and Social Psychology, 74,* 629-45.

Rusting, C.L., & Nolen-Hoeksema, S. (1998). Regulating responses to anger: Effects of rumination and distraction on angry mood. *Journal of Personality and Social Psychology, 74,* 790-803.

Sander, F., & Goldberg, S.B. (1994). Fitting the forum to the fuss: A user-friendly guide to selecting an ADR procedure. *Negotiation Journal, January,* 49-68.

Scanzoni, J.H. (1982). *Sexual bargaining: Power politics in the American marriage* (2nd ed.). Chicago: University of Chicago Press.

Schafer, S. (2000, October 31). Misunderstandings @ the office. *Washington Post,* p. E1.

Schelling, T. (1960). *The strategy of conflict.* New York: Oxford University Press.

Schneider, A.K. (2002). Shattering negotiation myths: Empirical evidence on the effectiveness of negotiation style. *Harvard Law Negotiation Review, 7,* 143-231.

Schweder, R.A., & Bourne, E. (1982). Does the concept of the person vary cross-culturally? In A.J. Marsella & G. White (Eds.), *Cultural conceptions of mental health and therapy* (pp. 97-137). Boston: Reidel.

Scott, J.C. (1985). *Weapons of the weak: Everyday forms of peasant resistance.* New Haven, CT: Yale University Press.

Scott, K. (2003, June 24). McCartney ends feud, lets song credits be. *Globe and Mail,* p. A10.

Seguin, R. (2002). Crees, Quebec sign historic deal. *Globe and Mail,* p. A7.

Sexual Harassment, Education and Complaints Centre, York University. (2003). *Procedure for dealing with complaints of harassment or discrimination.* Toronto: York University.

Shipler, D.K. (2001, May 27). A conflict's bedrock is laid bare. *New York Times,* p. 14.

Silbey, G., & Merry, S. (1986). Mediator settlement strategies. *Law and Public Policy, 8,* 7-32.

Simmel, G. (1950). The sociological significance of the third element. In K. Wolff (Ed.), *The sociology of Georg Simmel* (pp. 145-169). London: Collier-Macmillan.

Simmel, G. (1955). *Conflict: The web of group affiliations.* Translated by R. Bendix. Glencoe, IL: Free Press.

Simmel, G. (1959). *The sociology of George Simmel.* Translated and edited by K. Wolff. New York: Free Press.

Slim, R.M. (1993). Turkey, Syria, Iraq: The Euphrates. In G.O. Faure & J.Z. Rubin (Eds.), *Culture and negotiation: The resolution of water disputes* (pp. 135-155). Newbury Park, CA: Sage.

Smart, C. (1976). *Women, crime and criminology.* London: Routledge.

Smart, C., & Smart, B. (1978). Women and social control. In C. Smart & B. Smart (Eds.), *Women, sexuality and social control* (pp. 1-7). London: Routledge & Kegan Paul.

Smeesters, D., Warplop, L., Avermat, E.V., & Corneille, O. (2003). Do not prime hawks with doves: The interplay of construct activation and consistency of social value orientation on cooperative behaviour. *Journal of Personality and Social Psychology, 84,* 972–987.

Smith, D. (2004, June 9). Stern to NHL: Be nice. *Toronto Star,* p. C9.

Smith, E.B. (2003, May 2). Fastow charges may be used as leverage. *USA Today,* p. 2.

Smyth, L.F. (1994). Intractable conflicts and the role of identity. *Negotiation Journal, 10,* 311-321.

Stark, R. (1992). *Sociology* (2nd ed.). Toronto: Thompson.

Statistics Canada. (2002). *Technical report on the analyses of small groups in the General Social Survey.* Ottawa: Canadian Centre for Justice Statistics.

Steil, J.M., & Hillman, J.L. (1993). The perceived value of direct and indirect influence strategies: A cross-cultural comparison. *Psychology of Women Quarterly, 17,* 457-62.

Stockholm International Peace Research Institute. (2004). *Yearbook.* Stockholm.

Stone, D., Patton, B., & Heen, S. (1999). *Difficult conversations.* New York: Viking.

Straus, M.A. (1980). Resources and power. In M.A. Straus & G.T. Hotaling (Eds.), *The social causes of husband–wife violence* (pp. 188-207). Minneapolis, MN: University of Minnesota Press.

Stulberg, J., & Bridenback, M. (1981). *Citizen dispute settlement: A mediator's manual.* Tallahassee, FL: Supreme Court of Florida.

Sumner, W.G. (1906). *Folkways.* Republished (1959). New York: Dover.

Swann, W. (1987). Identity negotiation: Where two roads meet. *Journal of Personality and Social Psychology, 53,* 1038-1051.

Sydie, R.A. (1987). *Natural women and cultured men.* New York: Methuen.

Tannen, D. (1990). *You just don't understand: Men and women in conversation.* New York: Ballantine.

Tannen, D. (1993). *Gender and conversational interaction.* New York: Oxford University Press.

Tannen, D. (1994, October). But what do you mean? *Redbook,* pp. 121-123.

Tannen, D. (1998). *The argument culture: Moving from debate to dialogue.* New York: Random House.

Thernstrom, M. (2003, August 24). Untying the knot. *New York Times Magazine,* pp. 38-44.

Thomas, W.I. (1966). The relation of research to the social process. In I.M. Janowitz (Ed.), *W.I. Thomas on social organization and social personality* (pp. 289-305). Chicago: University of Chicago Press.

Thorne, B., & Henley, N. (1975). Difference and dominance: An overview of language, gender and society. In B. Thorne & N. Henley (Eds.), *Language and sex: Difference and dominance.* Rowley, MA: Newbury House.

Ting-Toomey, S. (1988). Intercultural conflict styles: A face-negotiation theory. In Y.Y. Kim & W.B. Gudykunst (Eds.), *Theories in intercultural communication* (pp. 213-235). Thousand Oaks, CA: Sage.

Toch, H. (1969). *Violent men: An inquiry into the psychology of violence.* Chicago: Aldine.

Traub, J. (2005, January 30). The new hard-soft power. *New York Times Magazine,* pp. 28-29.

Triandis, H. (1989). Cross-cultural studies of individualism and collectivism. *Nebraska Symposium on Motivation,* 41-133.

Triandis, H., Bontempo, R., Villareal, M.J., Asai, M., & Lucca, N. (1988). Individualism and collectivism: Cross-cultural perspectives on self–ingroup relationships. *Journal of Personality and Social Psychology, 54,* 323-338.

Tyler, T.R., & Lind, E.A. (1992). A relational model of authority in groups. In M. Zanna (Ed.), *Advances in experimental social psychology: Vol. 25* (pp. 115-192). New York: Academic Press.

Tyler, T., Lind, E.A., Ohbuchi, K.-I., Sugawara, I., & Huo, Y.J. (1998). Conflict with outsiders: Disputing within and across cultural boundaries. *Personality and Social Psychology Bulletin, 24,* 137-146.

Ulin, P.R., Cayemittes, M., & Metellus, E. (1993.) *Haitian women's role in sexual decision-making: The gap between AIDS knowledge and behavior change.* Durham, NC: Family Health International.

Universal Declaration of Human Rights. (1948). Adopted and proclaimed by General Assembly resolution 217A(III).

Ury, W. (1991). *Getting past no: Negotiating your way from confrontation to cooperation.* New York: Bantam.

Ury, W., Brett, J., & Goldberg, S. (1993). *Getting disputes resolved: Designing systems to cut the costs of conflict* (2nd ed.). San Francisco: Jossey-Bass.

Ver Steeg, N. (2003). Yes, no and maybe: Informed decision making about divorce mediation in the presence of domestic violence. *William and Mary Journal of Women and the Law, 9,* 147-204.

Versi, A. (2004). Coping with culture clash. In E. Angeloni (Ed.), *Annual review: Anthropology* (pp. 23-24). Guilford, CT: McGraw-Hill.

Walby, S. (1990). *Theorizing patriarchy.* Oxford: Basil Blackwell.

Walker, A. (1996). Couples watching television: Gender, power and the remote control. *Journal of Marriage and the Family, 58,* 813-823.

Wallihan, J. (1998). Negotiating to avoid agreement. *Negotiation Journal, July,* 257-268.

Walton, R.E., & McKersie, R.B. (1965). *A behavioral theory of labor negotiating.* New York: McGraw-Hill.

Watkins, M., & Winters, K. (1997). Intervenors with interests and power. *Negotiation Journal, April,* 119-142.

Watson, C. (1994). Gender vs. power as predictor of negotiation behaviour and outcomes. *Negotiation Journal, April,* 375-386.

Weber, M. (1904–1905). *The Protestant ethic and the spirit of capitalism.* Republished (1956), T. Parsons (Trans.). New York: Charles Scribner's.

Weingart, L.R., Thompson, L.L., Bazerman, M.H., & Carroll, J.S. (1990). Tactical behaviour and negotiation outcomes. *International Journal of Conflict Management, 1,* 7-31.

Werner, T., & Risen, J. (1998, May 25). Policy makers, diplomats, intelligence officers all missed India's intentions. *New York Times,* p. 16.

West, C., & Zimmerman, D.H. (1987). Doing gender. *Gender and Society, 1,* 125-51.

Westley, W. (1953). Violence and the police. *American Journal of Sociology, 59,* 34-41.

Wheatcroft, A. (2004). *Infidels: A history of conflict between Christendom and Islam.* New York: Random House.

White, J. (1992). The pros and cons of getting to yes. In S. Goldberg, F.E. Sander, & N. Rogers (Eds.), *Dispute resolution: Negotiation, mediation and other processes* (2nd ed., pp. 45-48). Boston: Little, Brown.

Williams, J.E., & Bennett, S.M. (1975). The definition of sex stereotypes via the adjective checklist. *Sex Roles, 1,* 327-337.

Williams, J.E., & Best, D.L. (1990). *Measuring sex stereotypes: A thirteen nation study.* Beverly Hills, CA: Sage.

Williams, S. (2003). *Karla: A pact with the devil.* Toronto: Random House.

Wilmot, W.W., & Hocker, J.L. (2001). *Interpersonal conflict.* New York: McGraw Hill.

Wilson, M., & Daly, M. (1992). Till death do us part. In J. Radford & D.E. Russell (Eds.), *Femicide: The politics of woman killing* (pp. 83-98). New York: Twayne.

Wilson, M., & Daly, M. (1994). Spousal homicide. *Juristat, 14,* 1-14.

Wingood, G.M., & DiClemente, R.J. (1998). Partner influences and gender-related factors associated with non-condom use among young adult African American women. *American Journal of Community Psychology, 26,* 29-51.

Winslade, J., & Monk, G. (2001). *Narrative mediation: A new approach to conflict resolution.* San Francisco: Jossey-Bass.

York University Faculty Association. (1999). *Communique, 11.*

Young, H., Knippenberg, A., Ellemers, N., & de Vries, N. (1999). The asymmetrical perception of men and women. *Group Processes and Intergroup Relations, 2,* 259-78.

Zartman, I.W. (1975). Negotiations: Theory and reality. *Journal of International Affairs, 9,* 69-77.

Zartman, I.W. (Ed.). (1983). *Ripe for resolution: Conflict and intervention in Africa.* Oxford: Oxford University Press.

Zartman, I.W. (1993). A skeptic's view. In G.O. Faure & J.Z. Rubin (Eds.), *Culture and negotiation: The resolution of water disputes* (pp. 17-21). Newbury Park, CA: Sage.

Index

adjudication
    defined, 122
    evaluation, 125-126
    gender theory, and, 215-217
    mini-trial, 124-125
Adler and Silverstein's power-balancing
    intervention, 163
agreeableness, and negotiation, 226-227
Alternative Dispute Resolution Institute of
    Canada (ADRIC), 110
anchoring, 225
arbitration
    baseball arbitration, 118
    binding and non-binding, 114
    defined, 113-114
    evaluation, 119-120
    judges, and, 114-115
    mediation, and, 117-118, 119
    Ontario *Arbitration Act, 1991*, 121, 132-134
Arbitration Act, 1991 (Ontario), 121, 132-134
aspiration, level of, 164, 230-232
Association for Conflict Resolution (ACR),
    110

balance of power
    effects on negotiation, 155-156
    mediators, and
        imbalance assessment, 157-159
        motivational orientation, 156-157
        resource education, 160-161
bargaining, 94
baseball arbitration, 118
BATNA, 48-49, 142, 150, 163

Bennett and Hermann's power-balancing
    intervention, 161
"big five" personality traits, 222, 238-240
binding arbitration, 114
brainstorming, 94

CANOE, *see* five-factor (CANOE) theory of
    personality
caucusing, 96
cognitive ability, and negotiation, 227-228
cognitive conflicts, 17-19
collectivist cultures, 173-174
co-mediation, 109-110
communications theories
    meanings, 183-184
    styles, 184-187
compromise, 42, 94
concession–convergence model, 43
conflict
    analysis, *see* conflict analysis
    conflict–control procedure continuum, 4
    definitions
        integrative definition, 8-11
        mutual elements, 5-6
        objective interaction definitions, 6-7
        subjective feelings definitions, 7-8
    dysfunctional conflict, 2-3
    escalation, stages of, 75-76
    ethnic conflicts, 2
    functional conflict, 2
    resolution, *see* conflict resolution
    social phenomenon, as, 1
    terminology of, 3

conflict (cont.)
 types of
  cognitive conflict, 17-19
  identity conflict, 19-21
  interest conflict, 1, 13-14
  realistic conflict, 21
  unrealistic conflict, 21
  value conflict, 14-17
conflict analysis
 discovery, 22-25
 illustration of, 27-29
 prominent source, 25-26
 solution, 26-27
conflict–control procedure continuum, 4
conflict resolution
 adjudication
  defined, 122-124
  evaluation, 125-126
  gender theory, and, 215-217
  mini-trial, 124-125
 approaches to, 31-32
 arbitration
  baseball, 118
  binding and non-binding, 114
  defined, 113-114
  evaluation, 119-120
  judges, and, 114-115
  mediation, and, 117-118, 119
 collectivistic and individualistic cultures,
  174
 Costa Rican model, 174-177
 elicitive model, 196
 First Nations model, 177-178
 guidelines, process selection, 126-130
 mediation
  defined, 79-82
  ethics, 110-113
  gender theory, and, 212-215
  ground rule, 83
  models of, 84-110
  process, 82
  roles, 83
 mediation–arbitration, 120-121
  evaluation, 122

negotiation
 distributive negotiation, 39-40
 failure, reasons for, 73-76
 gender theory, and, 206-212
 impression management, 37-38, 41
 integrative negotiation, 40-41
 models of, 41-73
 struggle, 32-36
  evaluation, 36-37
  gender theory, and, 205-206
Costa Rican model of mediation, 174-177
cultural–situational theory, 193-194
culture
 conflict resolution, and, 171
 cultural–situational theory, 193-194
 defined, 170-171
 elicitive model, use of, 196
 ethnocentrism, 189-191
 in-groups and out-groups, 187-189
 practitioner advice, 194-196
 relativity, 169-170
 situational factors, 187
 stereotyping, 191-193
 theories
  communications, 183-187
  evaluation, 196-197
  value orientations, 172-183
cyclical–development negotiation
 cyclical process
  alternation, 65-67
  evaluation, 72
  information exchange, 65
 developmental process
  agreement, execution of, 72
  arena, creation of, 67-69
  arena, search for, 67
  differences, narrowing of, 69-70
  evaluation, 72-73
  field, exploration of, 69
  final bargain, 71
  final bargaining, preliminaries to,
   70-71
  outcome, ritualization, 71-72
  stepping stones, 68

dynamic, 64
    terminology, 61-64

distributive negotiation, 39-40
dysfunction conflict, 2-3

educational model of mediation, 180
elicitive model of conflict resolution, 196
Ellis process theory of power, 148-154
empowerment, 99
ethnic conflicts, 2
ethnocentrism, 189-191, 195
extroversion, and negotiation, 227

Family Mediation Canada (FMC), 110
First Nations mediation model, 177-178
five-factor (CANOE) theory of personality
    (FFT), 222-223
functional conflict, 2
fundamental attribution error, 194, 228

gender
    conflict resolution, and
        adjudication 215-17
        mediation, 212-215
        negotiation, 206-212
        struggle, 205-206
    defined, 199-200
    practice implications, 219
    theories of
        evaluation, 217-218
        interactionist–situational theory, 203
        socialization theory, 201-203
        structural theory, 204
Gewurtz's power-balancing intervention,
    162-163
Gulliver's process theory of power
    external factors, 146-147
    modifications to, 148-150
    outcomes, 147
    resources, 144-146
    use of resources, 146

hard on problem focus, 54

Haynes's power-balancing intervention, 162
high-context style, 184

identity conflicts, 19-21
impression management, 37-38, 41
individualistic cultures, 172-173
in-groups, 187
integrative negotiation, 40-41
interactionist–situational theory of gender,
    203, 217-218
interest-based mediation
    defined, 90
    evaluation, 97-98
    facilitation, 97
    stages, Bennett and Hermann model
        agenda setting, 93
        contracting, 91
        information gathering, 91-92
        intake, 90-91
        issue identification, 92
        issue resolution, 93
        review, 97
interest classification, 93
interest conflicts, 1, 13-14
interests, relationship between, 94
interpersonal orientations, 229-230

judges, 114-115
judicial review, 114
June bug study, 234-236

low-context style, 184

mediation
    arbitration, and, 117-118
    cultural differences, 179
    defined, 79-82
    ethics, 110-113
    gender theory, and, 212-214
        violence and abuse, effect of, 214-215
    ground rule, 83
    models of
        co-mediation, 109-110
        interest-based mediation, 90-98

mediation (cont.)
    models of (cont.)
        narrative mediation, 102-109
        rights-based mediation, 84-90
        transformative mediation, 98-102
    process, 82
    roles, 8
    Uniform Mediation Act, 131-132
mediation–arbitration
    defined, 120
    evaluation, 122
    process, 121
mediators
    objectives
        conflict resolution, 26-27
        conflict discovery, 22-25
        prominent source determination,
          25-26
    power-balancing interventions
        Adler and Silverstein, 163
        aspiration levels, maintenance of, 164
        BATNA, perceptions of, 163
        Bennett and Hermann, 161
        ethical considerations, 164
        Gewurtz, 162
        Haynes, 162
        Moore, 162
    power imbalances, and
        imbalance assessment, 157-159
        motivational orientation, 156-157
        resource education, 160
    power of, 165
    roles, 83
metacognitive processing, 56
mini-trial, 124
Moore's power-balancing intervention, 162
motivational orientations, 228-229, 230

narrative mediation
    defined, 102-103
    evaluation, 108
    process
        construction, alternative story,
          107-108

        deconstruction, conflict-saturated
          story, 105-107
        engagement, 105
negotiation
    distributive negotiation, 39-40
    failure, reasons for, 73-76
    gender theory, and, 206-209
        communication, 210
        fair salaries, 209
        negotiation power, 211-212
    impression management, 37-38, 41
    integrative negotiation, 40-41
    models of
        cyclical–developmental negotiation,
          61-73
        positional bargaining, 42-50
        principled negotiation, 50-60
    personality, and
        actual negotiations, 223-224
        agreeableness, effect on, 226-227
        cognitive ability, effect on, 227-228
        extroversion, effect on, 227
        simulated negotiations, 224-228
non-binding arbitration, 114

objective standards, 95
options, creation of, 55-57
outcomes, culture and, 180-183
out-groups, 187

personality
    "big five" personality traits, 222, 238-240
    defined, 221-222
    five-factor (CANOE) theory of
        personality (FFT), 222-223
        evaluation, 237
    negotiations, and
        actual negotiations, 223-224
        agreeableness, effect on, 226-227
        cognitive ability, effect on, 227-228
        extroversion, effect on, 227
        simulated negotiations, 224-228
    situational factors
        aspiration, level of, 230-232

interpersonal orientations, 229-230
motivational orientations, 228-229
social value orientations, 232-233
theory, evaluation of, 237
struggle, and, 233-236
personality clash, 224
positional bargaining
compromise and formula, 42-46
efficiency, 48-50
evaluation, 50
morality of, 46
steps involved, 42
power
balance between parties
effects of, 155-156
ethical considerations, power
balancing, 164-165
gender inequality, and, 211-212
imbalances, assessment of, 157-159
mediator interventions, 161-164
practical implications, 156-157
resource differences, 160-161
resource uses by mediators, 161, 165
defined
multidimensional definitions, 138
parties' use of resources, 139-140
process definitions, 138
relational definitions, 140-141
resource definitions, 138
unidimensional definitions, 137-138
process theories
Ellis process theory, 149-154
evaluations, 166
Gulliver's process theory, 144-147
modifications to Gulliver's theory,
148-150
resource–process theory, 150
resource theories, 141-143
evaluations, 166
power-balancing interventions
Adler and Silverstein, 163
aspiration levels, maintenance of, 164
BATNA, perceptions of, 163
Bennett and Hermann, 161

ethical considerations, 164
Gewurtz, 162
Haynes, 162
Moore, 162
power imbalance assessment questionnaire
(PIAQ), 158
principled negotiation
defined, 50-51
evaluation, 60
hard on problem focus, 54
interests, reconciliation, 54-55
objective standards, use of, 57-59
options, creation of, 55-57
problem-solving approach, 59
separation, person from problem, 52-54
wise agreement, and, 51-52
problem-solving approach, 59
process theories of power
Ellis process theory, 149-150
Ellis process theory application
conflict, 151
external factors, 154
outcomes, 153
resources, 151-152
use of resources, 152-153
evaluation, 166
Gulliver's process theory
external factors, 146-147
outcomes, 147
resources, 144-146
use of resources, 146
modifications to Gulliver's theory, 148-
150
proximal values, 14, 15-16

realistic conflicts, 2
recognition, 99
resource differential questionnaire (RDQ), 158
resource–process theory of negotiation power,
150
resource theories, 141-143, 166
rights-based mediation
communication frame, 86-87
defined, 84-86

rights-based mediation (cont.)
    evaluation, 89-90
    human rights, and, 84
    settlement frame, 86-87

situational factors, 228-233
social value orientations, 232-233
socialization theory of gender, 203, 217
stereotyping, 191-193, 195
structural theory of gender, 204-205, 218
struggle
    defined, 32-33
    evaluation, 36-37
    gender theory, and, 205-206
    likelihood, factors increasing, 36
    personality, and, 233-234
    punishing struggle tactics, 34

Ting-Toomey's value orientations theory,
    174-175
transformative mediation
    approach, 99-100
    concepts, 99
    defined, 98
    evaluation, 102
    model and theory, 101
    process, 100

ultimate values, 14
Uniform Mediation Act, 110, 131-132
unrealistic conflicts, 21

value conflicts, 14-17
value orientations theory
    collectivism, 173-174
    conflict resolution, and, 174
    Costa Rican model, 174-177
    First Nations model, 177-179
    individualism, 172-173
    mediation models, comparison of, 179
    outcomes, cultures and, 180-182
    Ting-Toomey's value orientations theory,
        174-175

Acknowledgments

The following publishers and institutions have been generous in giving their permission to reproduce works in this text. If we have inadvertently overlooked any acknowledgment, we offer our sincere apologies and undertake to rectify the omission in any future editions.

American Psychological Association Barry, B., & Friedman, R.A. (1998). Bargainer characteristics in distributive and integrative negotiation. *Journal of Personality and Social Psychology, 74,* 345-359.

Association for Conflict Resolution Association for Conflict Resolution. (2001). *ACR's Uniform Mediation Act (UMA) principles.* Washington, DC: Association for Conflict Resolution. http://www.ACRnet.org/uma/principles.htm.

Blackwell Publishing Adapted from F. Sander, F., & Goldberg, S.B. (1994). Fitting the forum to the fuss: A user-friendly guide to selecting an ADR procedure. *Negotiation Journal, January,* 49-68, at 59.

Elsevier Inc. Gulliver, P. (1979). *Disputes and negotiations: A cross-cultural perspective* (p. 122). Burlington, MA: Academic Press. Reprinted with permission from Elsevier.

Houghton Mifflin Company Fisher, R., Ury, W., & Patton, W. (1991). Chart from *Getting to yes* (2nd ed.). Boston: Houghton Mifflin. Copyright © 1981, 1991 by Roger Fisher and William Ury. Reprinted by permission of Houghton Mifflin Company, New York. All rights reserved.

Mennonite Central Committee Lajeunesse, T. (1990). Cross-cultural issues in the justice system: The case of aboriginal peoples of Canada. *Conciliation Quarterly Newsletter, 9,* 6-13.

Sage Publications Ting-Toomey, S. (1988). Intercultural conflict styles: A face-negotiation theory. In Y.Y. Kim & W.B. Gudykunst (Eds.), *Theories in inter-cultural communication* (pp. 213-235). Thousand Oaks, CA: Sage.

Torstar Syndication Services Powell, B., & Small, P. (2004, May 28). Tragedy over a $10 cover. *Toronto Star,* p. B1. Reprinted with permission— Torstar Syndication Services.

Torstar Syndication Services Smith, D. (2004, June 9). Stern to NHL: Be nice. *Toronto Star,* p. C9. Reprinted with permission—Torstar Syndication Services.